Stills, Reels and Rushes
Ireland and the Irish in 20th Century Cinema

About the Author

Michael Gray is the film critic for The Irish Echo newspaper in New York City, and is a contributor to Cineaste and Film Ireland magazines. He welcomes comments, questions, and/or bitter recriminations about Stills, Reels and Rushes at :
filmgripes@hotmail.com

Stills, Reels and Rushes

Ireland and the Irish in 20th Century Cinema

Michael Gray

ASHFIELD Press

This book was typeset by
Claire Rourke for

BLACKHALL PUBLISHING
26 Eustace Street
Dublin 2
Ireland

e-mail: blackhall@tinet.ie

ISBN: 1 901658 21 X

A catalogue record for this book is available
from the British Library.

Printed in Ireland by
Betaprint Ltd

CONTENTS

Acknowledgements viii

Introduction xiii

A Century of Irish Films

The Lad from Old Ireland (1910) 2
Rory O'More (1911) 4
The Colleen Bawn (1911) 6
For Ireland's Sake (1914) 10
Ireland a Nation (1914) 12
Regeneration (1915) 16
O'Neil of the Glen (1916) 20
When Love came to Gavin Burke (1917) 22
Knocknagow (1918) 24
In the Days of St Patrick (1920) 28
Will Reilly and his Colleen Bawn (1920) 30
The Four Horsemen of the Apocolypse (1921) 34
Irish Destiny (1926) 38
The Public Enemy (1931) 42
The Bowery (1933) 46
Man of Aran (1934) 50
Captain Blood (1935) 54
Guests of the Nation (1935) 56
The Informer (1935) 58
The Dawn (1935) 60
Beloved Enemy (1936) 62
Ourselves Alone (1936) 66
Irish and Proud of it (1936) 68
Angels with Dirty Faces (1938) 70
The Islandman (1938) 74
Blarney (1939) 76
I See a Dark Stranger (1946) 78
Captain Boycott (1947) 82
Odd Man Out (1947) 84
Another Shore (1948) 86
Daughter of Darkness (1948) 88
Luck of the Irish (1948) 92
Saints and Sinners (1949) 94
No Resting Place (1951) 96
The Quiet Man (1952) 98

Happy Ever After (1954) 100
Jacqueline (1956) 102
The Rising of the Moon (1957) 104
The Story of Esther Costello (1957) 106
Rooney (1958) 108
Darby O'Gill and the Little People (1959) 110
Home is the Hero (1959) 112
Shake Hands with the Devil (1959) 114
This Other Eden (1959) 116
A Terrible Beauty (1960) 118
The Quare Fellow (1962) 120
Dementia 13 (1963) 122
Girl with Green Eyes (1963) 124
Young Cassidy (1965) 126
Ulysses (1967) 128
Paddy (1969) 132
Quackser Fortune has a Cousin in the Bronx (1970) 134
Ryan's Daughter (1970) 136
Images (1972) 140
The Mackintosh Man (1973) 142
Zardoz (1974) 144
Caoineadh Airt Uí Laoire (1975) 146
Portrait of the Artist as a Young Man (1977) 148
Poitín (1978) 152
Maeve (1981) 154
Traveller (1981) 156
Angel (1982) 158
Ballroom of Romance (1982) 160
Anne Devlin (1984) 162
Cal (1984) 164
Four Days in July (1984) 166
Pigs (1984) 168
Lamb (1985) 170
Budawanny (1987) 172
The Dead (1987) 174
Clash of the Ash (1987) 178
Reefer and the Model (1988) 180
Da (1988) 182
Hush-A-Bye-Baby (1989) 184
My Left Foot (1989) 186
Hidden Agenda (1990) 188
The Field (1990) 190
December Bride (1990) 194
The Commitments (1991) 196
The Miracle (1991) 200
The Crying Game (1992) 202
Into the West (1992) 204
You, Me and Marley (1992) 206
In the Name of the Father (1993) 208

The Snapper (1993) 210
War of the Buttons (1994) 212
Ailsa (1994) 214
The Secret of Roan Inish (1994) 216
Guiltrip (1995) 218
A Man of No Importance (1995) 220
The Eliminator (1996) 222
Michael Collins (1996) 224
Some Mother's Son (1996) 228
This is the Sea (1996) 232
I Went Down (1997) 234
The Butcher Boy (1998) 238
Divorcing Jack (1998) 240
The General (1998) 242
This is my Father (1998) 246
I Could Read the Sky (1999) 250

Bibliography 253

Indexes
Films 254
Names 256

ACKNOWLEDGEMENTS

The author and Ashfield Press would like to thank the following people and companies for giving their permission to use the stills reproduced in this book. Every effort has been made to contact all copyright holders for their permision to use the stills featured. If a copyright holder has been inadvertently overlooked, we will be happy to make the appropriate arrangements at the earliest opportunity.

Cathal Black

Carlton International Media Ltd

Joe Comerford

Jane Gogan

Goldcrest Films International

Samuel Goldwyn

Margo Harkin

Hot Property Films

Little Bird

Merlin Films Group Ltd

Michael Johnston

Arthur Lappin

Pat Murphy

Steve Pyke

RTÉ

Bob Quinn

Temple Films

Warner Bros

ACKNOWLEDGEMENTS

I'd like to thank the following people, without whose help I could not have completed this book:

My research team (The Chuck Brindle Rapid Response Unit) Mel Gray, Philip Gray, and Denis Gray; and for advanced research, Mel Gray and Paul Power.

Paul White of A&L Goodbody, for legal counsel.

Sunniva O'Flynn, Liam Wylie and Emma Keogh at the Film Archive of the Film Institute Of Ireland.

Philip Gray BSc, director of Film Base, Dublin.

Marjorie Sweeney at Film Forum NYC, Eliza O'Grady at Ireland House NYC, Kathleen Dickson at the British Film Institute, London, Michelle Galvin in Killarney, Teresa Hogan in Dublin, and John Buckley at LaSalle College, Philadelphia for archival material.

Robert Monks at the National Library, Dublin.

Niamh Barrett at Clarence Pictures, Dublin.

John McHugh, BBC London.

Jim Halpin, a great titler of books, and Mel Gray, a great deviser of ratings.

Peter Shelton for technological firepower.

Niall and Margaret, facilitators at the finale.

The late Liam O'Leary for getting me interested in all this in the first place.

The following film-makers gave generously of their time to help with my research:

Cathal Black
David Caffrey
Neil Jordan
Pat Murphy
Paul Quinn
Fergus Tighe

For Mary
(who remembers everything, and never has to look anything up)

INTRODUCTION

Ireland was a late starter in the world of cinema. Though quick off the mark to exhibit moving images – Dublin audiences were terrified by footage of incoming steam locomotives at Dan Lowrey's Star of Erin Theatre within months of the first Lumiére Brothers' projections in Paris in December 1895 – thirteen years would pass before the city had its own film theatre. Opened in 1909 by an unlikely entrepreneur, an exiled writer named James Joyce, the Volta screened imported Italian dramas in the absence of domestic product. Another year would pass before a film was actually made in the country. Sidney Olcott's 1910 drama The Lad from Old Ireland is generally credited with being the first fiction film shot on Irish soil (previous cinematic efforts consisted of travelogue and newsreel footage), and its international success led to a period of prolific productivity by the director, working on location in Kerry in the years leading up to the World War I.

Output during the silent and early sound years was characterised by promising, if rarely commercially sustainable, beginnings by local independent companies, airing romances with socio-political subtexts, and one-off Irish-themed features by British and US film-makers that portrayed Ireland with dubious accuracy. The dormant period of World War II was followed by a gathering of momentum that led to the establishment, finally, of an indigenous film studio, allowing full production to be completed in situ and giving native directors the opportunity to represent (and misrepresent) Ireland on-screen. This momentum faltered, largely for financial reasons, during the 1960s and 1970s, until the final flourishing of the industry brought commercial success, international acclaim and numerous awards for Ireland's top film-makers in the closing decades of the 20th century.

Stills, Reels and Rushes charts that uneven course through the century, examining one hundred of the most important fiction films of Ireland's people, places and Diaspora made during that time period. From modest beginnings to formidable finale – the pre-independence nationalist rebel-rousers made in Ireland and robust action adventures of the Diaspora abroad during the silent era the corny pastoral melodramas that established Ireland's enduring reputation beyond its shores as a land of belligerent redheads, superstitious rustics and volatile gunmen; and the mature later works that constitute a remarkable synthesis of Ireland's renowned literary heritage and thespian stagecraft – this anthology covers the full spectrum. Not all of the films included here are Irish, but all of them reflect crucial aspects of the Irish experience at home and abroad through the artifice of the 20th century's most popular mass media, cinema and television. In some instances, Ireland's spectacular terrain is used solely as a location for metaphoric or iconic purposes by directors of internationally financed films that have no other Irish content. The specifics of film finance and the nationality of the film production team, key factors in defining the 'Irishness' or otherwise of a particular feature, are of far greater concern to the few who make films than the many who watch them, and need not be argued further here. As film-making becomes a more expensive and supranational medium, fewer and fewer films will fit narrow definitions of Irishness, though they may be written, set, and filmed on the island.

The effort to encompass the broadest possible range of genres and themes, distributed fairly across the whole century, will inevitably exclude worthy features from the list, in a time-frame that saw more films made in and around Ireland in its last two decades than in the previous eight. But the fact that a film was made at all in the turbulent and newly independent nation in the 1920s or 1930s makes it a more valuable record of its place in the century than a perfectly competent entertainment from the crowded field of sixty years later. Each of the one hundred films included here is given a review and synopsis, with the emphasis on a detailed description of the narrative for less familiar films, particularly those that are rarely screened or broadcast and are unavailable on video (two films from the silent period no longer exist in any format, and for these I relied on research into contemporary periodicals and the sources cited in the bibliography). More recent films are presented with less narrative detail and more analysis, in the belief that readers will know something of the plot already. The reviews and overviews are illustrated throughout by stills from the films, further elucidating the less-celebrated dramas of yesteryear and bringing vividly to mind the more recent works.

Stills, Reels and Rushes ends as it began, with a film about the Irish immigrant experience; in between can be found the timeless masterpieces and satirical caricatures, the trash-culture bloodbaths and gripping political dramas that made Ireland's mark in a century of cinema. From Ailsa to Zardoz, from Olcott and Ingram to Jordan and Sheridan, these are the reels that shaped how the world sees us and how we see ourselves.

Michael Gray
Dublin
November 1999

AUTHOR'S NOTE

The cast lists given with each film are reproduced faithfully from the film credits. In some cases this has caused discrepencies between the spellings of certain actors' names.

RATINGS SYSTEM

A watchable film for good location footage and/or interesting cast credits.

A worthy effort, well put together.

A notable film, with good performances and visuals.

A very good film, with admirable performances, worthy of repeated viewing.

An outstanding cinematic achievement, and a sublime synthesis of screenwriting, acting, cinematographic and directorial talent.

1

THE LAD FROM OLD IRELAND
(1910) US silent b&w 10 mins approx

(Still courtesy of The National Library)

Production Team

Producer .... Kalem Co/USA
Director .... Sidney Olcott
Screenplay .... Gene Gauntier
Cinematography .... George Hollister

Cast

Sidney Olcott .... Terry O'Connor
Gene Gauntier .... Aileene
Thomas O'Connor .... The landlord
Arthur Donaldson .... Parish priest
J P McGowan .... Election agent
Robert Vignola .... Election agent
Jane Wolfe .... Society woman
Agnes Mapes .... Aileene's mother
Laurene Santley ....

THE LAD FROM OLD IRELAND
(1910) US silent b&w 10 mins approx

Prior to 1910, most of the films made in Ireland consisted of non-fiction reels of scenery and current events, intended for local audiences. The first fiction film made there that achieved international renown was made by Kalem, a US company that had a reputation for realistic action films shot on location. Following a string of hits directed by Sidney Olcott (among them his 1907 version of *Ben Hur*), Kalem assigned its top director the project of filming abroad to ensure authentic scenic contexts for its features. Olcott had started in film in 1904 with Mutograph, and worked as studio manager, actor and director at Edison's Biograph, before joining Kalem. A Canadian with Irish parents, Olcott chose Ireland as his first stop, going there with a small crew in the summer of 1910 to shoot *The Lad from Old Ireland*, written by Gene Gauntier, about a poor farmboy who leaves his home to find success in America.

In this pioneering film, labourer Terry O'Connor (Sidney Olcott) sails for the US, leaving behind his broken-hearted girlfriend, Aileene (Gene Gauntier) with her mother (Agnes Mapes) on the family farm. He vows to return when he has done well. When he arrives in New York, Terry starts work in construction, and before long he has risen to an eminence that makes him forget his sweetheart back home. Terry enters the world of politics, and wins the election for Mayor of the city. While celebrating in his tuxedo with society women, his jubilation is tempered by a letter he belatedly receives from Aileene back in County Cork. The envelope in which it arrives has a series of New York addresses written on it and crossed out, starting downtown and ending on the upper east side, indicating Terry's rise through the city neighbourhoods. The letter relates the decline of Aileene's fortune – her family can't pay the rent and eviction is inevitable. Terry resolves to help, and boards a ship for Ireland.

On the ocean, he fantasises about Aileene, and she appears on deck in a vision. She vanishes when he tries to kiss her. Terry lands in Ireland, to warm greetings from the locals, and travels to Aileene's cottage by jaunting car, arriving just as the landlord (Thomas O'Connor) appears to evict the poor women. Aileene begs for mercy, while soldiers remove the furniture. An old woman offers some coins to appease the landlord, but he's unimpressed. Terry arrives and enters, politely doffing his hat, to an anguished scene. He shouts at the landlord, waving a wad of money to pay the rent owed. The delighted landlord removes his own hat at the sight of cash. Terry commands him to leave the house at once. In the local church on Sunday, the priest (Arthur Donaldson) announces the engagement of Aileene and Terry.

The theme of the rich emigrant returning to save his poor sweetheart had a broad appeal for Irish people, and went over well in Boston, Chicago and New York. The commercial success of the film prompted Kalem to send Olcott, Gauntier and Hollister to Ireland again in 1911 with a larger crew to make a series of Irish-themed films. Over a four-year period, Olcott made more than two dozen films in Ireland, to become the most important film-maker in the country in the years leading up to the First World War.

RORY O'MORE
(1911) US silent b&w 10 mins approx

(Still courtesy of the Irish Film Archive of the Film Institute of Ireland)

Production Team

Producer .... Kalem Co/USA
Director ....Sidney Olcott
Screenplay ....Gene Gauntier
based on Samuel Lover's 1836
novel of the same name
Cinematography .... George Hollister

Cast

Jack J Clark .... Rory O'More
Gene Gauntier .... Kathleen
Robert Vignola .... Black William
J P McGowan .... Commander of the
English troops
Arthur Donaldson.................. Father O'Brien
Anna Clark .... Rory's mother

RORY O'MORE
(1911) US silent b&w 10 mins approx

On their second visit to Ireland in 1911, the Kalem Company crew established a base at Beaufort, County Kerry to shoot a series of costume dramas based on events from Ireland's past and famous plays from Irish theatre. Among them was *Rory O'More*, loosely based on the life of one of the leaders of the 1641 Rising against the English.

Jack J Clark plays the title character, a dashing rebel on the run from the British authorities in County Kerry. The soldiers are kept apprised of his whereabouts by an informer, Black William (Robert Vignola), who wants the £100 reward for O'More's capture. Rory's girlfriend Kathleen (Gene Gauntier) warns him about the price on his head, and he decides to leave for the hills. Kathleen gives him a head start by stalling the troops who are searching for him, flirting with their commanding officer (J P McGowan). But they catch up on Rory, and he has to swim across a lake in a hail of musket fire to avoid arrest by the redcoats. One of the soldiers follows him into the lake, but gets into difficulties in deep water, and calls out for help. The noble Rory, torn between making a getaway while his enemy drowns, and rescuing the hapless soldier, turns back and saves him. The commanding officer nabs Rory, but is so impressed by his valour, that he is willing to let him go. However, under duress from the greedy informer Black William, he arrests the rebel and puts him in jail.

Rory is locked in a gloomy cell to await his trial. The judge finds Rory guilty, and dons a black veil to indicate that the rebel is to receive the maximum sentence – death by hanging – but Rory remains defiant, declaring to the assembled crowd, "If to fight for Ireland be a crime, I am guilty." Rory's mother (Anna Clark) and Kathleen are distraught by the verdict and they visit the priest, Father O'Brien (Arthur Donaldson), for help. Father O'Brien hatches a plan.

Rory is marched to a gallows built in front of a high wall. He mounts the scaffold with the priest and the executioner, and Father O'Brien gives him the Last Rites. As the hangman manoeuvres Rory into position over the trapdoor, Father O'Brien surreptitiously removes a knife from his sleeve and cuts the ropes that bind Rory's hands. Rory vaults the high wall to escape, and the redcoats fire a volley of shots at him, fatally wounding the priest. Behind the wall Rory finds a horse that the priest has left there for him, and he gallops away to safety. A note from the priest directs him to go to Crager's Point on the coast, where Kathleen is waiting for him with a boat to take them abroad, to America.

For this return to Ireland, Olcott and Gauntier chose a more overtly political theme than they had done the previous year. This briskly-paced drama brought to the fore Olcott's Irish nationalist sympathies, latent in the class issues of *The Lad from Old Ireland*, and introduces on-screen that perennial villain of Irish history, the informer. Olcott's interest in the cause of Irish nationalism would produce increasingly incendiary films over next two years, leading to complaints by the English authorities to Kalem in the US, and censorship of his work in Ireland.

THE COLLEEN BAWN
(1911) US silent b&w 30 mins approx

(Still courtesy of the British Film Institute)

Production Team

Producer ....Sidney Olcott/
Kalem Company
Director..Sidney Olcott
Screenplay .... Gene Gauntier
from the stageplay
by Dion Boucicault
Cinematography ....George Hollister

Cast

Gene Gauntier .... Eily O'Connor,
'the Colleen Bawn'
J P McGowan .... Hardress Cregan
Sidney Olcott ....Danny Mann
Jack J Clark .... Myles na Copaleen
Arthur Donaldson........................ Father Tom
Alice Hollister................................Anne Chute
Robert Vignola ....Mr Corrigan
Agnes Mapes .... Mrs Cregan
Anna Clark...Sheelah
George Fisher .... Kyrle Daly

THE COLLEEN BAWN
(1911) US silent b&w 30 mins approx

The plays of Dublin-born dramatist Dion Boucicault provided a rich source of material for the Kalem Company's historic costume dramas during their second visit to Ireland in 1911. Among them was *The Colleen Bawn*, adapted for the screen by Gene Gauntier. This tale of secret love and attempted murder centres on a romance between a landed gentleman, Hardress Cregan, and a beautiful peasant girl, Eily O'Connor, known as 'the Colleen Bawn'. Olcott filmed *The Colleen Bawn* against a backdrop of beautiful Kerry scenery, with helpful title cards inserted throughout the course of the film to identify the various scenic spots in front of which the silent players equivocate, gesticulate and remonstrate.

Hardress Cregan (J P McGowan) meets the Colleen Bawn (Gene Gauntier) at a country inn (shot at Beaufort, County Kerry), and dances a stately jig with her to the music of local fiddlers. They two are mutually attracted, and despite warnings from her priest, Father Tom (Arthur Donaldson), that class differences will ruin their romance, they marry in secret at her mother's grave. The clandestine ceremony is performed by a defrocked priest and witnessed by Cregan's deformed servant, Danny Mann (Sidney Olcott). Hardress' mother (Agnes Mapes), unaware of her son's secret nuptials, tries to marry him off to his wealthy cousin Anne Chute (Alice Hollister), to save the heavily mortgaged Cregan estate from the greedy clutches of their creditor, Mr Corrigan (Robert Vignola). Hardress shows no interest in Anne, and is quite unperturbed that she has another suitor, Kyrle Daly (George Fisher). The scheming Corrigan discloses to Mrs Cregan that her son has a secret lover, who he visits nightly. Mrs Cregan confronts Hardress about this, and, taken aback by his mother's question, he admits to a mistress but not a wife.

Hardress has installed the Colleen Bawn in the cottage of Danny's mother, Sheelah (Anna Clark), at Muckross Head, across the lake from the Cregan mansion. The lovers signal to each other from the windows with candles and lamps to arrange trysts. The conniving Danny, apparently attempting to help his master, ends up causing him trouble when he shows a note to Anne that Eily had given him for Hardress, and pretends that it is intended for Kyrle Daly. Anne is furious that her suitor is apparently dallying elsewhere. Meanwhile, at the celebrated Gap of Dunloe, the crafty Corrigan tries to bribe Myles na Copaleen (Jack J Clark), Eily's lovelorn admirer, with bags of money to reveal the identity of Hardress' mistress. Myles angrily rejects his offer, too smitten by the Colleen Bawn to betray her.

Myles, an enthusiastic amateur distiller, visits Sheelah's cottage with a keg of poitín, to the delight of Eily, Father Tom and Sheelah. Over the half-door, Eily spots Hardress coming down the lane towards the cottage, and the others retire to the back room to leave the lovers alone. Hardress tries to cajole Eily into handing over their marriage certificate, so that she has no proof of his commitment to her. Myles emerges heroically from the back room to intercept it, and gives Hardress a stern lecture. Hardress, thwarted by Eily's valiant protector, leaves in a huff. Father Tom, concerned about

7

Eily's interests, advises her to keep her marriage certificate on her person at all times.

Danny meets Hardress later and offers to help him out by doing away with the Colleen Bawn. Hardress throttles him furiously, then gallops away on his high horse. Anne, indignant about Danny's misleading information, goes to Muckross Head to confront Eily about her alleged note to Daly. When Eily refuses to elaborate, Anne gives up on Daly and resolves to marry Hardress instead. She arrives at the stately portico of the Cregan residence to declare her intentions to Mrs Cregan and her son, just as Hardress receives a note sent by Eily, in which she threatens to kill herself if she doesn't see him that night. She believes herself to be the cause of his ruin and can't bear to live with that thought.

Meanwhile, Danny pursues his plan to murder the Colleen Bawn, without his master's consent. He convinces her, under a false pretext, to go with him to Devil's Island, where he tries to drown her by throwing her in the lake. The irrepressible Myles, busy making poitín at his secret still on the island, spots the dastardly servant and shoots him. Danny falls wounded in the water, but manages to swim to his boat and row homewards. He takes to his bed, badly injured. Sheelah finds Eily's cloak by the lakeshore the next day, and shows it to Hardress, who assumes that she committed suicide, as she had threatened to do in her note. The spineless Hardress consents to marry Anne without a further thought for the Colleen Bawn, and the wealthy cousin immediately pays off the mortgage, leaving Corrigan bitterly disappointed that he doesn't get the house.

As Hardress' wedding day approaches, Danny's condition has deteriorated, and on his deathbed he blurts out to his mother Sheelah that he murdered Eily. She fetches Father Tom to hear his last confession, which the eavesdropping Corrigan overhears. Corrigan runs of to get some soldiers to arrest Hardress, since Danny's version of the story implicates his master. Father Tom pays a visit to Myles' cottage, suspecting that Myles knows what really happened, and is surprised to find Eily there very much alive, looked after by the gallant distiller after he rescued her from drowning in the lake.

As Corrigan attempts to have Hardress jailed for murder, Mrs Cregan provides an alibi clearing her son of blame. Father Tom and Myles arrive with Eily, and a sort-of-happy ending follows, in which Mrs Cregan gives her blessing to the dubious union of her feckless son and Eily, and the duped Anne seems content to settle for the dangled suitor Daly, without demanding the money back for the mortgage payments.

The Colleen Bawn is based on the true story of the murder of a sixteen-year-old Limerick girl named Ellie Hanley in 1819. The reporter who covered the trial for the local paper wrote a book about it, which became the basis for Boucicault's play. A title card in the film claims that the bed in which Danny Mann expires originally belonged to Daniel O'Connell, renowned Irish orator, pacifist and lawyer, who defended the accused in the original court case.

THE COLLEEN BAWN
(1911) US silent b&w 30 mins approx

Boucicault's lively dramas and robust social satires were hugely successful on the US stage in the late-19th century, and, in bringing them to the screen, Olcott was virtually guaranteed an audience for stories that were already very familiar to theatre goers on both sides of the Atlantic. The prolific director would go on to film two more Boucicault plays, *Arrah-Na-Pogue* and *The Shaughraun*, in the same year, before departing for the Middle East to shoot *From the Manger to the Cross*, the first American-made screen epic of the life of Christ. For this biblical spectacular, Olcott cast Gene Gauntier, his Colleen Bawn, as the Virgin Mary, and Jack J Clark, his Myles na Copaleen, as Joseph.

FOR IRELAND'S SAKE
(1914) US b&w silent 25 mins approx

Sidney Olcott, director of *For Ireland's Sake*
(Still courtesy of The National Library)

Production Team

Producer .... Sidney Olcott
Director .... Sidney Olcott
Screenplay .... Sidney Olcott
Cinematography .... George Hollister

Cast

Gene Gauntier .... Eileen Donaghue
Jack J Clark .... Marty O'Sullivan
Madam Norina .... Mrs Bridget Donaghue
Sidney Olcott .... Father Flannigan

FOR IRELAND'S SAKE
(1914) US b&w silent 25 mins approx

Sidney Olcott continued to stoke the flames of Irish nationalism with *For Ireland's Sake*, a rebel drama filmed in Kerry and set around the time of the 1798 Rising. The film stars Olcott's preferred leading lady Gene Gauntier as Eileen Donaghue, a patriotic Irish girl. Her 'gosoon' Marty O'Sullivan (Jack J Clark) is a blacksmith, seen hammering glowing metal at his anvil into pikes for the rebels. Surprised at this seditious work by a squad of British soldiers, Marty flees across the countryside with the redcoats close behind. He meets Eileen who helps him with a clever ruse: she conceals him in the folds of her ample cloak, and gives the soldiers wrong directions when they ask her where he went.

Marty goes to a shebeen, and when soldiers arrive outside he seems certain to be caught. With nowhere else to hide, he climbs into the chimney shaft before the soldiers enter. The fire is lit, and he can barely keep from coughing. One of the soldiers flirts with Eileen, then stirs the embers in the hearth. Marty loses his grip and falls down the chimney covered in soot, landing in front of the soldier. A brawl breaks out between the shebeen customers and the redcoats in which the customers get the upper hand, sending the soldiers back to the barracks without their weapons.

The triumphant civilians conceal the soldiers' muskets in a haystack for future use and Marty goes with Eileen to her mother's cottage to wash up, playfully kissing Mrs Donaghue (played by the exotically named Madam Norina) with his sooty face.

At the barracks, the commanding officer is furious that his men have been humiliated and disarmed by a group of shillelagh-toting peasants. He sends his soldiers to search the local cottages looking for Marty and the weapons, and they put a torch to the haystacks without realising that the guns are hidden there. Marty takes refuge in a cave across the lake and Eileen brings him food. A soldier spots Eileen landing her boat at the lakeside, and the next time she crosses to see Marty she is followed by redcoats who arrest the lovers and put them in jail. Eileen's distraught mother runs for the priest, Father Flannigan (Sidney Olcott) when she hears the news, and the two of them go to visit Marty and Eileen in their cells. The priest smuggles a file to Marty the next day as they await sentence after their trial. That night Marty cuts his way to freedom through the bars of his cell window, singing loudly to disguise the rasping sound of metal on metal.

He frees Eileen, and they run to Glen Castlemare, where they are reunited with Father Flannigan and Eileen's mother. Marty impetuously asks Eileen to marry him, and the priest whips out his prayer book to give God's blessing to the union. He also makes Marty toss away a rifle that he had taken from a prison guard as he made his escape. The next morning, Marty and Eileen board a ship bound for America.

Working as his own producer independently of Kalem, the financiers of his first location shoots in Ireland, Olcott remained resistant to pressure from the British authorities to desist from filming rebel-rousing themes. Off-screen, rumours persisted that he played his part for the cause by importing from America 'prop' rifles for his films that were actually the real thing, for use by Kerry Volunteers against the forces of the Crown.

IRELAND A NATION
(1914) US silent b&w 50 mins

Production Team

Producer .... MacNamara Feature Film Company

Director .... Walter MacNamara

Screenplay .... Walter MacNamara

Cast

Barry O'Brien .... Robert Emmet

P J Bourke ....

Fred O'Donovan ....

Barney Magee ....

Patrick Ennis ....

Dominick Reily ....

IRELAND A NATION
(1914) US silent b&w 50 mins

The failed risings of 1798 and 1803 were popular subjects with film-makers in the years leading up to Ireland's independence, and the story of one of the heroes of those years, Robert Emmet, provided enough dramatic value to generate three films during this period. Walter MacNamara's version of the events of this time, *Ireland a Nation*, featured Emmet's visit to France to enlist Napoleon's aid for the Irish cause, and Emmet's return to Ireland to prepare the United Irishmen for the upcoming rebellion.

Originally a five-reel film, the first and final reels of *Ireland a Nation* have been lost and no complete copies of the orginal remain. Existing prints of the film open with Michael Dwyer's men at the old watch tower in County Wicklow, and, amid scenes of the men drilling, catching an informer and being sold out to the infamous Major Sirr, at Dublin Castle, we see a recreation of Emmet's visit to Napoleon to solicit his aid for the Irish cause ("England's Difficulty is Ireland's Opportunity" declares a title card). The diminutive Corsican dictator promises to send ships, guns and men to Ireland, raising the hope of freedom in the United Irishmen back home.

The action returns to Ireland as redcoats scour the countryside for rebels, and come upon a group of Catholics attending a forbidden mass by the banks of a swiftly flowing river. When the redcoats are sighted by a lookout, the congregation starts dancing vigorously, pretending it's a ceili that the soldiers have come upon, and not a clandestine religious ceremony. Dwyer's men are then seen committing to the cause of Ireland with Emmet (Barry O'Brien), and going on manoeuvres at scenic locations in Glendalough (St Kevin's church and the round tower are featured). A group of Dwyer's men is cornered in a cottage in Wicklow, and one of them, Sam MacAllister, is wounded. He bravely sacrifices himself by drawing the fire of the redcoats to allow his comrades to escape in the smoke and confusion. They then make their getaway through the woods.

Another legendary character of that era, Anne Devlin, housekeeper for Emmet and his men in Dublin, is also featured. She is accosted by an informer who tries to bribe her for information about Emmet's hiding place, and she clatters him across the jaw for his impertinence. The informer later spots Emmet talking to Devlin and fetches the army to arrest him, but Emmet has already left to bid farewell to his fiancée, Sarah Curran, before leaving for France. The officer in charge offers a thousand pounds to Devlin to betray Emmet, and when she refuses, she is lashed with sally rods. The soldiers put a noose around her neck, and dangle her from the axle of a cart, almost killing her. She is distraught from her ordeal, but bravely gives nothing away to her inquisitors.

Emmet has another narrow escape at Sarah Curran's palatial residence. A squad of soldiers arrives looking for him seconds after he leaves. But his luck runs out and he is soon caught at Harold's Cross. The defiant patriot leader is brought before Major Sirr at Dublin Castle, and is then jailed as an emissary of France. In a courtroom scene, Emmet's fighting words stir the people in the public gallery, as he declares to the judge, Lord Norbury, that he "has nothing to say that will alter your predetermination". The snivelling informer piously kisses *The Bible* and testifies against Emmet. The judge quickly arrives at his decision, and Emmet is sentenced to hang. Emmet, unbowed, boldly states that he tried to achieve for Ireland that which Washington did for America. He makes his famous request that his epitaph remain unwritten until Ireland is free, and soon Sarah Curran, who is briefly allowed to see him before the execution, is seen placing flowers on an unmarked grave.

The scene flashes forward to a scene of a long-haired maiden chiselling Emmet's gravestone, implying that Ireland is free. She gazes pensively at the monument and then strums a nearby harp. The action returns to the time of Emmet's execution and the informer is shown getting his just desserts when Anne Devlin arranges to meet him by the river, sending in her stead a United Irishman dressed in her cloak. The disguised rebel meets the informer at the appointed time and throws him in the river. Anne Devlin is then shown making an apocryphal escape abroad. The historic recreations end with scenes from 1829 of Daniel O'Connell reproaching himself "that he has lived to see Ireland a province".

Director Walter MacNamara spent months making *Ireland a Nation*, shooting the exterior scenes at the locations described above. The interior scenes were shot in England at Kew Bridge Studios in London.

The original film, released in 1914, was re-released in 1920 with an epilogue of additional newsreel footage. The extra scenes include Eamonn De Valera's fundraising visit to America in 1919 (the Free State leader is featured wearing a snappy new boater), shots of the Black and Tans being inspected by British Prime Minister Lloyd George before setting sail for Ireland, and the funeral of Irish patriot and Lord Mayor of Cork, Terence MacSwiney, who died on hunger strike in London's Brixton Prison in 1920. The funeral cortege through the city streets is shown shadowed by British armoured cars to quell unrest from the placard-bearing protestors.

Though the original version of the film was released in the US in 1914, the first attempt at showing it in Ireland in 1915 was thwarted when the distributors sent the print by ship, on the ill-fated *Lusitainia*. The film finally made its Irish debut a year later, in January 1916, with some scenes removed that were deemed likely to inflame anti-English sentiments in the cinema audience. The film was banned in 1917 when the English authorities feared that the overtly nationalist

IRELAND A NATION
(1914) US silent b&w 50 mins

bias of the film would have a negative effect on the drive to recruit Irish men for the British army, to fight against Germany in the First World War. The surviving film remains a peculiar mix of melodramatic scenes of dubious historical accuracy from the early-19th century, and fascinating newsreel footage of the main protagonists involved in the struggle for independence around the time of the First World War and later.

REGENERATION
(1915) US silent b&w 73 mins

Production Team

Producer .... William Fox
Director .... Raoul Walsh
Screenplay .... Raoul Walsh, Carl Harbaugh
from the autobiographical novel
My Mamie Rose by Owen Kildare
Cinematography .... Georges Benoit

Cast

Rockcliffe Fellowes .... Owen Conway
Anna Q Nilsson .... Marie Deering
William Sheer .... Skinny the Rat
Carl Harbaugh .... Assistant DA Ames
James Marcus .... Jim Conway
Maggie Weston .... Maggie Conway
Johnny McCann .... Owen Conway (aged 10)
Harry McCoy .... Owen Conway (aged 17)
Peggy Barn ....

REGENERATION
(1915) US silent b&w 73 mins

Irish-American director Raoul Walsh shot his seminal silent gangster movie *Regeneration* in the streets of his native New York, establishing himself as a director of hard-edged action drama in his own right after learning his trade under D W Griffith. The honours for creating the gangster film as a cinematic genre belong to Griffith for the short he made three years earlier, *The Musketeers of Pig Alley*, but Walsh is generally credited with making the first full-length gangster feature with *Regeneration*.

Walsh co-wrote the screenplay with actor-writer Carl Harbaugh, adapting from the autobiographical novel *My Mamie Rose* by Owen Kildare. Kildare's life story is a tale of salvation from illiteracy and crime on the streets through the love of a kind-hearted woman. The screenplay follows the life of an Irish slum-dweller, from deprived childhood to juvenile deliquency and eventual reform. A poor young boy named Owen (Johnny McCann) is orphaned when his mother dies. As she is carted off to the cemetery in a humble wicker casket, Owen sits dejected in their shabby tenement. Maggie Conway (Maggie Weston) a ragged washerwoman from the apartment across the hall, takes pity on him and adopts him. Mrs Conway treats Owen well, but her husband Jim (James Marcus) gets violent when he's drunk and beats the boy. Owen takes to the streets, and learns to live by his wits and his fists. As a teenager Owen (Harry McCoy) gets a reputation down the docks for being a good fighter, and by the age of 25 he is the leader of his own gang.

Meanwhile uptown, New York Assistant District Attorney Ames (Carl Harbaugh) starts a campaign to crack down on crime. At a dinner party in the Deering residence, social butterfly Marie Deering (Anna Q Nilsson) remarks to Ames and her other guests how awfully interesting it must be to see some real-live gangsters. The DA offers to show them some. He takes them downtown by hansom cab to Grogan's Beer Hall, where negro minstrels and dancers entertain an audience of Bowery hoodlums, among them Owen Conway (Rockcliffe Fellowes) and his gang. Some of the thugs recognise the DA and accost him for cramping their style, brandishing in his face newspaper reports of his war on crime. Ames' guests are terrified. Owen notices Marie, and intervenes to save the DA from a brutal beating. Ames and his entourage make a hasty exit from Grogan's, but before they go back uptown Marie is transfixed by the words of a firebrand activist addressing a crowd in the street, demanding hospitals and schools for the neighbourhood. He implores the people to give their time as volunteers for the poor, and stirs Marie's conscience, inspiring her to become a social worker in a Settlement House.

The workers at the Settlement House organise a riverboat excursion up the Hudson, and Marie kindly invites Owen and his gang along when she sees them malingering on the dockside. As the evening progresses the tenement dwellers are enjoying themselves dancing on deck. Then disaster strikes: a gang member named Skinny (William Sheer) drops a lit cigarette end on a frayed coil of rope, setting the boat on fire. The passengers jump overboard in panic, capsizing the lifeboats. But all are saved when a tug from the Shamrock Towing Company comes to the rescue, as the riverboat burns to the water line. Owen and Marie cross paths again at the Settlement House, when Marie's staff needs some muscle to help Mrs Flaherty get her baby back from her violent brute of a husband. Owen is called in to help, and he duly flattens Flaherty, rescues the baby, and brings him safely to his mother at the Settlement House. Maire is so delighted that she rewards Owen by teaching him to read and write. Soon the social worker and the street thug develop a warm rapport, much to the annoyance of the DA, who has designs on Marie.

Owen's increasing involvement with Marie and the Settlement House leave an opening for devious gang member Skinny to take over the leadership of the Conway mob. But when Skinny knifes a cop, he comes to his old leader for help. Marie is horrified when she finds out that Owen has shielded Skinny from the police, and she is convinced that he has lapsed back to his old ways. The DA is delighted, certain that she'll have nothing more to do with Conway.

While Owen consults his priest for advice, Marie searches for him at the gang's basement hideout. Skinny takes her upstairs, locks her in a room, and molests her. A friend of Owen's hears her screams and runs to get the cops. While the police subdue the gang in the basement with nightsticks, Owen runs upstairs to save Marie. Skinny heads out the window for the fire escape when Owen arrives, and shooting back at Owen, he hits Marie. She dies beatifically from her wounds a few days later. As Owen and the cops search for Skinny, the murderer packs in a hurry to go on the lam. Owen tracks him down before he gets away, and, in a blind rage, tries to strangle him; but the saintly Marie appears in a vision, interrupting him in mid-throttle, and makes him realise that killing Skinny would be wrong. Skinny makes a daring escape bid out the window, climbing across a clothesline in the tenement courtyard. From below, Owen's friend from the Settlement House fires a gun and hits Skinny, who falls to his death.

The film concludes with a scene in which the grieving Owen pays tribute at Marie's graveside to her pure and noble spirit, and pledges to live the rest of his life as the changed man she made him.

Regeneration remains a stark testament to the hardships Irish immigrants faced in the crowded, filthy slums of urban America in the early years of the 20th century. Director Walsh tackles head-on the violence, drunkeness and illiteracy that were the norm in poor neighbourhoods, and elicits an extraordinary performance, in the adult Conway role, from his star Rockcliffe Fellowes. A Canadian actor with the machismo and pouty insolence of a young Brando, Fellowes exudes charisma in subtle shades of sympathy and menace, marred only a little by the primitive editing. In marked contrast, Anna Q Nilsson, a pre-Garbo Swedish import, delivers a range of facial histrionics that might be viewed more appropriately from the cheap seats of a vaudeville theatre. Nilsson would go on to become a charity worker in real life, when the

REGENERATION
(1915) US silent b&w 73 minutes

talkies and a riding accident ended her film career.

Regeneration's fire on the river is all but extraneous to the plot of the film, but it gave Walsh the opportunity to shoot exciting scenes of pandemonium on deck as the smoke engulfed the boat and the passengers headed en masse for the water. Legend has it that when the negative cutters scrutinised the scenes of female passengers jumping overboard with their abundant petticoats flying up over their heads, they discovered that some of the women weren't wearing any underwear. Artists were engaged to hand-paint ladies' bloomers onto each individual frame to restore modesty.

The riverboat fire scenes were more than likely based on a real-life New York disaster from a few years earlier, involving the greatest loss of life the city has ever seen in one accident. In the summer of 1904, an East River paddleboat called the *General Slocum* caught fire, and more than a thousand passengers bound for a church picnic lost their lives, mere yards from the New York shoreline.

O'NEIL OF THE GLEN
(1916) IRL silent b&w 30 mins approx

THE
FILM COMPANY of IRELAND LTD.
Telegraphic Address: Fileaire, Dublin.   Telephone: Dublin 4487.
EXCLUSIVES THAT PAY! PAY! PAY!
'NOUGH SAID WHEN THE PAY-BOX SPEAKS!
BUY FILMS THAT DRAW Crowded Houses Every Night!
"O'NEIL OF THE GLEN" (In Prologue and THREE ACTS).
Played by Irish Players and produced in prettiest spots in Ireland.
FIRST FILM RELEASED by the FILM COMPANY OF IRELAND
Drew crowded houses all the week to one of the largest Picture Houses in Dublin, notwithstanding tropical heat   THE EXHIBITOR'S VIEW: Mr. F. R. Sparling, Bohemian Picture House, Dublin (where "O'Neil of the Glen" was shown exclusively August 7th to 13th) wrote to the Film Company:—"I have been
PACKED SOLID ALL THE WEEK.
Absolutely whole-hearted appreciation by all who saw it, and the
MUSIC AT THE PAY-BOX has kept time with the Orchestra throughout.
THE FILM COMPANY OF IRELAND,
34, Dame Street, Dublin,
Now offers in this splendid Film SOLE BRITISH and COLONIAL RIGHTS.
FOUR SPARKLING IRISH COMEDIES FOR RELEASE IN SEPTEMBER:
"THE MISER'S GIFT" TWO REELS "WOMAN'S WIT" TWO REELS
"FOOD OF LOVE" TWO REELS "UNFAIR LOVE AFFAIR" TWO REELS
The Company is at present engaged in producing the following photo-plays:
"BLARNEY," "THE GIRL FROM THE GOLDEN VALE,"
(Tipperary Romance.)
"THE UPSTART," "TREASURE TROVE," "THE BYE-WAYS OF FATE," "WILLIE REILLY," "The IRISH GIRL."
BOOK AT ONCE—
FILM COMPANY OF IRELAND, LTD.,
34, Dame Street, Dublin.

(Still courtesy of The National Library)

Production Team
Producer .... Film Company of Ireland
Director .... Fred O'Donovan
Screenplay .... Mr W T Lysaght
adapted from a story
by Mrs M T Pender

Cast
J M Kerrigan .... Magroome
Brian Magowan .... Don O'Neil
Fred O'Donovan .... Graves
Nora Clancy .... Nola Tremaine
J M Carre .... Tremaine
J Smith ....
R V Justine ....

O'NEIL OF THE GLEN
(1916) IRL silent b&w 30 mins approx

The first native company to make Irish shorts and features was the Film Company of Ireland, founded by entrepreneur and returned emigrant J M Sullivan. After some initial setbacks (attributable largely to the fact that they set up offices in what is now O'Connell Street a few weeks before the 1916 Easter Rising), the FCOI produced a series of comedies and romances featuring prominent players from the Dublin theatres. The output continued steadily between 1916 and 1920, gradually developing a more nationalist subtext as the political mood of Ireland shifted during the War of Independence. An early offering, *O'Neil of the Glen* deals with a romance between two young people who must come to terms with a dark secret that undermines their love.

O'Neil, a man of considerable means, has foolishly left control of his assets in the hands of his profligate solicitor Tremaine (J M Carre), and becomes angry when he finds out that Tremaine has squandered the lot, leaving him with nothing. He visits Tremaine to demand redress, and when the solicitor refuses to remedy the problem to his satisfaction, O'Neil decides to leave. As he is about to go, Tremaine shoots him to avoid the consequences of his financial mismanagement.

As O'Neil lies dying he is too feeble to name his killer, but his angry manservant Magroome (J M Kerrigan) swears revenge before O'Neil's son, as his father expires. The son, Don O'Neil (Brian Magowan), grows up and falls in love with Tremaine's daughter Nola (Nora Clancy), rescuing her from an accident that almost cost her her life, not knowing that her father is his father's murderer. But she has another suitor – the malevolant Graves (Fred O'Donovan), who has come in possession of information from Tremaine's private diary that lets him know that Tremaine is the killer of O'Neil senior. He blackmails Tremaine with this information so that Tremaine will allow him to propose to his daughter, and the weak Tremaine consents. But Nola refuses his offer. Graves become furious, and directs his attention to his rival, Don O'Neil. He tries to kill him but doesn't succeed. As a last resort to turn the lovers against each other, he bursts out with the news to Nola that her father had killed Don's father many years previously. She is so shocked that she moves far away. But her love for Don proves stronger than the tragic circumstance of their childhood, and the couple reunites.

Director J M Kerrigan made his acting debut with this romantic melodrama for the Film Company of Ireland, and would go on to direct more than half a dozen light comedies and romances for the company in that same year. He later achieved international recognition in Hollywood as a character actor, most notably in John Ford's *The Informer* in which he played Gypo Nolan's drinking partner Terry, and *Gone with the Wind*, as the cruel millowner Gallagher. Fred O'Donovan had previously made a name for himself on the Irish stage in Synge's *The Playboy of the Western World*, in the title role of pseudo-patricidal Christy Mahon. He worked occasionally as director for the FCOI, and continued his sporadic screen-acting career over the next three decades with *Ourselves Alone*, *The Vicar of Bray* and *Another Shore*.

WHEN LOVE CAME TO GAVIN BURKE
(1917) IRL silent b&w 40 mins approx

Fred O'Donovan, director of *When Love Came to Gavin Burke*
(Still courtesy of The National Library)

Production Team

Producer .... Film Company Of Ireland
Director .... Fred O'Donovan
Screenplay .... Fred O'Donovan

Cast

Fred O'Donovan .... Gavin Burke
Nora Clancy .... Kate O'Malley
Oonah Halpin .... Grace (child)
Brian Magowan .... Jack Devine
Valentine Roberts .... Tom Ryan
Kathleen Murphy .... Queenie Coleman
Stephen Gould .... John Ronan

WHEN LOVE CAME TO GAVIN BURKE
(1917) IRL silent b&w 40 mins approx

Abbey actor Fred O'Donovan made his directorial debut for the FCOI as well as playing the title role in *When Love Came to Gavin Burke*, a story shot on location in the Irish countryside, in which love triumphs over money.

An attractive young woman named Kate O'Malley (Nora Clancy) has two suitors, a poor hard-working farmer named Gavin Burke (Fred O'Donovan) and a wealthy merchant and hotelier named John Ronan (Stephen Gould). She doesn't fancy the hardships that the future holds if she marries Gavin, so she opts instead to marry John. Gavin is left inconsolable. He gives up on romance and sets his mind to business, becoming, after many years of hard work, a prosperous merchant. John Ronan, by contrast, has fared badly, and lost all his money after taking to the drink. The only consolation in Kate's life, as her husband becomes more dissolute, is their daughter Grace (Oonah Halpin).

Grace falls ill and has to be taken to the doctor by her father. On the way he falls from his horse near Gavin's house and is fatally injured. Grace runs to Gavin's house for help, but nothing can be done, and her father is already dead. The wealthy but lonely Gavin is charmed by the little child, and, when he finds out who she is, he decides to adopt her as an act of revenge against her mother for jilting him. He strikes a cruel bargain with the impoverished Kate – that he will raise the child himself in comfort, if the mother promises never to see her again. Kate reluctantly goes along with this scheme, believing it is in Grace's best interest. Grace grows up, and as a young adult faces the same dilemma that her mother did many years earlier. She has two admirers, one poor, the other not, but unlike her mother she follows her heart's desire and marries the penniless Jack Devine (Brian Magowan). His rival, Tom Ryan (Valentine Roberts) becomes insanely jealous and tries to kill Jack, but only succeeds in making Grace's love stronger.

As Grace's wedding day approaches, Kate desperately wants to give her daughter some expensive gifts. Reduced by this time to working as a maid in the hotel that her late husband had owned when they were first married, Kate steals some money from her employer. Gavin is blamed, and, given the chance to clear his name by identifying the real culprit, he decides to spare Kate the humiliation of being branded a thief. He also softens in his attitude towards her, and lets her attend Grace's wedding. When he sees how lonely she looks as the young newlyweds depart on their honeymoon, his heart softens even more and he realises that he still loves her. After giving all his money to his adopted daughter and her new husband, Gavin and Kate are once again on equal footing. They both realise that love is far more important than money, and when he asks her to marry him this time, she happily consents.

This rural melodrama marked a jump in scale for the FCOI from the frivolous three-reel comedies and shorts that had previously been the norm for the company. The screening in Ireland of epic films from the US would soon inspire FCOI founder James M Sullivan to produce even more ambitious works from the canon of 19th century Irish literature by Charles Kickham and William Carleton.

KNOCKNAGOW
(1918) IRL silent b&w 90 mins approx

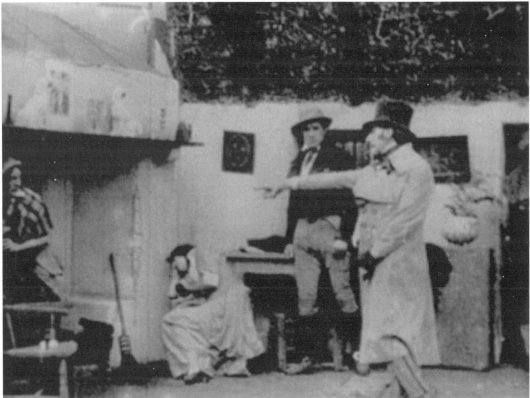

(Still courtesy of the Irish Film Archive of the Film Institute of Ireland)

Production Team

Producer .... FCOI / James M Sullivan
Director .... Fred O'Donovan
Screenplay .... Mrs N F Patton
from the novel of the same
name by Charles Kickham

Cast

Brian Macgowan .... Mat 'the Thrasher'
O'Donovan
Fred O'Donovan .... Arthur O'Connor
Arthur Shields .... Phil Lahy, the tailor
Brenda Burke .... Honor Lahy
Kathleen Murphy .... Norah Lahy
J M Carre .... Pender
Alice Keating .... Bessie Morris
Breffni O'Rourke .... Billy Heffernan
Valentine Roberts .... Father O'Carroll
Patrick O'Donnell .... Barney 'Wattletoes'
Broderick
Dermot O'Dowd .... Maurice Kearney
Nora Clancy .... Mary Kearney
George Larchet .... Henry Lowe
Charles Power .... Sir Garrett Butler
Miss Rooney .... Nellie O'Donovan
Moira Breffni .... Peg Brady
Cyril Cusack .... Mick Brian's son

Charles Kickham's sprawling, unwieldy novel *Knocknagow* was one of the bestselling Irish books of the late-19th century, and its undiminshed popularity in the early years of the 20th made it a prime target for cinematic treatment. Inspired by the success of the American epics of D W Griffith, the Film Company of Ireland adapted the book for the screen to create one of the country's most ambitious native productions of the silent era. The screenplay, written by Mrs N F Patton, shifts the setting of the Kickham's 1873 novel to 1847, at the end of the famine years, giving the film a more volatile timeframe than the original. Set in County Tipperary, the film is a melodrama involving a complex tangle of rural romances set against a tense backdrop of evictions and land clearances by a conniving landlord's agent.

Mary Kearney (Nora Clancy), the attractive young daughter of prosperous tenant farmers in Knocknagow, County Tipperary, has two admirers. One of them, Henry (George Larchet), is the nephew of her parents' landlord, Sir Garrett Butler (Charles Power). The other, Arthur (Fred O'Donovan), is a sensitive seminary student. He tries to meet with Mary on Christmas Day but the unreliable servant, Barney (Patrick O'Donnell), fails to deliver his note to her. His attraction to Mary makes him realise that he's not suited for celibacy and doesn't have a true vocation for the priesthood - the only heavenly thing he wants to study is "the blue in Mary's eyes". He discusses the problem with his mentor Father O'Carroll (Valentine Roberts), who advises him to study medicine instead. He backs up this suggestion by offering to pay the tuition fees.

Mat O'Donovan (Brian Magowan), ace sportsman, star of the Knocknagow hurling team and popular man-about-town, visits the local tailor Phil Lahy (Arthur Shields, brother of Barry Fitzgerald), a tippler with a consumptive daughter (Kathleen Murphy), to collect a jacket Lahy is making for him to wear to a wedding. Pender (J M Carre), the landlord's agent and the villain of the piece, arrives at the tailor's shop while Mat is there and insults the Lahys, prompting him to defend them. Mrs Lahy prevents Mat from striking Pender. The ill-tempered land agent leaves, vowing to get revenge on Mat. Pender hatches a devious plan to evict many of the village farmers under his control, including Mat. Mat tells him that he may take the fields that he rents but he can't take the house since he owns it freehold.

Pender brings an eviction team to the Brians' cottage and evicts the family, throws their goods on the street and burns their house down, while the bailiffs hold back an angry mob with poles. The Brians and their son (a very young Cyril Cusack) are left homeless and take shelter in a ditch. The angry Mick Brian finds a gun belonging to Kearney and plans to shoot Pender to avenge the loss of his house, but he can't bring himself to do it and throws the gun into a pond. The gun had been sent by Kearney to Mat for repair but Mat's careless servant Barney lost it en route.

Meanwhile, Mat wears his new jacket to Ned Brophy's wedding, and he and his friends dance in the barn, blissfully unaware of the evictions of their friends and

KNOCKNAGOW
(1918) IRL silent b&w 90 mins approx

neighbours. Pender continues his fiendish work, evicting the Hogans, a family with a son decorated for bravery in the Queen's army. Mat runs into some romantic dischord when he is led to believe that the woman he loves, Bessie Morris (Alice Keating), is still carrying on with a dragoon she met in Clonmel a year earlier. Mat has a fight with Bessie, beats up the dragoon, and decides to leave Ireland to make a new start in America. Pender observes the proceedings and decides to use them to his advantage.

When Pender realises that Mat plans to emigrate, he decides to steal the rent money from his absentee empoyer, Sir Garrett, and blame Mat for the crime. He hatches a plot with Bessie's dragoon, offering him £100 for his help in framing Mat. Pender plants evidence incriminating the gallent hurler as he packs to leave and says his farewells. Mick Brian is upset at Mat's departure and la-

(Still courtesy of the Irish Film Archive of the Film Institute of Ireland)

ments, "What curse is on this land of ours when men like Mat Donovan are forced from its shores?" But Mat does not get far – he is arrested off the boat in Liverpool and brought back in handcuffs to jail in Ireland. He spends Christmas behind bars in Clonmel Prison. Bessie, distressed by Mat's incarceration but convinced of his innocence, decides to leave Ireland herself for the USA, where her father already lives. Kearney and Mat's servant Barney provide an alibi for Mat and he is released from jail. There's a big turnout at the Kearney residence to welcome Mat home. Kearney himself makes a stirring speech ful of veiled references to Irish independence, to denounce the injustice that Mat suffered.

Swanning about in Italy, the landlord Sir Garrett tells his daughter about happy, carefree Knocknagow, but his nephew Henry arrives with the harsh truth about Pender's land clearances, done in Sir Garrett's name. He lets him know that poor women and children are being driven from their hovels to perish by the roadside and dramatically paints a vivid picture of burning cottages and destitute peasants.

Sir Garrett returns in haste to his estate as Pender is about to evict the Kearneys for late payment of rent, and is met with a hostile reception from Kearney for driving decent people into a state of poverty. Sir Garrett has Pender arrested, to the delight of the evicted tenants. Pender cringes and begs for mercy, in the traditional manner of the defeated scoundrel. Mat resumes his interrupted trip to the US and travels across

KNOCKNAGOW
(1918) IRL silent b&w 90 mins approx

the country in search of his beloved Bessie. When he eventually finds her way out in the west, Mat convinces her to leave the fine mansion of her father and return with him to live in a humble thatched cottage at Knocknagow. Mat brings her back as his bride and they find that, in their absence, their friends Mary Kearney and Arthur O'Connor have also married (little effort is made to portray America convincingly - the 'far west' where Mat finds Bessie has a backdrop of castellated granite walls of rhododendron bushes, not unlike Tipperary).

The bitter social grievances folded between layers of romantic trifle in *Knocknagow* gave considerable cause for concern to the British authorities at a time when Sinn Féin candidates were sweeping the elections in Ireland and the struggle for independence was getting out of the control of the London government. *Knocknagow* fared well commercially in the US in Irish immigrant communities, and also in Britain to the alarm of reviewers disturbed by its unapologetically nationalist tone.

IN THE DAYS OF ST PATRICK
(1920) IRL silent b&w 69 mins approx

(Still courtesy of the British Film Institute)

Production Team

Producer ....General Film Company
                          of Ireland / Norman Whitten
Director .... Norman Whitten
Screenplay .... Mr McGuinness
Cinematography .... J Gordon Lewis

Cast

Ira Allen .... St Patrick
Vernon Whitten .... St Patrick as a child
Gilbert Green ...... St Patrick as an adolescent
Alice Cardinall .... Conchessa Patrick's ma
Dermot McCarthy .... Calpurnius
Alice Keating .... Lupita
J B Carrickford .... St Martin
Ernest Matthewson .... Bishop Tussach
George Brame .... Pope Celestine
George Griffin .... King Laoghaire
Maude Hume .... Queen
Mary Murnane .... Foster mother
Patrick McDonnell ... Foster-father of Patrick
Herbert Mayne .... Gornias, blind hermit
Eddie Lawless .... Milcho
T O'Carroll Reynolds .... Niall
Charles Doyle .... Dichu
C Byrne .... Benignus

IN THE DAYS OF ST PATRICK
(1920) IRL silent b&w 69 mins approx

The most lavish screen epic made in Ireland during the silent era was Norman Whitten's historic five-reeler of the life of Ireland's patron saint. *In the Days of St Patrick* charts his progress from childhood in Wales, slavery in Ireland, and his eventual escape, to return as a missionary and lead the benighted natives of the island away from paganism to a life of wholesome Christianity.

Whitten's film opens in the early part of the 5th century. Young Patrick (Vernon Whitten) and his sister Lupita (Alice Keating) are living in fosterage in Wales, where the holy lad performs his first miracle by turning blocks of ice into fuel for the fire. The Welsh coast and hinterland are attacked by Irish pirates, and Patrick is hauled away by Niall of The Nine Hostages (T O'Carroll Reynolds, looking like Genghis Khan with hoop earrings and pointy helmet) and brought to Ireland, where he is sold at a slave auction. He is bought by Milcho, King of Dal Riada, who puts him to work as a swineherd. Patrick endures the ordeal with an unwavering Christian faith, and learns the language of this heathen nation. After six years he makes his escape with foreign traders, following a tip from an angel that he'd find their ship at Killala Strand. Though happy to be free, he is haunted by visions of Irish children leading sinful pagan lives, so he resolves to improve their spiritual lot. He studies for the priesthood in France, at Marmoutier, and is later appointed bishop by Pope Celestine in Rome.

Patrick then sets forth for Ireland armed with a strong Christian faith and an ability to put manners on serpents. He visits the aged Milcho, his former owner, who is terrified by this new religion and sets his own house on fire. The most important pagan festival of the year approaches, and by tradition, Laoghaire, High King of Ireland, lights the first bonfire of Bealtaine at Tara. As soon as it is visible, all the chieftains light their beacons until every hilltop in Ireland is ablaze. Unaware of this custom, Patrick lights an Easter fire at Slane ahead of the optimum pagan time, infuriating Laoghaire. He demands an explanation from Patrick, who seizes the opportunity to preach his Christian teachings to Laoghaire's court. Patrick survives a poisoning attempt by Laoghaire's druid, and destroys the stronghold of idolatry at Mag Slecht. In classic patrician garb, he gives the snakes their marching orders (two kinds are featured – the rubber joke shop variety, and larger serpents that look like draught excluders from behind front doors in the windy hallways of Ireland). The ailing saint is then shown on his deathbed, his life's work complete.

Director Whitten followed the dramatised scenes of the saint's life with modern footage of places associated with his missionary journey through the island. Masochistic pilgrims with their best slacks rolled up to mid-thigh are shown climbing the unforgiving shale pile of Croagh Patrick on their knees. Cardinal Logue, less than camera-ready, is also shown, blinking vacantly at the camera like he'd just been woken up from his afternoon nap to get his picture taken. These contrasting scenes leave the modern viewer with the abiding impression that when the ancient pagans swapped the splendours of Laoghaire's Tara with its tapestries, chariots, burnished shields and dancing maidens, for the burlap-clad asceticism of the missionaries' religion, Ireland became a duller place indeed.

WILLY REILLY AND HIS COLLEEN BAWN
(1920) IRL silent b&w 90 mins approx

(Still courtesy of the Irish Film Archive of the Film Institute of Ireland)

Production Team

Producer .... Fim Company of Ireland/
                      John MacDonagh
Director .... John MacDonagh
Screenplay .... Dr D A Moriarty
        from the novel by William Carleton

Cast

Brian Magowan .... Willy Reilly
Frances Alexander .... Helen Folliard
        ("known throughout the land as
                    the Collen Bawn")
Dermot O'Dowd .... Squire Folliard
Richard Sheridan .... Tom the Fool
Barrett MacDonnell .... Red Rapparree
Séamus MacBlante ..... Sir Robert Whitecrafte

WILLY REILLY AND HIS COLLEEN BAWN
(1920) IRL silent b&w 90 mins approx

Director John MacDonagh wastes no time in establishing the fact that the main characters of this 18th century romantic drama are of different religions – handsome, dashing Willy Reilly is a Catholic gentleman ("not one of the Queen's Reillys") and Squire Folliott is a Protestant – a difference which causes problems for the Squire when his daughter meets Willy and they fall in love. Willy Reilly (Brian Magowan) rescues Squire Folliard (Dermot O'Dowd) and his servant, lost on a moor and held at gunpoint by the dastardly Red Rapparee (Barrett MacDonnell) and his gang. Willy sends Red Rapparee on his way, and escorts the Squire home safely to his house. There he meets the squire's daughter, the beautiful Helen Folliard (Frances Alexander), known throughout the country as 'the Colleen Bawn'. Willy is smitten by her.

During the night, Red Rapparee climbs the battlements and fiendishly tries to abduct Helen. Willy is forewarned of Red's attack by the ubiquitous servant Tom the Fool (Richard Sheridan), who overhears every scheme in the film. Willy foils the abduction attempt, and Helen's heart is won over by his gallantry. Willy soon finds that he has a rival for Helen's hand – Sir Robert Whitecrafte (Séamus MacBlante), "notorious as a Catholic hunter during the penal laws". Sir Robert hears of Helen's fondness for Willy, and hatches a cunning plot with Red Rapparee to discredit her Catholic suitor – the highwayman agrees to tell the squire that he was paid by Willy to do the hold up, allowing Willy to effect a sham rescue, ingratiate himself with Folliard, and then court his daughter. The squire invites Sir Robert to dinner at his house that night where he meets Willy Reilly. Sir Robert is so rude to Willy that Helen leaves the table in disgust, and Willy is not far behind. Left alone with the unwitting squire, Whitecrafte tells him of the spurious plot between Red Rapparee and Willy, and brings in Red, who has been waiting ouside, to verify the story. The Squire is very perplexed, and paces in the wood-panelled splendour of his mansion wondering what to do. The Squire declares to Sir Robert that Willy must be hunted down if he is guilty of perpetrating this outrage.

Tom the Fool overhears this exchange, and warns Helen that Willy is in danger. She sends him with a note to Willy, who is relaxing at home with his wolfhounds. Willy bids farewell to the Colleen Bawn, grabs the deeds to his house, and goes on the run. He meets with a sympathetic Protestant clergyman, Reverend Brown, who, appalled at Whitecrafte's excesses, helps Willy transfer ownership of his house to a trusted friend named Hastings. This transfer theoretically prevents Whitecrafte from legally confiscating the property; but, unaware that this has taken place, Whitecrafte burns Willy's mansion.

Squire Folliott announces that Helen will marry Whitecrafte in one month, leaving her in despair. Her maid conveys the news to Willy, who is hiding at one of his tenant's cottages. He disguises himself as a gardener to get close to the Folliott residence, and Helen is delighted to see him, but he is soon spotted.

Helen and Willy decide to elope, but en route they are caught by Sir Robert. Squire

Folliott drags his daughter home where she resumes her posture of despair. Helen had given Willy her jewelry for safe-keeping, and he's jailed on the false charge of stealing it, a hanging crime in those days. Seeing how badly affected his daughter is after Willy's arrest, Folliott visits him in jail with a final offer of salvation – if he changes his religion, charges will be dropped, otherwise he faces the rope. Willy remains defiant and unbending.

Meanwhile, Whitecrafte's outrageous behaviour has incensed Reverend Brown enough to send Hastings to Dublin, to obtain a warrant for the scurrilous arsonist's arrest. By the time he comes back, the wedding guests are assembled to see the reluctant bride Helen numbly greet her repugnant groom. Hastings and Brown arrive in the nick of time with a warrant for Whitecrafte's arrest as they are about to be married. Soon both Sir Robert and Red Rapparee find themselves up before the same judge who would shortly decide Willy Reilly's fate. The judge takes the hardline, dons his black veil, and sentences the scoundrels to be hanged.

Willy Reilly is placed on trial for his life, and the Colleen Bawn testifies in his favour concerning the jewels. She waits anxiously outside, and when she hears the

(Still courtesy of the Irish Film Archive of the Film Institute of Ireland)

WILLY REILLY AND HIS COLLEEN BAWN
(1920) IRL silent b&w 90 mins approx

(Still courtesy of the Irish Film Archive of the Film Institute of Ireland)

juryman pronounce Willy guilty, she loses her reason, not realising that it is for the lesser offence of abducting a minor, and not the hanging offence of stealing her jewels. Willy is sentenced to seven years in exile, news he handles stoically. But the insane and inconsolable Colleen Bawn believes him dead.

Seven years pass and he returns home, to be told by Reverand Brown that the Colleen Bawn never recovered from the shock. At Folliott's, the Squire greets him warmly, hoping Willy can restore his daughter's reason, and he apologises for the stubborn pride that caused the problem in the first place. Willy embraces Helen and she becomes her old self. A brief epilogue shows them sitting happily at the fireplace in Squire Folliott's with a baby daughter for Willy and Helen, and the old Squire puffing contentedly on his pipe.

THE FOUR HORSEMEN OF THE APOCALYPSE
(1921) US silent b&w w/col tint 132 mins approx

Production Team

Producer .... Metro
Director .... Rex Ingram
Screenplay .... June Mathis
                                based on the novel by
                                Vicente Blasco Ibañez
Cinematography .... John Seitz
Editor .... Grant Whytock

Cast

Rudolph Valentino .... Julio Desnoyers
Alice Terry .... Marguerite Laurier
Joseph Swickard .... Julio's father
John Sainpolis .... Wounded husband
Nigel de Brulier .... Tchernoff, the mystic
Bowditch Turner ....
Wallace Beery ....
Alan Hale ....
Jean Hersholt ....
Edward Connelly ....
Stuart Holmes ....
Ramon Samaniegos ....
Beatrice Dominguez .... Tango Dancer
Pomeroy Cannon .... Madariaga
                                                'the Centaur'

THE FOUR HORSEMEN OF THE APOCALYPSE
(1921) US silent b&w w/col tint 132 mins approx

A daring anti-war statement released less than three years after World War I ended, *The Four Horsemen of the Apocalypse* is the epic masterpiece of the silent era that made a star of a bit-part player named Rudolph Valentino and raised to the level of art a medium that had been widely perceived until then as a passing fad. The critical and commercial success of the film elevated its director, Rex Ingram, to the same league as the top artists of the silent cinema, Erich von Stroheim and D W Griffith, and would cement his reputation in Hollywood as a resolute perfectionist. This triumvirate of ambitious film-makers dared to take the subject matter of screenplays above the level of tearjerkers, slapstick comedies and damsel-in-distress three-reelers that were the norm at the time, and challenged audiences with themes that required serious thought. Ingram's work matched Griffith's for scale but surpassed him in its seamless sophistication, and was to influence von Stroheim's legendary, sprawling *Greed* three year later.

Rex Ingram was born Reginald Hitchcock in Ireland, in 1893. The son of a clergyman, he spent his childhood in the Dublin suburb of Rathmines and his teen years in the rectory at Kinnity, County Offaly, before emigrating to the US. He studied sculpture at Yale, developing skills that would serve him well later on in his career for storyboarding, costumes and set design. He moved to Hollywood to work in film, changing his name to Ingram, his mother's family name, as he considered Hitchcock to be unpalatable to the public (in the late-1920s he was to advise an aspiring English director named Alfred Hitchcock to do the same). A series of successes with films set in exotic locales and the support of screenwriter June Mathis earned him a spot in the director's chair for *The Four Horsemen of the Apocalypse*, the rights to which had just been bought by Metro from its author, Spanish writer Vicente Blasco Ibañez. Mathis was also largely instrumental in casting the unknown Valentino in the lead role, despite strong opposition from the studio, which would have preferred an established star.

The film begins at a hacienda in Argentina run by a formidable patriarch, Madariaga (Pomeroy Cannon), known as 'the Centaur', whose two daughters are married to European immigrants, one from Germany, the other from France. The grandfather can't abide the Teutonic branch of the in-laws, and his favourite in the extended family is from the French side – his grandson, Julio (Rudolph Valentino). Julio is a suave playboy whose romantic credentials are established in the immortal scene in a taverna in Bueños Aires' Boca quarter, in which he dances a sensuous tango with a local girl (Beatrice Dominguez). When the Centaur dies, the two branches of the family divide his fortune and return to France and Germany respectively. In France, Julio's father Marcelo Desnoyers (Josef Swickard) becomes obsessed with antiques and purchases a chateau at Villeblanche to house his collection. Julio remains a dissolute libertine, living as an artist and scrounging money and jewellery from his mother to pay for his bohemian lifestyle. He also teaches tango to the wives of wealthy Parisians, and has an affair with one of them, Marguerite Laurier (Alice Terry). Marguerite's husband is a friend of his father's, and a scandal ensues that is interrupted by the outbreak of the First World War.

Marguerite's husband enlists, and she becomes a nurse. Laurier (John Sainpolis) is blinded in battle and his wife, feeling guilty about her affair, nurses his injuries without him realising her identity. At his Paris studio, Julio is visited periodically by his ascetic neighbour Tchernoff, (Nigel de Brulier), a visionary who shows him an ancient tome that makes a clear connection between the horrors of the Great War and the dread predictions of the *Book of Revelations*. As the German army advances through France, Villeblanche is destroyed by artillery, and Marcelo is forced to accommodate the victori-

ous Germans, among them his nephew, in his chateau. Julio eventually joins the French army, to his father's delight, and fights at the front, where he is killed in battle. In the final scenes of the film at a war cemetery, the mystic, Christ-like Tchernoff gestures at a field of white crosses stretching as far as the eye can see, and declares "I knew them all!"

The recurrence of Ingram's film in best-of lists the world over is due in no small part to his perfectionism as director and his active involvement in camerawork, art direction, lighting and set design. He demanded a lot of his cast and crew, drilling the extras for hours so that their marching would be believable in the epic battle

(Still courtesy of The National Library)

scenes, and he was known to send the actors to foreign language lessons – despite the fact that the film was silent – to get in character for their parts as French artists or German soldiers (and to make the film credible for lip-readers in the audience in countries where those languages were spoken!). And to ensure authenticity in military matters, Ingram hired his brother, Colonel F C Hitchcock, to advise on uniforms and weaponry. The film features hand-tinted colour fantasy scenes, horrific depictions of hell, and battle carnage on a scale not seen since Griffith's *Birth of a Nation* six years earlier. Ingram's skill with scenes of epic proportion was matched by his ability with intimate exchanges. The subtlety and sophistication of the love scenes between Valentino and Alice Terry were in marked contrast with the standards of the contemporary cinema, which usually painted its emotions in clumsily broad strokes. Terry, the daughter of a County Kildare farmer named Taaffe who emigrated to the States before she was born, would later become Ingram's wife.

Though his success with *The Four Horsemen of the Apocalypse* would give him enormous budgets to work with and a free hand in choosing subject matter in subsequent studio projects, Ingram quickly tired of Hollywood. Finding his artistic will too frequently at odds with the commercial exigencies that dominated the US movie industry even then, Ingram left for Europe in 1923 and began operating in the south of France. He assumed control of the Victorine studio in Nice with US backing, and began making films again on his own terms, most notable among them *Mare Nostrum* and *The Magician*, based on the life of Aleister Crowley.

His output dwindled towards the end of the silent era as his themes became gradually less marketable, and he was virtually inert in the film world from the early sound era up to his early death in 1950.

IRISH DESTINY
(1926) IRL silent b&w 50 mins approx

(Still courtesy of the Irish Film Archive of the Film Institute of Ireland)

Production Team

Producer	Eppel Films/Ireland
Director	Dr Isaac Eppel
Screenplay	Dr Isaac Eppel
Cinematography	Joe Rosenthal

Cast

Paddy Dunne Cullinane	Denis O'Hara
Frances MacNamara	Moira Barry
Clifford Pembroke	Mr O'Hara
Daisy Campbell	Mrs O'Hara
Brian Magowan	Gilbert Beecher
Cathal MacGarvey	Shanahan, the jarvey
Evelyn Henchey	Kitty Shanahan
Kit O'Malley	Captain Kelly, IRA commandant
Tom Flood	Intelligence Officer, IRA HQ
Derek Eppel	Schoolboy
Simon Eppel	Cigar smoker at Vaughan's Hotel

IRISH DESTINY
(1926) IRL silent b&w 50 mins approx

As the War of Independence escalates in Ireland, the peaceful village of Clonmore is disrupted by the arrival of the notorious Black and Tans, a motley group of irregulars drafted in to quell the unrest in Ireland in the years after the First World War. They raid the houses of local people searching for arms. At the O'Hara household, Mrs O'Hara (Daisy Campbell), a woman of delicate disposition and failing eyesight, is very distressed by the raids, and frets about her son Denis (Paddy Dunne Cullinane), who has joined the IRA to fight these brutal intruders. Denis is engaged to local teacher Moira Barry (Frances MacNamara), and divides his time between courting Moira and fighting with the IRA against the British. In one such skirmish, an IRA group ambushes a convoy of British soldiers on a country road, killing several in a brief exchange of fire. Denis' commanding officer Captain Kelly (Kit O'Malley) finds a despatch on the body of a fallen soldier, issued by Curragh Command and intended for Army GHQ in Parkgate Street, outlining a plan to make a raid that night on Vaughan's Hotel, the venue for a secret IRA meeting. Captain Kelly directs Denis to ride to Dublin immediately to warn his comrades of the raid.

Denis borrows the jarvey Shanahan's (Cathal MacGarvey) fastest horse, and bids farewell to Moira before setting off for Dublin. As he leaves, the horse pulling Moira's jaunting car goes out of control and bolts, and she passes out. Denis gives chase and catches the horse before Moira is hurt. Torn between his concern for the unconscious girl and his duty to get to Dublin before the curfew, Denis leaves Moira in the care of Beecher (Brian Magowan), an affable sort but secretly a poitín maker, who comes on the scene of the accident. Unbeknownst to Denis, Beecher has devious designs on his fiancée. When Moira comes to, Beecher tries to convince her that Denis saw her plight, yet abandoned her, and only for Beecher's intervention she would have been injured. She doubts Denis' love for her on hearing this, but resists Beecher's attempts at forcing himself on her. Beecher surmises Denis' motive for going to Dublin, and informs the Tans.

Galloping at high speed through the countryside to avoid detection by sentries on the roads, Denis is challenged as he approaches the city by a soldier stationed on a bridge, and they exchange fire. As Denis gallops away, he is chased by another soldier on a motorcycle. Denis shoots him, and commandeers his bike. He continues on the motorcycle, rounding St Stephen's Green at high speed, down Grafton Street, around College Green and along O'Connell Street to Parnell Square. He stops at Vaughan's Hotel and as he is about to enter, waiting soldiers accost him. He pulls his gun and the soldiers shoot him.

Denis' horse, meanwhile, makes its way back to Clonmore to the jarvey's stables, distressing the jarvey's daughter Kitty (Evelyn Henchey), who believes he is dead. She breaks the news to Moira, who is in turn devastated. An envoy arrives at the O'Hara household announcing that Denis has been shot in Dublin, and Mrs O'Hara loses her sight completely from the shock. But Denis survives the shooting, and he manages to smuggle a letter out with the help of a sympathetic nurse who tends his wounds at a military hospital. As soon as he is well enough, he is imprisoned with other republicans in the Curragh, County Kildare.

In the Curragh Camp, a relay of prisoners digs a tunnel and when they break through outside the barbed wire compound, hundreds of them escape, including Denis. The British search the countryside for the fugitives, deploying a squadron of biplanes (here the film-makers use stock footage of aircraft flying over completely different terrain) to aid the ground patrols. On the run, Denis pauses for refreshment and directions at scenic locations like the Sugarloaf Mountain in County Wicklow. As he approaches Clonmore, he meets Kitty, Moira's friend, who tells him that Moira has gone with Beecher to help a wounded volunteer. But the wounded volunteer story is just a ruse by Beecher to get Moira into his car, and he takes her away to the disused mill in which his poitín still is located. Beecher ties her to a column and both he and his drunken, misshapen assistant molest her. Beecher accuses the helpless Moira of leaking information to the IRA regarding his association with the Tans. A fight breaks out between Beecher and one of his henchmen, in which the henchman is killed. A cigarette falls from the dead man's mouth, setting ablaze the straw on the floor. The mill catches fire (flames are hand-painted cartoonishly onto the frames of film). Denis and Kitty gallop up to the blazing mill, and arrive in the nick of time to beat up Beecher and rescue Moira.

A title card informs us that "as a result of the the burning of the Custom House, the bloody ambuscades and the horrors of guerilla warfare, overtures were made to the Irish republicans". The ensuing truce with the British restores peace to Clonmore, and the populace is seen dancing in the streets. Mrs O'Hara is delighted to have her son back, if not her eyesight, and the War is over. *Irish Destiny* was shot in Dublin and County Wicklow, and the village of Enniskerry was used as the location for the fictional Clonmore. The producer Eppel was a cinema owner in Dublin and despite the success of this republican romance in Ireland and in Irish-American communities, he made no other films.

(Still courtesy of the Irish Film Archive of the Film Institute of Ireland)

(Still courtesy of the Irish Film Archive of the Film Institute of Ireland)

THE PUBLIC ENEMY
(1931) US b&w 83 mins

Production Team

Producer .... Warner Brothers/
Darryl F Zanuck
Director .... William Wellman
Screenplay .... Kubec Glasmon, John Bright
(from a story by Harvey F Thew)
Cinematography .... Dev Jennings
Editor .... Edward M McDermott
Musical Score .... David Mendoza,
conductor, Vitaphone Orchestra

Cast

James Cagney .... Tom Powers
Mae Clark .... Kitty
Jean Harlow .... Gwen Allen
Beryl Mercer .... Ma Powers
Edward Woods. .... Matt Doyle
Joan Blondell .... Mamie
Donald Cook .... Mike Powers
Mia Marvin .... Jane
Leslie Fenton .... Nails Nathan
Robert Emmett O'Connor .... Paddy Ryan
Murray Kinnell .... Putty Nose
Snitz Edwards .... Miller
Rita Flynn .... Molly Doyle
Frank Coghlan Jr .... Tom (as a boy)
Frankie Darro .... Matt (as a boy)
Purnell Pratt .... Officer Powers
Robert E Homans .... Officer Pat Burke

THE PUBLIC ENEMY
(1931) US b&w 83 mins

The massive influx of Irish immigrants to the poor neighbourhoods of urban America in the early years of the 20th century generated a range of Hollywood-Irish types – cops, firemen, priests and gangsters – that would endure for decades and eventually become clichés. In Wellman's Prohibition-era classic *The Public Enemy*, actor James Cagney, in his first starring role, launched the Irish-American gangster prototype with an uninhibited ferocity that would become his trademark, and set the standard for other tough-guy actors to follow. The son of an Irish-born bartender in New York's lower east side, and a former poolhall racker himself, Cagney was no stranger to the inner-city slums that are the setting for *The Public Enemy*. In this violent drama, Cagney plays a ruthless thug named Tom Powers who learns early on that it's easier to make money from crime than to come by it honestly.

His brother Mike (Donald Cook) is more high-minded about living within the law – he works on the streetcars by day and studies at night ("learnin' how to be poor" sneers Tom derisively). Their doting Irish Ma (Beryl Mercer) loves them both, and deludes herself that Tom earns his money legally. Tom's partner-in-crime since early childhood is Matt Doyle (Edward Woods). The pair switch allegiances from an early mentor, a fence named Putty Nose (Murray Kinnell), when a fur heist he organised goes wrong and he leaves them stranded (the livid Tom vows to "give it to that Putty Nose right in the head" the next time he sees him). They align themselves instead with Paddy Ryan (Robert Emmett O'Connor), a crooked operator who runs a saloon.

By this time the US has entered the First World War, and upstanding citizen Mike Powers enlists. Preparing to leave for Europe, Mike warns Tom that he'd better straighten out and stay home to look after Ma. An incensed Tom resents Mike's lecturing and accuses him of pilfering from the streetcar company, calling him a "nickel snatcher". Mike thumps his brother but Tom doesn't retaliate.

In 1920, Prohibition creates new opportunities for Tom and Mike, and Paddy Ryan greedily outlines a profitable future for them. They hook up with a bootlegger, 'Nails' Nathan (Leslie Fenton), and strong-arm speakeasy owners into buying Nathan's illicit booze. Mike Powers, who seems to have taken his time getting back from a war that ended in 1918, arrives home a wounded veteran. He's brought up to date on his brother's escalating criminal lifestyle by Officer Burke (Robert E Homans). Ma and Tom lay on a welcome-home party for Mike, with a beer-keg placed on the dinner table, blocking the diners' view of each other. Tom and Mike argue about the dirty money that bought the beer, and Tom accuses his brother of being a killer in the war:

"Your hands ain't so clean. You didn't get them medals for holding hands with them Germans!"

Tom storms out, and goes to the hotel where he and Matt have been shacking up with their girlfriends, fast molls Kitty (Mae Clark) and Mamie (Joan Blondell). In his hotel room the next morning, Tom arrives for breakfast in a bad mood. His girlfriend Kitty questions his need for a drink at that hour, and they argue. In one of the cruelest scenes in gangster cinema, Tom gives Kitty her vitamin C the hard way, impulsively grabbing a half-grapefruit and viciously smashing it in her face.

Soon Tom is on the lookout for a new girlfriend and he takes up with the glamourous Gwen Allen (Jean Harlow). She accompanies him to a celebration announcing Matt's wedding to Mamie, at which gathering Tom spots Putty Nose. Tom and Matt follow Putty Nose from the party to his apartment, seeking revenge for the fur heist double-cross. Tom makes Putty Nose beg for his life at gunpoint. Putty Nose tries to appeal to a sentimental side that the hardened Tom no longer has, by reminding the boys how he used to entertain them at the piano. Tom callously plugs him twice point-blank, in mid-tune at the keyboard.

Tom's relationship with his brother deteriorates when he tries to give his mother a wad of cash that Mike refuses. Tom rips the money in two and tosses it at Mike, then leaves in a huff for Gwen's hotel to get his mothering from her instead. At the hotel, Matt interrupts a tender scene as Gwen cuddles tough-guy Tom to her bosom, bearing the news that their boss Nathan has been thrown from his horse and killed. Shaken by the news, Tom leaves Gwen immediately, and she smashes a glass in the fireplace in frustration at his coldness to her.

After the lavish funeral for the gangland boss, Tom, still attired in his best duds, goes to the stables to buy Nathan's horse and shoots it dead in its stall. Nathan's death gives rival bootlegger Schemer Burns an opening to monopolise the illegal booze racket. When Nathan's brewery is torched and Paddy's saloon bombed, Paddy orders his men into hiding until he can regroup. Matt and Tom hide out at a safehouse run by a madam named Jane (Mia Marvin), who seduces the sexually uptight Tom when he's drunk. When she reminds him playfully about it the next day, he angrily slaps her face, and leaves the safehouse in defiance of Paddy's orders to lie low. Matt follows him and is gunned down by killers from Burns' gang who are hiding in a nearby building. Tom escapes, and sets out to avenge Matt's death by taking on the entire Burns gang at their headquarters, the Western Chemical Company. Marching into their lair he takes out most of the gang with both guns blazing, but is himself badly wounded. He staggers from the building in a torrential downpour, and falls down bleeding into the gutter, almost dead. But Tom is tough and he survives.

His mother and brother visit him in the hospital and they are at last reconciled. Tom, bandaged from head to toe, resolves to move back in with Ma as soon as he recovers, but Burns' remaining gang kidnaps him from the hospital. Paddy Ryan offers Burns' mob a deal – he will get out of the rackets and let them take over if they return Tom home that night. The gang obliges, dumping Tom's near-dead body at the doorway of the Powers' apartment. He falls dead to the floor as Mike looks on, aghast.

The Public Enemy makes some attempt to examine the social forces that cause criminal types to develop, rather than present the adult criminal as a fully formed law-

breaker who has always been that way. Following a mealy mouthed disclaimer stating that the film does not intend to glorify criminals, *The Public Enemy* opens in 1909 with a prologue in which the young Tom and Matt are shown as mischievous boys, playing pranks and pilfering, before they fall in with a bad crowd and begin their life of crime. Note that the tall dark-haired boy (Frank Coghlan Jr) in the prologue is the more vicious of the two, and the shorter boy (Frankie Darro) the quieter one – the adult parts had originally been cast with tall, dark Edward Woods as the volatile thug and Cagney as the sidekick, but the roles were reversed (after the prologue was shot) when the studio replaced the original director with William Wellman, who recognised Cagney's superior ability to project seething malice. Despite convincing forays into comedy, romance and song-and-dance, Cagney would be forever associated with the gangster persona that assaulted American cinema audiences in 1931, and he would later reprise this frenetic psychopath in Michael Curtiz's *Angels with Dirty Faces* and Raoul Walsh's *White Heat*.

THE BOWERY
(1933) US b&w 92 mins

Production Team

Producer .... 20th Century Pictures Inc/
Darryl F Zanuck
Director .... Raoul Walsh
Screenplay .... Howard Estabrook,
James Gleason,
from the unpublished novel
Chuck Connors by Michael L Simmons,
Bessie Roth Solomon
Cinematography .... Barney McGill
Editor .... Allen McNeill
Musical Score .... Alfred Newman

Cast

Wallace Beery .... Chuck Connors
George Raft .... Steve Brodie
Jackie Cooper .... Swipes McGurk
Fay Wray .... Lucy Calhoun
Pert Kelton .... Trixie Odbray
Herman Bing .... Max Herman
Oscar Apfel .... Ivan Rummel
Ferdinand Munier .... Honest Mike
George Walsh .... John L Sullivan
Lillian Harmer .... Carrie A Nation
Charles Lane .... The doctor
Harold Huber .... Slick
Fletcher Norton .... Googy
Warren Hymer .... Lumpy Hogan
Esther Muir .... The tart
John Bleifer .... The mute
Tammany Young .... Chuck Connor's
henchman

THE BOWERY
(1933) US b&w 92 mins

Set in the late-19th century in the teeming slums of downtown New York, Irish-American film director Raoul Walsh's **The Bowery** follows the rivalry of Chuck Connors (Wallace Beery) and Steve Brodie (George Raft), two denizens of the eponymous street who like to gamble. The film opens with an angry exchange between the pair over a broken window at Connors' tavern, interrupted by a fire alarm which prompts a bet. Both are volunteer firemen, and each bets $100 that he can get to the scene in his fire truck and put out the fire before the other does.

The fire is in Chinatown, and Brodie's crew arrives there first, only to find Swipes McGurk (Jackie Cooper), a friend of Connors, sitting on a keg over the fire hydrant, hogging the water supply until Chuck gets there and preventing Brodie's crew from using it. A fight breaks out between the rival crews when Connors' truck arrives, and the building burns down, with the Chinese occupants still trapped inside. Brodie is furious and resolves to get back at Connors for this chicanery. Two thugs from Jersey, Slick and Googy, offer to help him out by killing Connors for $500, but Steve doesn't want Connors taken care of to that extent so he slaps them around.

Chuck saves innocent Lucy Calhoun (Fay Wray) from the Jersey thugs, and puts her up in the apartment that he shares with Swipes. Swipes, unhappy with the new domestic arrangements, falls out with Chuck and moves in with Steve. Steve mistakenly believes that Lucy is Chuck's girlfriend, and to get back at Chuck he tries to seduce her. She rejects him initially but, before long, they fall in love.

Steve decides to open a saloon to rival Chuck's booze emporium, so he decides on a publicity stunt to attract attention – he plans to jump off the Brooklyn Bridge into the East River, hundreds of feet below. Chuck doesn't believe that he can survive such a jump, so he bets his saloon against a free funeral for Steve that he won't do it. Steve has no intention of actually jumping, so he rigs up a life-size mannequin dressed in his clothing, and arranges with Swipes to throw it off the Bridge while he waits in the water below. On the day of the jump, an excited crowd has gathered, but Steve and Swipes can't find the dummy, so Steve has to make the jump himself. He survives, and is carried shoulder high by a jubilant crowd.

As they approach Chuck's saloon, Chuck sees them parading around with his rival, and realises that Steve has actually done it. A band of temperance enthusiasts, led by Kansas crusader Carrie Nation (Lillian Harmer), arrives outside Chuck's tavern, armed with axes, and threatens to destroy the joint. Knowing he has lost the bet and the tavern with it, Chuck gives them the go-ahead to trash the place. Steve assumes ownership of the vandalised saloon, undertakes some repairs and reopens for business. Chuck, deprived of his source of income, is reduced to joining the army. He fights in the Spanish-American War, and when he comes back to New York he finds that Swipes has moved back into his apartment.

He meets the Jersey thugs, Slick and Googy, and they show him the dummy and convince him that Steve didn't really do the jump that lost Chuck his tavern. Chuck accuses Steve of faking the jump and angrily demands his saloon back. Steve, denying the accusation, starts a fight with him, in which he comes off the worse, resulting in assault and attempted murder charges against Chuck. The court case is droppped because Steve refuses to testify, but their fighting resumes when Chuck goes to visit Steve in hospital, and Swipes has to keep them from killing each other. The combative boys patch up their friendship, and their habit of challenging each other resumes: this time,

Chuck dares Steve to join him in fighting the Cuban War. They both enlist, as does Swipes, and off to war they go.

The Bowery represented a return of sorts to the old New York turf Walsh had previously shot in 1915, while making **Regeneration**. But, unlike the earlier gangster silent, *The Bowery* was shot mostly in the studio. Walsh reconstructed the squalid New York street of the title and its infamous saloon McGurk's Tavern on a California soundstage, using two of the bar counters from the original premises to create an authentic setting. For atmosphere, Walsh added 25 chorus girls he nicknamed 'the Beef Trust', and hired a few dozen extras to leer at them. The director only went to New York to shoot the Brooklyn Bridge jump scene ("there wasn't a Brooklyn Bridge any nearer," said Walsh, by way of explaining to 20th century his 6,000 mile round-trip journey with cast and crew). Friction between Walsh's stars, Raft and Beery, made life difficult for the director during the shoot. Their intense dislike of each other resulted in several of the mock fights in the film turning into the real thing, with black eyes and bruises for the extras on both sides. Raft had mob ties dating back to his young days working as a driver for gang boss Owney Madden's outfit in New York during Prohibition, and when henchmen were needed for minor roles, Raft made sure Madden's boys got the job. These professional bruisers had trouble restricting themselves to fake punches on camera, and gave Beery the works when the burly actor started to punch their boy Raft for real.

THE BOWERY
(1933) US b&w 92 mins

By the time he made *The Bowery*, Raoul Walsh was already a Hollywood veteran with twenty years experience in front of and behind the camera. An actor in *Birth of a Nation* (he played Abraham Lincoln's assassin John Wilkes Booth), this former cowboy had been turning out westerns since the pioneering days of the silent era under Griffith, and would continue to produce masculine, no-nonsense features well into his late-seventies.

Born in New York City a few years before the time in which *The Bowery* is set, Walsh's background of Irish and Latin parentage – his father was a tailor from Dublin who had to leave the country after getting mixed up in some Fenian activity, and his mother was Spanish-Irish from New York – would have given him enough ammunition to stereotype at least two ethnic groups convincingly. But he was an equal opportunity offender, and in *The Bowery* he takes a potshot at most of the immigrant types that thronged Gotha's turn-of-the-century slums, the caricatures becoming steadily more ridiculous the further he gets away from perceived Anglo-American norms. Walsh had no equal in Hollywood when it came to tough, boisterous action movies that never slowed down long enough to allow introspection, and subtlety was not his strong point. Jack Warner said of his attempts at portraying romance, "To Raoul Walsh, a tender love scene is burning down a whorehouse."

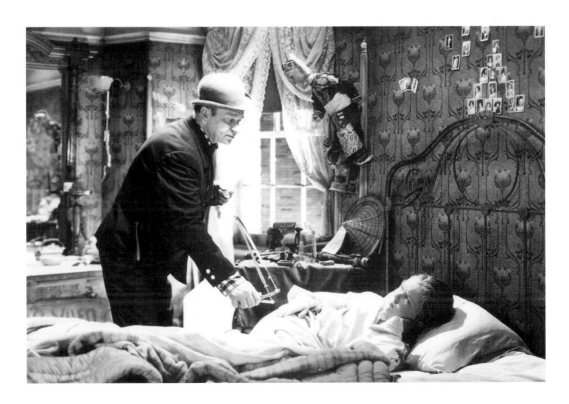

MAN OF ARAN
(1934) UK b&w 76 mins

(Still reproduced courtesy of Carlton International Media Ltd)

Production Team

Producer	Gaumont/Gainsborough/ Michael Balcon
Director	Robert J Flaherty
Assistant Director	Pat Mullin (John) of Aran
Screenplay	Robert J Flaherty and Frances Flaherty
Cinematography	Robert J Flaherty
Musical Score	John Greenwood (based on folk songs of the Aran Islands)

Cast

Coleman 'Tiger' King	Man of Aran
Maggie Dirrane	His wife
Michael Dillane	Their son
Pat Mullin	Shark hunter
Patch Ruadh 'Red Beard'	Shark hunter
Patcheen Faherty	Shark hunter
Tommy O'Rourke	Shark hunter
'Big Patcheen' Coneely	Canoeman
Stephen Dirrane	Canoeman
Pat McDonough	Canoeman

MAN OF ARAN
(1934) UK b&w 76 mins

Legend has it that pioneering documentary film-maker Robert Flaherty was inspired to film on the Aran Islands when a fellow passenger on a transatlantic journey told him about the hardships of life there, in a barren environment where farmers had to mix sand, seaweed and what little earth could be found between the cracks in the rocks to yield a single bucket of topsoil to grow their potatoes.

Flaherty had made his name as a film director in 1922 with *Nanook of the North*, an internationally acclaimed documentary about man's struggle to survive in the severe climate of the Arctic. He made the film on location in extremely difficult conditions, using real people rather than actors to dramatise events from the daily lives of the Inuit. At the time, spending lengthy periods in remote outposts of civilisation was unheard of, and the film established his reputation as a ground-breaking film-maker willing to go to extreme lengths to complete his work. The subject of mankind tackling nature head-on remained an abiding fascination with the Irish-American director, and Flaherty travelled to the Aran Islands, a few miles from the mainland on Ireland's tempestuous western seaboard, to make a film of the islanders' lives. Using local people as actors, he recreated notable scenes from their recent past to paint a vivid portrait of a world that was already disappearing by the early-1930s.

Flaherty depicts the islanders on land, working their rocky acres to raise a few meagre crops, and at sea, setting out in currachs on fishing expeditions. His two leading players, Maggie Dirrane and Tiger King, are both amateurs and native islanders. Maggie plays a farmer, and gives an impressive performance as she portrays the anxieties of waiting for the menfolk to get back safely from fishing, and the joys of working together as a family in the rare good weather of summer. Tiger, the island's blacksmith in real life, plays her husband, and is the leader of the currach crew on the fishing trips. Maggie and Tiger are seen in a number of interlinked scenes, engaged in back-breaking work to sustain their humble existence – hauling seaweed to the potato patch, breaking stones to clear and level the land, and digging for earth in narrow rock crevices to generate a few rows of soil to grow their staple food, potatoes. The family has an indomitable cheerfulness that shines through despite the difficulties of their existence.

The frailty of the islanders in the face of the elements is palpable, as they row through treacherous waves and wrestle the fishing nets back on board their flimsy currach, the traditional cowhide-and-tar boat that is still made on the island. Flaherty underlines this vulnerability by shooting his cast at a distance, with very few close-ups. The dark-clad islanders often appear as tiny silhouettes against the lighter backdrop of enormous cliffs and surging seas that threaten to drown them at any second. In his efforts to show the perils of island life as realistically as possible, Flaherty often imperilled both cast and crew to make his footage convincing. In one particularly striking scene, as the fishermen and women of the island frantically try to drag their nets ashore in rough waters, Maggie Dirrane is almost swept out to sea when the

MAN OF ARAN
(1934) UK b&w 76 mins

waves catch her petticoats. One of the boatmen saves her by pulling her ashore by her hair – not the sort of scene that can be rehearsed beforehand. The end of the fishing trip from which the currach crew returns after getting caught in a storm also placed the cast at risk. Mother and son are shown frantic with worry at their cottage, waiting for the missing menfolk to return. At last their currach is sighted in the distance, being thrown about by the raging surf. The sea is a white foaming mass against which the dark, struggling figures of the fishermen are starkly outlined. The men in the boat attempt to reach the shore but are continually dragged back out by the swirling waves. Their next attempt is successful but their precious currach is lost and only a fishing line, harpoon and an oar are saved. The sea rages on as Tiger and family climb wearily back up the cliff. In one of the few close-ups of the entire film, Tiger's face is shown, haunted yet defiant as he looks out

(Still reproduced courtesy of Carlton International Media Ltd)

onto the crashing waves and jets of spray which took his boat and his means of livelihood, and almost took his life as well.

One of the high points of this visually remarkable film is the shark hunt. Tiger King and his crew pursue the huge basking shark relentlessly in their tiny currach, and after two days the enormous creature succumbs exhausted to their patient efforts. The islanders greatly value the precious shark oil to light their lamps in the dark months of winter, and there is a mood of jubilation as the 40 foot shark is hauled ashore by a group of islanders. The mother and son immediately set about stripping the gigantic carcass, and rendering its liver in a huge cauldron.

The primitive cycle of existence that had remained immutable on the Aran Islands for centuries would soon be gone, in a rapidly changing Ireland of rural electrification, urbanisation, and mechanised mariculture. Flaherty's stunning cinematic achievement is an invaluable social and historic document of that cycle, without which we would have little visual evidence of a culture that was disappearing even as he filmed it. Flaherty has been faulted over the years for presenting as documentary footage a film that is in reality a re-creation of incidents that had occurred many years previously. But *Man of Aran* fits more accurately in the genre of docudrama, a term which didn't exist when the film was made, and the recreated scenes feel no less real (and no less dangerous) than they might have been had Flaherty shot these events as they happened a generation earlier.

Man of Aran remains a stunning cinematic achievement, remarkable not as an anthropological scrutiny of a beleaguered ethnic community, but as a declarative testament to man's determination to survive against the most hostile forces that nature can muster. Flaherty's film won the Best Foreign Film Award from the National Board of Review (USA) in 1934, and in the same year won the Mussolini Cup for best foreign film at the Venice Film Festival. *Man of Aran* is still screened regularly during the summer months on Inis Mór, and the stories associated with the making of the film have become part of the local folklore for generations of Aran islanders.

(Still courtesy of the Irish Film Archive of the Film Institute of Ireland)

Robert Flaherty, director of *Man of Aran*

CAPTAIN BLOOD
(1935) US b&w 120 mins

Production Team

Producer .... First National Pictures/
Harry Joe Brown/Jack Warner
(executive producer)
Director .... Michael Curtiz
Screenplay .... Casey Robinson
(from the book of the same name
by Gabriel Sabatini)
Editor .... George Amy
Musical Score .... Erich Wolfgang Korngold

Cast

Errol Flynn .... Dr Peter Blood
Olivia de Havilland .... Arabella Bishop
Lionel Atwill .... Colonel Bishop
Basil Rathbone .... Captain Levasseur
Ross Alexander .... Jeremy Pitt
Guy Kibbee .... Henry Hagthorpe
Henry Stephenson .... Lord Willoughby
Robert Barrat .... John Wolverstone
Hobart Cavanaugh .... Dr Bronson
Donald Meek .... Dr Whacker
Jessie Ralph .... Mrs Barlowe
Forrester Harvey .... Honesty Nuttall
Frank McGlynn Sr .... Revered Ogle
Holmes Herbert .... Captain Gardner
David Torrence .... Andrew Baynes
J Carroll Naish .... Cahusac
Pedro de Córdoba .... Don Diego

CAPTAIN BLOOD
(1935) US b&w 120 mins

Errol Flynn's first lead role made a star of the devilish Tasmanian and set him up for a rollicking career as Hollywood's leading swashbuckler until his wild social life got the better of him. In this Caribbean pirate drama set in the 1680s, Flynn, the grandson of Irish immigrants to Australia, plays an Irish surgeon named Peter Blood plying his trade in Jacobean England. Blood is arrested by Crown forces when he's caught treating the wounds of anti-Royalists injured in a skirmish with the King's army. He is deported to the West Indies, where he is sold into slavery for £20 to Arabella Bishop (Olivia de Havilland), beautiful niece of a senior officer in the British forces at Port Royal. Blood uses his medical knowledge to gain favour with the gouty governor of the island, and his charm to flirt with Arabella, who has an ethical conflict about being attracted to a man she owns. During an attack on Port Royal by Spanish galleons, Blood escapes from his captivity on a stolen ship with a crew of his fellow slaves and, over the next few years, makes a name for himself as Captain Blood, the most feared pirate in the Caribbean.

On a return journey to England, Arabella is captured by a rival pirate and Captain Blood gallantly rescues her. He intends to return her to the safety of Port Royal and the home of her uncle, though she fears for his life if he sails into a harbour filled with British naval vessels. Meanwhile, back in England, the defeat of James II and the accession of King William to the throne (a change of personnel which benefitted few Irishmen), results in a pardon for Blood, and he becomes governor of the island on which he had been a slave. When she enters the governor's mansion in Jamaica, Arabella finds Captain Blood sitting with his feet on the the governor's desk, ready to court her on a more equal basis.

Errol Flynn was cast in the title role when the original lead, Robert Donat, backed out after a row with Warner Brothers. Flynn threw himself into the first day of filming, fortified with a bottle of brandy to tone down a fever from which he was suffering. With flailing cutlass and billowing blouse, the drunken Flynn nearly fell overboard several times and forgot all his lines, but improvised exuberantly. He was promptly hauled up before Jack Warner to explain his behaviour. Warner was notorious for his disapproval of drinking on the set, and Flynn expected to get his marching orders. But Warner was so impressed by the footage he saw of Flynn's performance that he begrudgingly declined to make an example of him. Flynn romped away with the whole film, leaving his seasoned fellow cast members Lionel Atwill and Basil Rathbone in the dust, and establishing himself overnight as Hollywood's top choice for dashing romantic roles. From the opening scenes in Jacobean England to the finale in Jamaica, Flynn lives the role like there's nothing more exhilarating in the world than playing a pirate in a lavish adventure film.

GUESTS OF THE NATION
(1935) IRL silent b&w 49 mins

(Still courtesy of the Irish Film Archive of the Film Institute of Ireland, used courtesy of Michael Johnston)

Production Team

Producer .... George H Brown
Director .... Denis Johnston
Screenplay .... Mary Manning
from the short story of
the same name by Frank O'Connor
Cinematography .... Joe Manning,
Harold Douglas, Michael Farrell
Editor .... Máirín Hayes

Cast

Barry Fitzgerald .... British soldier
captured by the IRA
Frank Toolin ....
Cyril Jackson .... Charles Maher
Georgina Johnson ....
Shelah Richards .... Bicycle Courier
Cyril Cusack .... IRA man, imprisoned
Donald Beaven ....
Robert Collis ....
Edward Levy ....
William Fassbender ....
Cissy Cunningham ....
Tony MacAn ....
Lionel Dymoke ....
Hilton Edwards ....
H Fine ....
Niall Montgomery ....
Frank O'Connor .... IRA member

A silent film shot some eight years after the first sound films were made, *Guests of the Nation* opens with the date 1921 scrawled in chalk on a steel door. The War of Independence in Ireland is at its peak, the city of Dublin is in flames, and a ragtag crew of Irish rebels, some in uniforms and some in civvies, engages the British army in guerilla combat. Royal Irish Constabulary emblems are torn down at a police barracks and the Irish tricolour is raised, the urgency of the scene conveyed by the use of hand-held cameras. Three policemen are captured and taken from the barracks, but one escapes to tell his comrades of the whereabouts of the IRA unit. A Rolls Royce armoured car gives chase to the IRA men, and, in an exchange of fire, two of the rebels are captured.

The commandant of the IRA sends a despatch by bicycle messenger (Shelah Richards) to alert two of the volunteers to report for duty. They are assigned the task of guarding the two British captives. Their charges seem cheerful despite their predicament, and they pass the time smoking and playing cards. The woman in whose cottage they are being held views both prisoners and guards with suspicion. The IRA men and the Englishmen get on well together, finding their enemies to be genial human beings, and the atmosphere in the cottage is relaxed at first. One of the English prisoners (an oddly miscast Barry Fitzgerald) keeps the household entertained by belting out tunes on a button accordion. They all enjoy the antics of the old lady's kitten, and the big feeds of flowery spuds garnished with butter that she regularly serves to both guards and prisoners. The passage of time is shown by the filling ashtrays and many clock windings as the guards anxiously await news of the fate of their comrades in jail in Dublin.

The tension grows when the word comes through from Dublin that the IRA men are to be hanged. A directive arrives at the cottage from the head of the IRA stating that the two English prisoners must be executed as a reprisal. The guards are morose, but they keep the news from their prisoners. One guard decides to cycle to Dublin to try to stop the hangings. He arrives at the prison shortly after dawn. A crowd keeping vigil outside Kilmainham Gaol kneels in prayer. He realises that he's too late, and the IRA men are already dead. He returns to the cottage for further orders.

After a last supper of batch loaves and more spuds, the two prisoners are told to put on their uniforms and get ready to leave. They realise that their number is up when the guards refuse to allow the musician to bring the accordion with him. The pair are marched to a hillside where their graves are dug. One asks for a blindfold and the other pleads for his life with the guards. They carry out their onerous duty and return to the cottage, shattered by the experience. The old woman prays, and the camera pans to the discarded accordion, symbol of the conviviality destroyed by the deeds of war.

Frank O'Connor, author of the short story on which the film is based, made a brief cameo appearance as a Flying Column volunteer. In the newspapers of the time he declared himself well satisfied with the film version of his story, and felt it compared favourably with the work of Russian directors in vogue at the time. This film would remain director Denis Johnston's only foray into film-making.

THE INFORMER
(1935) US b&w 91 mins

Production Team

Producer .... RKO/John Ford
Director .... John Ford
Screenplay .... Dudley Nichols
          from the book by Liam O'Flaherty
Cinematography .... Joseph H August
Musical Score .... Max Steiner

Cast

Victor McLaglen .... Gypo Nolan
Heather Angel .... Mary McPhillip
Preston Foster .... Dan Gallagher,
                        IRA Commandant,
Margot Grahame .... Katie Madden
Wallace Ford .... Frankie McPhillip
Una O'Connor .... Mrs McPhillip
Joe Sawyer .... Bartley Mulholland
Fred O'Donovan .... Terry
Neil Fitzgerald .... Tommy Connor
Donald Meek .... Pat Mulligan
D'Arcy Corrigan .... Blind man
Leo MacCabe .... Donahue
Gaylord Pendleton .... Daley
Francis Ford .... Flynn
May Boley .... Madame Betty
Grizelda Harvey .... Lady

THE INFORMER
(1935) US b&w 91 mins

The informer of the title is a simple-minded brute named Gypo Nolan (Victor McLaglen), who has fallen out with the IRA in Dublin in 1920 over his failure to carry out an execution. Low on funds, Gypo is led into temptation when he bumps into his old friend and ex-comrade, Frankie McPhillip (Wallace Ford) in a cafe. Frankie has a price on his head – there's a £20 reward for turning him in – and life on the run is exhausting him. He tells Gypo that he wants to visit his mother (Una O'Connor) and sister Mary (Heather Angel). The dim-witted Gypo walks the streets restlessly, torn between friendship with Frankie, and desire for the reward, enough money to win the love of his favourite girl Katie (Margot Grahame) and pay the fare to take them both to America.

Gypo succumbs and betrays Frankie, collecting the £20 from the army barracks after the Tans have surrounded McPhillips' house and shot Frankie dead. At Frankie's wake, the IRA offers to reinstate Gypo if he names the informer, and he blames an innocent man named Mulligan (Donald Meek). Haunted by Frankie's face on the reward posters as he wanders through the grimy, claustrophobic city, the dark forebodings of Gypo's conscience close in on him like a rank mist. He hits the town with the reward money, making instant friends at fancy bars by buying rounds of drinks. Katie's reassurance of her devotion to him does little to ease Gypo's anxieties, and IRA observers note his tense behaviour and sudden prosperity with suspicion.

Within hours he squanders all of the reward money. The IRA take him to a kangaroo court to charge him with Frankie's betrayal, after Mulligan has produced a credible alibi, and Frankie's sister has let it be known that only Gypo knew that Frankie was at his mother's house. Gypo is too drunk and too dim-witted to talk his way out of it. He is sentenced to death but breaks free before the execution can be carried out, and flees to Katie's flat. His former IRA comrades track him there and shoot him. He staggers, fatally wounded, to the church across the street, where he comes upon Frankie's heartbroken mother praying, and begs her forgiveness with his dying breath.

The ebullient Victor McLaglen stamped his authority on the role of Gypo with such conviction that he carried the film to a level far above its drab, stagey, mise-en-scene, and won an Oscar for his performance. John Ford won an Oscar for Best Director (the first of four for the Irish-American master), and Dudley Nichols won for his screenplay. *The Informer* earned a fourth statuette for Max Steiner's musical score, but lost out to *Mutiny on the Bounty* for Best Picture. *The Informer* marked Ford and McLaglen's third film together. McLaglen, an English actor who made his name playing Irishmen, featured in Ford's silent *Mother Machree*, in 1928, as the 'giant of Kilkenny', and also appeared that same year in Ford's *Hangman's House*, the picture that gave John Wayne his screen debut. All three would reunite more than a quarter of a century later to make Ford's über-Irish nostalgia-fest, *The Quiet Man*.

Ford's version of *The Informer* was the second appearance on the big screen for Liam O'Flaherty's tale of friendship and nation betrayed. A silent version, made in 1929, starring Lars Hanson as Gypo, was later dubbed with risible Shakespearean accents that earned it a lambasting from contempororary critics in Ireland and Britain.

THE DAWN
(1935) IRL b&w 87 mins

(Still provided and reproduced courtesy of Michelle Galvin.)

Production Team

Producer .... Hibernia Films/Tom Cooper
Director .... Tom Cooper,
Screenplay .... Harry O'Donovan,
    Dr D A Moriarty, Donal O'Cahill
Cinematography .... James B S Lawler
Incidental Music...................... Pat Crowley's
    Dance Band

Cast

Brian O'Sullivan .... Brian Malone
Eileen Davis .... Eileen O'Donovan
Tom Cooper .... Dan O'Donovan
Donal O'Cahill............................ Billy Malone
Jerry O'Mahoney .... Commanding Officer
    of the Black and Tans
Bill Murphy .... Sergeant Geary RIC
James Gleeson .... John Malone
Marian O'Connell .... Mrs Malone

THE DAWN
(1935) IRL b&w 87 mins

In Kerry in the mid-1930s, local garage proprietor turned film-maker Tom Cooper assembled a group of local amateur actors to make *The Dawn*, a drama set during Ireland's War of Independence that deals with a stigma handed down through three generations of one family, and finally erased by the sacrifice of one of the sons.

The film opens with a prologue in which the grandfather of the film's main protagonist, Brian Malone (Brian O'Sullivan), is suspected of providing information to the British army with regard to the movements of local Fenian activists, because he's the only one missing from their unit when all his comrades are arrested. The Fenians are imprisoned and exiled, and the grandfather is ostracised 'til his dying day for an act of betrayal that he did not commit. The family bears the shame of being known as the descendants of an informer, a disgrace in Ireland down through the ages.

Time moves on and, in 1919, the activists are once again planning an insurrection against the British. Brian Malone, a volunteer in County Kerry, is deemed untrustworthy by his comrades when an old man who remembers his grandfather casts doubt on Brian's integrity. Brian becomes engaged to Eileen O'Donovan (Eileen Davis), whose brother Dan (Tom Cooper) is also an active member of the illegal organisation, and they have a pleasant courtship, unaware that the IRA is planning to kick him out. Brian's brother Billy (Donal O'Cahill), defends Brian, but is resolute about having nothing to do with the organisation himself.

At a meeting held to assess Brian's liability, Dan vouches for him, but Brian is expelled. Dan tells his sister to break the bad news to her fiancé, and promises to do everything he can to get Brian reinstated. At the Malone household, Brian is dejected after receiving the news, and his mother is concerned. Brian complains bitterly that they have nothing against his character and conduct, and Dan suggests that he lie low for a while. At home, Brian laments that he'd be better off dead, or in the Royal Irish Constabulary (not mutually exclusive propositions, as indicated by a recruitment poster defaced to read: "Join the RIC and see the next world").

Billy thinks his brother is daft, but Brian, bizarrely, joins the RIC anyway, and is deeply upset when Eileen won't answer the letters he sends from the training barracks. Eileen burns them instead. One of the IRA volunteers brings the news that a new lot has arrived at the local RIC barracks, wearing "peelers pants and khaki coats, the queerest brood of cuckoos you ever laid eyes on". An ideological colleague reminds him that they don't use that kind of bad language.

The RIC and Tans are shown at the barracks as a rowdy, undisciplined lot, swigging whiskey
 and threatening to fill the nationalists with lead. Suspects are marched out and shot ("Trying to escape!" laughs an RIC man). An ambush of a Tan convoy is shown in a rural area. By contrast, Brian is leading the quiet life on patrol elsewhere in the country, with nothing to do but read the paper. He reads about the violent activity at his home place, where a constable was wounded. Brian complains that it's too darn

quiet and requests a transfer back to his own area.

Meanwhile, in his hometown, intelligence information changes hands on both sides of the conflict. Two IRA men are ordered to collect a despatch from a person who remains anonymous, and Billy is seen slipping a note into a glove and handing it to the RIC men on the road. The local newspapers describe an attack on a barracks in Kerry, in which the building is burned and a republican leader freed. The paper lists the numbers of IRA at 200, to the amusement of the IRA boys reading the paper who had been among the handful involved in the attack. Reprisals and counter-reprisals are soon the order of the day as the authorities lose control of the situation.

Remarkable scenes are shown, shot in silhouette, of soldiers rounding up volunteers at gunpoint, with tar buckets and burning torches. Eileen tells Mrs Malone that she's been burning all the letters from Brian, and she lectures Billy about the company he's been keeping – the British. The IRA responds to the round-up by escalating its campaign, and they phone the RIC barracks to let them know that this is the first act of a tragedy.

Brian gets his transfer home, and when the RIC and Tans file out of the barracks to carry out house-to-house searches, he is among them. When they search the O'Donovan house, a perplexed RIC man finds a picture of Brian downstairs as his comrades search Eileen's room upstairs. Brian apologises for the intrusion, and Eileen coldly lets him know that he's just as welcome as the friends he brought. The O'Donovan family maid boldly douses a departing RIC man with a bucket of water as they leave the house, and Brian laments that he's fed up with everything and everybody. The IRA captures Auxiliary Captain Manning, who defies them to finish him off. His special code and signature are safe in the hands of the mysterious Brigade Intelligence Officer, and he realises that the IRA doesn't need him alive.

At an IRA meeting angry volunteers want Billy Malone court-martialled because he was seen giving information to peelers on the road. Dan defends Brian and Billy against his comrades, and forbids an official action against Billy because there isn't sufficient evidence of treason, declaring that, "Every man and woman in the country is entitled to freedom of opinion, per the Proclamation of Independence." He decides to report the whole matter to the Brigade IO. Again, Cooper shoots scenes in silhouette, showing informers giving notes to peelers.

At the RIC barracks, the drunken singing and card play is interrupted by the officer in charge announcing a raid on the IRA camp in the valley beyond Clanbridge at dawn. The Tans gleefully look forward to wiping the sleep from the IRA men's eyes, but doleful Brian thinks that they'll just make more martyrs for Ireland. "They'd cut your throat for tuppence," says one Tan about the IRA. "I'd cut theirs for nothing," says another.

Brian is deeply troubled about facing off against his old comrades, and has flashbacks to his mother telling him the story of his grandfather by the spinning wheel.

THE DAWN
(1935) IRL b&w 87 mins

He decides to rejoin the cause, and heads home, stealing rifles from the barracks as he leaves. He tells his dad about the plan to raid the IRA camp at dawn. Brian insists that they go and warn the IRA, and when Billy tries to stop him he gets called yellow for his trouble. Billy and Brian have an ugly stand-off in which Billy threatens Brian at gunpoint to stop him telling the IRA about the Tans' attack.

Their little brother wrestles the gun off Billy, and Brian and his dad head off, armed with revolvers, to warn the rebels at their hideout. Dan O'Donovan gets word by phone that Mr Malone and Brian are on their way to let them know about the Tans' operation – which they already know about from Manning's intelligence information.

Back at the RIC barracks, the Tans notice that their guns are missing. The volunteers are shown clearing a roadblock of boulders to let the Tans through to the ambush point, where the IRA will attack them. The IRA begin shooting, and they dynamite the RIC armoured car. Lots of Tans are shot in running combat. Dan spares the survivors, shouting contemptuously at them as Billy comes running across the fields in his pyjamas and is shot by RIC guys on bicycles. Dan finds a note on his fallen body that lets him know that the suspected informer Billy was secretly the Chief Intelligence Officer of the brigade. At the nearby IRA safe house, they assess the situation, and Mr Malone is very upset about Billy's death. Dan tries to explain but the bereaved father is too distraught to listen – his son was a covert IRA man, and he died trying to stop them from warning the rebels so as not to spoil the counter attack. Mr Malone finds some comfort when he realises that his son died a hero, and a cross is erected at the spot where Billy was shot.

The uneven story line – devised in the local pubs on Friday nights before shooting on Saturdays and Sundays – is more than compensated for by the enthusiasm that Cooper's amateur troupe brings to his film. Many of the cast were involved in IRA activities a decade and a half earlier, including Cooper himself, and were well familiar with their roles as IRA gunmen. The Black and Tans are less convincingly portrayed, but their remorseless villainy is pitched at about the level of villainy many Irish people perceive them to have to this day. Working with minimal resources, Cooper produced and directed an impressive independent feature, a cinematic *meitheal* that proved it was possible to launch a native film industry from scratch. Unfortunately, the challenge was not taken up by Irish film-makers, and *The Dawn* did not generate a legion of similar efforts. Despite box office success in Ireland and some attention abroad, Cooper himself only made one more film, *Uncle Nick*, since lost to posterity.

BELOVED ENEMY
(1936) US b&w 90 mins

(Still courtesy of the Irish Film Archive of the Film Institute of Ireland)

Production Team

Producer .... HowardProductions/
Samuel Goldwyn
Director .... H C Potter
Screenplay .... John L Balderston
Rose Franken
Cinematography .... Gregg Toland
Editor .... Sherman Todd
Musical Score .... Alfred Newman

Cast

Merle Oberon .... Helen Drummond
Brian Aherne .... Dennis Riordan
Karen Morley .... Cathleen O'Brien
Henry Stephenson .... Lord Athleigh
David Niven .... Gerald Preston
Jerome Cowan .... Tim O'Rourke
Donald Crisp .... Burke
Ronald Sinclair .... Jerry
Granville Bates .... Ryan
P J Kelly .... Rooney
Leo McCabe .... Connor
Pat O'Malley .... Callahan
Jack Mulhall .... Casey
Claude King .... Colonel Loder
Wyndham Standing .... Thornton

64

BELOVED ENEMY
(1936) US b&w 90 mins

This highly fictionalised life of Michael Collins was made only fourteen years after his death, but departs so far from reality that it was never likely to generate angry letters to the editor from people who think all features are documentaries. Brian Aherne stars as dashing rebel Dennis Riordan, the most wanted in man in Dublin during the War of Independence. He cycles around the city, impudently chatting with soldiers at roadblocks without getting caught. The British lack an accurate description of him, allowing him to play games with them that make him a hero to the people of Ireland. His guerilla war drives the British to negotiate a peace settlement, and they send an envoy, Lord Athleigh (Henry Stephenson), over from London. For some reason he brings his pretty daughter Helen (Merle Oberon) into this warzone.

An attempt on Athleigh's life endangers his daughter, but Riordan gallantly saves her. Undeterred by her brush with death, Helen is soon out again and meets an injured child. She takes him to his mother (Karen Morley), who reacts with hostility when she hears her English accent because her husband was killed by the British, then softens when she sees her heartfelt concern for her son. Riordan visits the O'Brien household, and offers to escort Helen safely to her hotel. She is smitten by him without realising the dangers inherent in this attraction. Riordan is less than informative about his anti-British activites, and they fall in love. But before long she joins the dots and realises that her father's nemesis and the man she's been kissing are one and the same man. She speaks of meeting him to Papa, and Riordan is almost caught. But he's sufficiently taken with Helen to want to see more of her, angering his comrades, one of whom, O'Rourke (Jerome Cowan) attacks him.

Helen admits to Riordan that she mentioned their relationship to her father, and he is almost caught by soldiers who followed her to their rendezvous point. Riordan resolves to forget her, and she returns to England with her father, promising never to see Riordan again. Athleigh goes home despairing of ever finding a peaceful solution, but Helen encourages him to persist, knowing a little about the potential for harmony between the two sides through her liaisons with Riordan.

A peace conference is begun in London, and Riordan is a pivotal member of the Irish delegation. He resumes his romance with Helen, who urges him to settle for a compromise when the talks are halted by intractable issues on both sides. A treaty is signed which brings peace, but gives the Irish a good deal less than they wanted. Riordan returns home, and Helen follows him, anxious for his safety when the extremists' bitter response to the deal becomes known. As Riordan gives a public speech, he is shot by his ex-comrade O'Rourke, and falls wounded. He manages to tell Helen that they can find happiness now that there is peace, even though he's just been shot.

History fans will find little to latch onto in this film, which barely concerns itself with factual accuracy in its cupid-inspired delirium. *Beloved Enemy* draws more from the alleged love affair Collins had with Lady Lavery, wife of artist Sir Charles Lavery (and beshawled model for the pre-decimal Irish pound note) than the factual details of his career as IRA leader, minister in the first Dáil government, and master of guerilla warfare.

OURSELVES ALONE
(1936) UK b&w 70 mins

(Still courtesy of the Irish Film Archive of the Film Institute of Ireland)

Production Team

Producer .... Alliance
Director .... Brian Desmond Hurst
Screenplay .... Dudley Leslie,
         Marjoire Deans, Denis Johnson
Cinematography .... Walter Harvey
Editor .... J Corbett
Musical Score .... Harry Acres

Cast

Antoinette Cellier .... Maureen Elliott
Niall MacGinnis .... Terence Elliott
Clifford Evans .... Connolly
Paul Farrell .... Hogan
Harry Hutchinson .... James Hennessey
John Loder .... Captain Wiltshire
John Lodge .... Inspector John Hannay
Tony Quinn .... Maloney

OURSELVES ALONE
(1936) UK b&w 70 mins

IRA volunteers commanded by dashing rebel Mick O'Day ambush a convoy of Crossley tenders and lorries during the War of Independence and free two prisoners, Moloney (Tony Quinn) and Connolly (Clifford Evans). When they convene later in Rooney's pub, the IRA men suspect that their comrade Hennessey (Harry Hutchinson) is leaking their plans to British Intelligence Officer Wiltshire (John Loder). The police search for the ambushers, who escape through the pub basement before they enter the premises. Wiltshire's colleague, Police Inspector Hannay (John Lodge) fears for the safety of his fiancée, local gentry lass Maureen Elliott (Antoinette Cellier), and advises her to phone the barracks with a specific message if she needs help. Maureen discovers that her brother Terence (Niall MacGinnis) is an IRA member, and when she overhears that the RIC is going to raid Ballyfinan House, an IRA hideout, she hurries over there to warn him. She is stopped by the police en route and brought to the barracks for breaking curfew. Her excuses about car trouble leave Hannay unconvinced and suspicious of her motives. The raid on Ballyfinan House goes ahead and the IRA are caught unawares as they review the case against Hennessey with their leader Mick O'Day (who is, in fact, Terence Elliott). Connolly and Moloney escape but most of their men are captured. Terence is arrested by Hannay, who is shocked to find that his future brother-in-law is the infamous O'Day, but tries to escape after they argue about Ireland. He is shot dead by Wiltshire.

To avenge Terence's death, Connolly and Hogan (Paul Farrell) go to Castle Elliott and force Maureen to lure Wiltshire into a trap. She phones him at the barracks and gets him to come over, and the IRA men tie him up. She also phones Inspector Hannay and leaves her cryptic message to let him know she's in trouble. The two IRA men flee with the captive Wiltshire and in Maureen's car, moments before Hannay arrives. Hannay realises from her concern for Wiltshire's safety that Maureen cares more about the Intelligence Officer than him. Hannay chases the getaway car and rescues Wiltshire, but Connolly and Hogan escape. He gallantly (or idiotically, depending on your point of view) ends his engagement to Maureen by pretending that it was he that killed her brother Terence, not Wiltshire, the man she really loves.

Ourselves Alone, released with the less political title *River of Unrest* in the US, shed even less light on the post-WWI conflict between Ireland and Britain than the standard Hollywood-Irish fare of its time, opting instead to use it as a volatile ethnic backdrop for an unlikely romance. Loder and future Connecticut governor Lodge give extraordinarily wooden performances on their respective corners of the film's romantic triangle, and Cellier is only marginally more lively on the third one. But the film is worth seeing for the police raid scene in Rooney's bar (*Knocknagow* director Fred O'Donovan plays Rooney). A 360° degree camera pan takes in the whole assembly of trenchcoated IRA men listening to tenor Cavan O'Connor as he sings 'The Rose of Tralee'. He follows with 'The Wearing of the Green', strolls casually around the bar gathering up his comrades' firearms, and, without missing a beat, hands them over to women sympathisers to conceal in their stockings before the police arrive. The RIC enter and search all the men present, only to come up empty-handed.

IRISH AND PROUD OF IT
(1936) IRL b&w 73 mins

Richard Heyward star of *Irish and Proud of It*

(Still courtesy of The National Library)

Production Team

Producer .... Crusade Films/
Donovan Pedelty
Director.............................. Donovan Pedelty
Screenplay .... Donovan Pedelty
and David Evans
(from a story by Dorothea Donn-Byrne)
Cinematography .... Geoffrey Faithfull
Editor .... Hans Nieter

Cast

Richard Heyward .... Donogh O'Connor
Dinah Sheridan .... Moira Flaherty
Jack Clifford .... O'Hara
Shaun Desmond .... Maloney
J Miles Marwyn .... McCartney
Charles Fagan .... Seargeant
Liam Gaffney .... Sean Deasy
Gwenllian Gill .... Mary Johnson
Jimmy Mageean .... Old Flaherty
George Pembroke .... Mike Finnegan
Herbert Thorpe .... Benny

Irish emigrant Donagh O'Connor (Richard Heyward) lives in England and possesses both business acumen and a fine tenor voice. A success in London, he never settled well in his adopted city and misses home, especially when he drinks and sings sentimental Irish songs. He takes an American client named McCartney (J Miles Marwyn) to a function at an Irish aviators' club, and bursts into song after a few, impressing his guest with his emotive voice. O'Connor announces dramatically that he really misses Ireland and would give half his money to be in Ballyvoraine, his home village, that very night. Some aviators take him up on this and they abduct him, tie him up in a sack, and fly him home. They dump him in a field near his village, still tied up. A farm girl, Moira Flaherty (Dinah Sheridan) finds him and is reduced to hysterical laughter by his plight. She frees him and takes him to her home. Her father (Jimmy Mageean), an amateur distiller, has been sampling his own product and is alarmed by the tuxedoed tenor, but recovers his manners and invites O'Connor for tea.

Idyllic Ballyvoraine has changed since O'Connor left. Ex-Chicago mobsters Finnegan (George Pembroke) and Benny (Herbert Thorpe), an Italian with Chico Marx tendencies, are running the local poitín business and forcing the publican, Maloney (Shaun Desmond) to buy third-rate booze for his bar. Maloney resists Finnegan's sales pitch despite getting thumped, and defiantly shows him an *Irish Press* headline declaring that the government plans to get rid of illegal distilling in the area.

O'Connor's arrival in the village stirs local curiosity. Finnegan suspects that the mysterious stranger might be an agent sent to find the illegal stills, and visits O'Connor with his henchman Sean Deasy (Liam Gaffney), Moira's boyfriend, to scare him. Moira defends him, having been charmed by his voice when he sang for her in the pub. She threatens to turn the gangster in if O'Connor gets hurt, and convinces him that the tenor is on the run from London and not a government spy. Finnegan changes his tune about O'Connor and he and Benny try to get the sweet-voiced visitor to perform at Maloney's bar, an offer O'Connor bluntly declines.

In London, O'Connor's secretary Mary (Gwenllian Gill) and McCartney are frantically looking for him – she because the business is in chaos, and he because he wants to make him a singing star on American radio. She finds out from the aviators about the prank they played, and flies to Ireland with McCartney to find O'Connor. Back in Ballyvoraine, O'Connor comes upon Finnegan's poitín still, and Finnegan delegates Benny to rub him out. Benny and O'Connor have a drink, and they sing Irish and Italian arias and drink poitín til Benny passes out. O'Connor, drunk but still mobile, escapes. He heads for the harvest dance where he meets the strained couple Moira and Sean, and diplomatically helps patch up their rift.

Finnegan arrives at the still to find Benny stocious and O'Connor gone. They look for him at at the dance and a brawl breaks out when Finnegan's men try to take O'Connor with them. O'Connor knocks out Finnegan as McCartney and Mary arrive with a radio contract. When the contrary O'Connor refuses to sign it, Mary belts him with a bottle, and he is bundled once more onto a plane, this time to Southampton to catch the *Queen Mary* to the US and become a radio star.

ANGELS WITH DIRTY FACES
(1938) US b&w 93 mins

Production Team

Producer ...... Warner Brothers/Sam Bischoff
Director .... Michael Curtiz
Screenplay .... John Wexley/Warren Duff
from a story by Rowland Brown
Cinematography .... Sol Polito
Editor .... Owen Marks
Musical Score .... Max Steiner

Cast

James Cagney .... Rocky Sullivan
Pat O'Brien .... Jerry Connolly
Humphrey Bogart .... James Frazier
Ann Sheridan .... Laury Martin
George Bancroft .... Mac Keefer
Billy Halop .... Soapy
Bobby Jordan .... Swing
Leo Gorcey .... Bim
Gabriel Dell .... Pasty
Huntz Hall .... Crab
Bernard Punsley .... Hunky
Joe Downing .... Steve
Edward Pawley .... Edwards
Adrian Morris...................................... Blackie
Frankie Burke .... Rocky (as a child)
William Tracey .... Jerry (as a child)
Marilyn Knowlden .... Laury (as a child)

ANGELS WITH DIRTY FACES
(1938) US b&w 93 mins

Echoing the prologue of Cagney's **The Public Enemy** seven years earlier, Michael Curtiz's punchy, hard-hitting crime drama *Angels with Dirty Faces* opens with urban scenes of juvenile mischief: two boys up to no good, teasing girls and stealing. Spotted thieving in a railroad yard, the boys are chased by cops; the taller of the two escapes, and the shorter one is caught. This incident seals their destinies – the taller boy is scared straight and goes on to become a priest, and the shorter one, refusing to rat on his pal, is sent to the Society for Juvenile Delinquents to begin a life of crime. When their paths cross again as adults, Father Jerry Connolly (Pat O'Brien) is a do-good priest in their old neighbourhood, trying to keep the current generation of tough boys (played by the 'Dead End Kids') out of jail; and gangster Rocky Sullivan (James Cagney) has just served three years for a crime in which a crooked lawyer named Frazier (Humphrey Bogart) is implicated. Rocky has kept his mouth shut about Frazier's involvement in return for a promise of $100,000 upon his release.

Back in the old neighbourhood, Rocky renews his friendship with Father Jerry when he visits his church where they served mass together as altar boys, greeting the priest with his catchphrase, "Whaddya hear? Whaddya say?" He also meets Laury (Ann Sheridan), a girl he used to tease as a kid, when he rents an apartment nearby. Things have changed while Rocky was inside. Frazier, now in cahoots with crime boss Mac Keefer (George Bancroft), has no intention of paying Rocky his money or cutting him in on any of his rackets. Instead, he plans to have him killed. On the street, Rocky's wallet is pickpocketed by the same kids that Father Jerry is trying to keep out of trouble. Rocky lets the kids know who they're dealing with, and they're awestruck. For Jerry's sake he gets them interested in basketball, which they had thought was a sissy sport when the padre proposed it. Rocky walks Laury home after the game, and, sensing that he's being followed, drops her off safely. He gets involved in a shootout with his pursuers, and realises it's a set-up by Frazier to get rid of him.

A furious Rocky abducts Frazier and cleans out his safe, discovering documents that link top city officials with Mac Keefer. Rocky uses Frazier as a bargaining chip to force Keefer to hand over his hundred grand, and when the crime boss sets the cops on him, blackmails him with the documents to call them off. Jerry goes looking for the kids when they fail to show up for a basketball game, and finds them swanking about in a pool hall with money that Rocky gave them, emulating his style. Rocky, meanwhile, is expanding his business to keep Laury in luxury. At Keefer's nightclub, he talks business with the owner, using the documents he stole from the safe as leverage. He demands, and gets, a 50 per cent cut of Keefer's operation. The newly prosperous Rocky makes an anonymous donation to the fund to build Father Jerry's recreation centre, but the priest rejects the dirty money when he realises its origin. Jerry confronts him about the damage he's doing to the kids by playing the lawless hero in the neighbourhood, but Rocky doesn't care.

ANGELS WITH DIRTY FACES
(1938) US b&w 93 mins

Father Jerry launches a fierce anti-corruption campaign, boldly taking a stand against his childhood friend and his crooked partners. Keefer and Frazier decide to kill the priest in retaliation, and when Rocky finds out he kills them both. As he flees from the murder scene, the cops corner him in an abandoned warehouse. Rocky wants to go down in a hail of gunfire, but he changes his plan when he runs out of bullets and the police let Jerry in to negotiate with him. He tries to escape using Jerry as a human shield, but is shot and arrested. The courts show no mercy to the unrepentant hoodlum, and he is sentenced to death for the double murder. Rocky remains defiant, promising to spit in the eye of his executioner, and his bravado on death row makes him more of a hero than ever to the street kids.

Jerry realises that he's losing these kids to crime, and he makes a last, desperate, plea to Rocky as he faces the electric chair. While Rocky wisecracks about his impending execution, Jerry begs him to throw away the only thing he has left – his defiance in the face of death – for the sake of the kids. Rocky refuses to drop the cocky strut and act scared. Snarling and full of hatred for the prison guards, he walks the long walk down the sombrely lit corridor to the death chamber. Max Steiner's score strikes an ominous, funereal tone, and Rocky bids a final farewell to Jerry. But as the warders are about to strap him in, he falls on the floor kicking and screaming, pleading pathetically for his life like a snivelling coward. Father Jerry's eyes well up in gratitude, his prayers answered, and the tough street kids are left with nothing but contempt for their former hero.

As the 1930s came to a close, Prohibition was long over, the mob had lost one of its most lucrative rackets, and Hollywood one of its most popular crime themes. But Cagney's wise-cracking, wired performance as Rocky Sullivan had lost none of the crackling energy that made him Hollywood's top gangster at the start of the decade. Curtiz's tautly directed crime classic pushes to the limit Cagney's violent thug persona, yet slaps enough social conscience on top in the form of Pat O'Brien's earnest priest to keep Production Code watchdogs at bay for glorifying an amoral anti-hero like Rocky Sullivan.

THE ISLANDMAN
(1938) IRL b&w 48 mins

Production Team

Producer .... INFC/Frank Duffy/
Victor Taylor
Director .... Patrick Keenan Heale
Screenplay .... Patrick Keenan Heale
from a story by
Donal O'Cahill/John Duffy
Cinematography .... Sidney Eaton
Editor .... J Neill-Brown
Musical Director .... Horace Sheldon

Cast

Cecil Ford .... Neal O'Moore
Eileen Curran .... Eileen Guheen
Brian O'Sullivan .... Liam O'Kane
Gabriel Fallon .... Father O'Sullivan
Daisy Murphy .... Peg
Gerard Duffy .... Boy
Paddy Carey .... Student
Brian Carey .... Student
Eugene Leahy .... Dancer
Séamus Moynihan .... Dancer

A pipe-smoking islander off the coast of Kerry regales a visitor with a story, shown in flashback, of a romance that occurred on the Great Blasket Island many years before, between a Dublin student and a local teacher. A bored Trinity medical student named Neal O'Moore (Cecil Ford) is inspired by reading Tomas O'Crohan's autobiography, *The Islandman*, to leave Dublin to visit Ó'Crohan's island, off the Kerry coast. Upon his arrival in Kerry after a scenic journey, he meets a local priest, Father O'Sullivan (Gabriel Fallon). When the priest finds out Neal is studying medicine, he asks him to take a look at the hand of an injured fisherman on the island, Liam O'Kane (Brian O'Sullivan). Neal takes care of the injury, and a ceili is held in his honour, at which he meets Eileen (Eileen Curran), a teacher in the island school. Eileen is engaged to Liam, and thanks Neal for taking care of her boyfriend. She does her party piece, singing 'Eileen Aroon', and the islanders dance jigs and reels.

Neal is attracted to Eileen and pesters her by hanging around, ostensibly to learn Irish, but really to be near her. He soon realises that she doesn't think he compares well with Liam. Dejected, he leaves the island and returns to Dublin to resume his medical studies. A year passes, and Neal finds life at university just as much of a chore as he did before his trip to the island. He is reminded of the Blaskets while listening to the wireless one day, when he hears Eileen singing 'Eileen Aroon'. He realises that he misses her, and decides to go back there to see her again.

During his absence, Eileen hopes he never comes back because he was disrupting things between her and Liam. Liam, however, liked the medical student more than she did and misses him madly. Neal returns, bearing a gift of a gramaphone and a record of Eileen singing. He resolves to be a better man than Liam at his own line of work. The priest is against this and advises him to go home, but Neal, determined to impress Eileen, ignores him and joins the crew of Liam's boat. He bonds with Liam by saving him from drowning in shark-infested waters after he gets into difficulties retrieving an oar. On their next fishing trip Liam falls overboard again and Neal rescues him, but he is badly injured on rocks. Liam is put to bed when they go ashore, and the islanders pray for him. Neal knows there isn't much hope. As the priest is about to give him his Last Rites, Liam feebly reaches for the hands of Eileen and Neal, and joins them together to consent to their romance after he's gone.

Made by a splinter group from the team that made *The Dawn* two years before, *The Islandman* was filmed on the Blasket Islands, in Trinity College and County Wicklow, with a cast of Gate Theatre actors and amateurs from the Cork Shakespeare Company. Also known as *West of Kerry*, the film and was released in the US as *Men of Ireland*. Given that it followed only four years after Flaherty's *Man of Aran* and uses the O'Crohan book as a reason for going to the Blaskets, *The Islandman* might have had more to say about the island than merely using it as a location for a trite love triangle. But the film shows impressive footage of currach racing, fishing, and local crafts, and is a valuable visual document of a lifestyle that ceased to exist when the entire population of the Blaskets was evacuated to the mainland in the 1950s.

BLARNEY
(1939) IRL b&w 62 mins

Jimmy O'Dea star of *Blarney*
(Still courtesy of The National Library)

Production Team

Producer	Harry O'Donovan/ O'D Productions
Director	Harry O'Donovan
Screenplay	Harry O'Donovan/ Jimmy O'Dea
Cinematography	C S Parker, C M P Richards
Editor	Tilly Day
Musical Score	Dermot MacMurrough

Cast

Jimmy O'Dea	Billy Brannigan
Hazel Hughes	Maura O'Connor
J H Edwin	Mr O'Connor
Noel Purcell	Sergeant Dolan
Rodney Malcolmson	Sergeant MacAleer
Myrette Morven	Annie Burke
Julie Suedo	Sadie Tyler
Ken Warrington	Albert Tyler
Jimmy Wildman	'Scutty' Whelan
Tome Dunne	'Bullock' Byrne

BLARNEY
(1939) IRL b&w 62 mins

Popular comedian of the Irish theatre Jimmy O'Dea had been making occasional screen appearances since the silent era, when he debuted in Norman Whitten's *Casey's Millions* in 1922. In 1938 he teamed up with director Harry O'Donovan to form their own production company and film *Blarney*, a satire written by O'Donovan about the peculiar effects of the partitioning of Ireland on those who live close to the border. Prominent in the story is a frontier customs post where "almost everything is dutiable except a sense of humour". Shot on location in the fishing villages of Carlingford and Greenore, Blarney features O'Dea (bearing some resemblance to Chaplin, in his bowler hat and tight little suit) in the role of Billy Brannigan, an out-of-work mechanic turned travelling salesman. Billy tries to make a living selling cough medicine from a suitcase in the border counties of Armagh and Louth. He runs into trouble when he bums a lift from a pair of jewel thieves, and accidentally gets his suitcase mixed up with theirs. When they throw him out of the car before fleeing from the cops, he ends up with the loot from their last job. Soon the thieves, Sadie (Julie Suedo) and Albert Tyler (Ken Warrington), are after him to retrieve their ill-gotten gains.

Billy meets an attractive barmaid, Annie (Myrette Morven), at the Border Inn, and falls in love with her. The proprietor of the bar, a man named O'Connor, has a beautiful daughter Maura (Hazel Hughes), who has two policemen making romantic enquiries about her, one a Garda from the South, Sergeant Dolan (Noel Purcell), and the other a Royal Ulster Constabulary man from the North, Sergeant MacAleer (Rodney Malcolmson). Maura prefers the RUC man, much to the annoyance of her father (J H Edwin), who would rather keep matters concerning his family on the southern side of the border. O'Connor thinks that a sergeant's pay won't support his daughter, and he makes it clear that a promotion for either officer would improve the chances of getting paternal approval for the courtship. As Maura's relationship with MacAleer grows, her father relents, and he accepts the inevitable. He blesses the union with the hope that the border will soon cease to be, and the disputes that brought it into being can be settled by friendly handshakes from both sides of the divide. Sergeant Dolan is left disappointed, but tries to save face by besting the Ulster officer in catching the jewel thieves.

In the finale, Billy helps the RUC man to catch the Tylers and retrieve the jewels on the northern side of the divide, guaranteeing promotion to the rank of District Inspector for MacAleer. The Garda sergeant stoically accepts defeat again and shakes hands across the border with his rival.

Released with the more pertinent title *Ireland's Borderline* in the United States, *Blarney* was to be the sole feature turned out by the O'Dea/O'Donovan production company, though O'Donovan had previously written a screenplay, *Jimmy Boy*, for O'Dea in 1935. O'Dea would go on to win international recognition for a lively performance as King Brian, monarch of the leprechauns, much later in his career in the Disney film *Darby O'Gill and the Little People*. His stage work at the now defunct Royal and Queens Theatres in Ireland has long since assumed the status of legend.

I SEE A DARK STRANGER
(1946) UK b&w 112 mins

Production Team

Producer ....Sidney Gilliat,
Frank Launder/
Individual Pictures (UK)
Director....................................Frank Launder
Screenplay ....Frank Launder,
Sidney Gilliat
Cinematography ....Willliam Allan,
Skeets Kelly
Editor .... Thelma Myers
Musical Score.............. William Allwyn/LSO

Cast

Deborah Kerr .... Bridie Quilty
Trevor Howard .... Lieut David Baynes
W O'Gorman ....Danny Quilty
Harry Webster .... Uncle Joe
Liam Redmond ....Uncle Timothy
Kathleen Murphy ....First Irishwoman
Josephine Fitzgerald ......Second Irishwoman
Eddie Golden .... Terence Delaney
Marie Ault .... Mrs O'Mara
Raymond Huntley .... J Miller
Tony Quinn ....Portrait museum guide
Brefni O'Rorke ....Michael O'Callaghan
John Salew .... Man in bookshop
James Harcourt .... Grandfather Edwards
Olga Lindo .... Mrs Edwards
David Ward .... Oscar Pryce
Garry Marsh ....Captain Goodhusband
Tom MacAulay .... Lieutenant Spanswick

I SEE A DARK STRANGER
(1946) UK b&w 112 mins

Impressionable young Bridie Quilty (Deborah Kerr), growing up in the village of Ballingarry in the west of Ireland, is so taken with the stories her locquacious father Danny (W O'Gorman) tells every night in the pub about his daring exploits against the British in the 1916 Rising, that she knows every word by heart. When she reaches the age of 21, she decides to emulate the old rogue and take up the struggle against the British herself. She heads for Dublin, and on the train she meets a German spy named Miller (Raymond Huntley). She takes an instant dislike to him, assuming he's British from the name tag on his luggage, the cruel set of his jaw, and the fact that he's reading *The Economist*. She tells him of her father's involvement in the Rising, more than 30 years earlier, and shares with him her hatred of all things English. Amused, he chides her with excessive belligerence for a citizen of a neutral nation.

At a portrait gallery in Dublin she meets Michael O'Callaghan (Brefni O'Rorke), a key figure in her father's rebel stories, who seems to have trouble remembering Danny Quilty. To his surprise she asks him to help her join the IRA to fight the British and end the partition of Ireland. O'Callaghan reminds her that Ireland has pursued only constitutional means to achieve this objective since the Treaty of 1921. He advises her to do the same, and to go back where she came from while she's at it. Perplexed, she finds inspiration in a portrait of Irish patriot Roger Casement in the Gallery, and goes to a bookshop to buy a German phrasebook with a view to learning the language and helping the Germans against the English.

Miller spots her in the bookshop, where he is surreptitiously meeting one of his fellow spies to hatch a plot to spring a colleague from jail in England. He enlists Bridie's help, and she moves to England to help free the prisoner, Oscar Pryce (David Ward). As a cover for her espionage, she works in a Devonshire hotel, gathering information from soldiers billeted there regarding the transfer of Pryce to a jail in London. Miller encourages Bridie to go out on a date with a hotel guest, a British Military Intelligence Officer named Baynes (Trevor Howard), while he sets in motion his plan to free Pryce. He helps Pryce to escape but the pair are shot by soldiers on patrol. Pryce is killed, and Miller badly wounded.

When Bridie returns to the hotel from her date with Baynes, she is shocked to find the injured Miller in her room, on the brink of death. Before he expires he discloses information about a mysterious notebook on the Isle of Man, as told to him by Pryce before he died. The sinister Miller enjoys a few final cigarettes and gives Bridie gruesome instructions regarding the disposal of his soon-to-be-dead body. Bridie pushes him down the town in a wheelchair, passing him off as the hotel manager's disabled grandfather, and tosses him over a cliff. Baynes is suspicious of Bridie's involvement in the night's skullduggery, and follows her the next day when she boards a train for Liverpool. From there, she proceeds by boat to the Isle of Man to find the notebook as Miller had described it, unaware that a pair of hilariously inept investigation officers (Garry Marsh and Tom MacAulay) are looking for her.

I SEE A DARK STRANGER
(1946) UK b&w 112 mins

The notebook contains secret information regarding the D-Day Invasion. Bridie burns it, fearing that thousands of English and Irish soldiers will be endangered if it falls into German hands. Baynes shows up at her hotel and declares his love for her. She declares that she is a retired German spy. The pair are abducted to Ireland by non-retired German spies, and they join a convoy of alarm clock smugglers, disguised as a funeral cortege, going to the border between Northern Ireland and the Free State. Bridie and Baynes escape from the Germans when custom officials intercept the convoy. They go to a pub and when some American soldiers arrive, Baynes realises that they are in Northern Ireland. Bridie refuses to leave when she finds out that she is on the northern side, but when police arrive looking for her, Baynes helps her to escape back across the border with the American soldiers on their way to a dance down south.

After the war Bridie and Baynes are reunited. They get married, and on their honeymoon night he books them into the Cromwell Hotel. She storms out in a huff

I SEE A DARK STRANGER
(1946) UK b&w 112 mins

when she finds out the name of the hotel, much to his astonishment.

Kerr plays the naïve but stubborn Bridie with a deadpan determination that generates much hilarity, thanks to Launder and Gilliat's eccentric script, and Howard's upper lip has never been stiffer. The following year, Kerr would extend her Irish repetoire to play Tipperary nun Sister Clodagh in the Powell/Pressburger film *Black Narcissus*, and Launder and Gilliat would return to work on location in Ireland with *Captain Boycott*.

CAPTAIN BOYCOTT
(1947) UK b&w 93 mins

(Still courtesy of Star Stills)

Production Team

Producer .... Sidney Gilliat,
Frank Launder/
Individual Pictures (UK)
Director.................................... Frank Launder
Screenplay .... Frank Launder,
Sidney Gilliat
Cinematography .... Oswald Morris
Editor .... Thelma Myers
Musical Score .... William Allwyn

Cast

Stewart Granger .... Hugh Davin
Kathleen Ryan .... Anne Killain
Noel Purcell .... Dan McGinty
Cecil Parker .... Captain Boycott
Robert Donat .... Charles Stuart Parnell
Niall MacGinnis .... Mark Killain
Liam Gaffney .... Michael Fagan
Bernadette O'Farrell .... Mrs Fagan
Mervyn Johns .... Watty Connell
Maureen Delaney .... Mrs Davin
Alaister Sim .... Father McKeogh
Liam Redmond .... Martin Egan
Edward Golden .... Harry Piggott

CAPTAIN BOYCOTT
(1947) UK b&w 93 mins

The man whose name entered the language as a synonym for organised social and economic isolation was the subject of one of the first films made in Ireland after World War II. Captain Charles Boycott was a notorious landlord's agent in the west of Ireland in the 1880s, and the true story of the collective action against him by his tenants, driving him to ruin, provided the basis for director Frank Launder's historic drama. The film features Stewart Granger in a lively performance as rebellious young tenant farmer and horse-racing fan Hugh Davin. Cecil Parker plays the villainous Captain Boycott, and a host of Abbey actors appear in the minor roles. Robert Donat makes a brief cameo as Charles Stuart Parnell, then at the peak of his power in Ireland before his affair with a married woman destroyed his career.

The agent of an absentee landlord in Lough Mask, County Mayo, Captain Boycott regards his tenants as a shifty, worthless lot. He raises the rent as high as he can to maximise profits, without a thought for the hardships the tenants inevitably suffer. Those who can't pay are forcibly evicted, and replaced by more compliant tenant farmers at still higher rates. The more volatile tenants plot secretly to remove Boycott by force, but are swayed by Parnell's policies of peaceful resistance.

One of the evicted tenants, Michael Fagan (Liam Gaffney), filled with rage at the loss of his holding, tries to kill the new renter (Niall MacGinnis) installed in his cottage, and is himself killed in the struggle. Emotions run high, and an armed insurrection against Boycott and his lackeys seems inevitable. An angry mob attacks him at a race meet (filmed at the now-defunct Mullingar racetrack) where the cash-poor land agent had hoped to win a bundle with a horse he obtained by unfair means from Davin. English soldiers rescue him and restore order. But the pacifist tactics of Parnell win out in the end, and the renters withold payments from Boycott until he's driven from the county, a broken man. Cecil Parker's Boycott is not quite the cartoon villain he first appears, despite the waxed moustache and gruff manner. He moves from intransigence to signs of sympathy for the tenants, adding another layer to a plot already textured by having Davin fall for the daughter (Kathleen Ryan) of that least popular of neighbours, the tenant who moves into the cottage of an evicted family.

The film was shot on location in Wicklow, Westmeath and Mayo, an experience that prompted producer Sidney Gilliat to add an addendum to W C Fields' famous caveat about acting with animals or children: "It is said that no actor can survive playing opposite a child or a dog. Let me add that it is just as lethal playing with the Abbey players. Apart from being able to act you off the screen, they can also drink you under the table!" The Abbey actors are in unusually restrained form, with the exception of the incorrigible Noel Purcell – as schoolteacher Dan McGinty, he foments revolution in the minds of his pupils with roguish charm and a Dublin accent that could be cut with a knife. Would-be dashing rebel Davin is put in his place on a regular basis by his nagging mother (Maureen Delaney), and lively dialogue and animal husbandry jokes recur during the course of the film, to lighten the tone of a historic drama based on real-life events in 19th century County Mayo.

ODD MAN OUT
(1947) UK b&w 116 mins

Production Team

Producer .... Carol Reed, Philip Samuel/
          Two Cities Films
Director .... Carol Reed
Screenplay .... F L Green, R C Sheriff
    from Green's book of the same name
Cinematography .... Robert Krasker
Editor .... Fergus McDonnell
Musical Score .... William Allwyn

Cast

James Mason .... Johnny McQueen
Kathleen Ryan .... Kathleen Sullivan
Robert Beatty .... Dennis
Cyril Cusack .... Pat
Roy Irving .... Murphy
Dan O'Herlihy .... Nolan
F J McCormick .... Shell
Robert Newton .... Lukey
Kitty Kirwan .... Granny
Maureen Delaney .... Theresa
Denis O'Dea .... Inspector
William Hartnell .... Fencie
Fay Compton .... Rosie Englishwoman
Beryl Measor .... Maudie English woman
W G Fay .... Father Tom

ODD MAN OUT
(1947) UK b&w 116 mins

James Mason stars as Johnny McQueen, an IRA leader on the run from jail in Belfast, in Carol Reed's crisp black-and-white suspense drama. Months of hiding out in a safe house run by Granny (Kitty Kirwan) has taken its toll of Johnny's mental health, and his men doubt his leadership abilities as they plan a payroll robbery at a Belfast mill. The robbery goes wrong, a cashier is killed, and Johnny is wounded as they try to escape from the scene after the alarm is sounded. Johnny falls from the speeding getaway car and the driver, Pat (Cyril Cusack), refuses to go back for him. Despite his injuries Johnny eludes the police as he wanders dazed through the backstreets of Belfast, the object of a massive manhunt. A passage is arranged for Johnny on a ship leaving Belfast docks that night, but his comrades Pat, Dennis (Robert Beatty), and Murphy (Roy Irving) have to track him down before the police do. His anxious girlfriend Kathleen (Kathleen Ryan) wants to go with them despite the dangers involved. Time (signified by the highly mobile Albert Clock, a Belfast landmark visible from almost every window in the film) is running out, and there's a price on his head that tempts a neighbour, Shell (F J McCormick), to turn Johnny in when he finds him. In a cryptic exchange with a priest, Father Tom (W G Fay), the nervous, agitated Shell debates whether to help Johnny to escape or to betray him for the reward.

While searching for their missing leader, Pat and Nolan (Dan O'Herlihy) unwittingly play into the hands of an informer, Theresa (Maureen Delaney). She phones the police with information they have given her about the safe house where Johnny stayed with Granny and his girlfriend Kathleen. The police arrive to arrest Pat and Nolan, starting a gunfight in which both are killed. Johnny takes refuge in the snug of a pub (a recreation of Belfast's famous Victorian gin palace, The Crown Bar) where he meets a charismatic artist (Robert Newton) who takes him to his studio to paint his dying portrait. Helped and hindered by this assortment of oddball characters, Johnny finally makes it to the docks only to meet a police patrol that fatally shoots both him and Kathleen, the woman who loves him.

Attempts at making and distributing films with IRA themes in the 1920s and 1930s often ran foul of the Chief Censor in Britain, an ex-army officer who had served in Ireland during the War of Independence and had little sympathy for the Irish. Later attempts to dramatise the deeds of the IRA tended to fare better when they were vague with details of the cause for which they were fighting. *Odd Man Out* evades the specifics of post-partition Belfast, giving away little about the clandestine organisation to which Johnny belongs or the city in which it conducts its violent campaign. However, it remains a triumph of style from the director who would go on to make *The Third Man* two years later. *Odd Man Out* features outstanding performances from Mason, Newton and veteran Abbey actor McCormick (in the penultimate performance of a sporadic film career that began in 1915), and was deemed the Best British Film at the 1947 British Film Academy Awards. Reed's chiaroscuro drama moves deftly from hard realism, to film noir flourishes, to surreal hallucination, as the mind of its ailing central character sinks into delirium and his wounded body seeps his life away on the snowy streets of Belfast.

ANOTHER SHORE
(1948) UK b&w 91 mins

(Still courtesy of the Irish Film Archive of the Film Institute of Ireland)

Production Team

Producer ...... Ealing Studios/Michael Balcon
Director .... Charles Crichton
Screenplay .... Walter Meade
          from the novel by Kenneth Reddin
Cinematography .... Douglas Slocombe
Editor .... Bernard Gribble
Musical Score .... Georges Auric

Cast

Robert Beatty .... Gulliver
Moira Lister .... Jennifer
Stanley Holloway .... Alaistair McNeil
Michael Medwin .... Yellow
Maureen Delaney .... Mrs Gleeson
Dermot Kelly .... Boxer
Michael Golden .... Broderick
Wilfred Brambell .... Moore
W A Kelly .... Roger
Sheila Manahan .... Nora
Fred O'Donovan .... Coghlan
Edie Martin .... Lady in park
Michael O'Mahoney .... Fleming
Bill Shine .... Socialite
Irene Worth .... Socialite
Desmond Keane .... Parkes

ANOTHER SHORE
(1948) UK b&w 91 mins

Robert Beatty stars as a workshy dreamer named Gulliver Sheils who lives in Dublin, and fantasises about escaping from his humdrum existence by moving to sunny Raratonga, in Tahiti. Lacking the 200 guineas to realise his dream, he comes up with a money-making scheme that quickly becomes an obsession. He imagines that if he hangs around for long enough at the dangerous traffic junction of Trinity College and Dame Street, he will eventually have the opportunity to save a wealthy pedestrian from injury in a car accident, and the grateful person will then reward him by paying his passage to the South Seas. He daydreams about what life would be like on the island as he bides his time waiting for such an accident to happen. Various distractions sidetrack him from his main objective as he waits for his plan to fall into place, most attractive among them being a beautiful girl named Jennifer (Moira Lister), who becomes smitten with the commitment-phobic Gulliver.

Eventually, his patience at the traffic-watch pays off, and he gets to assist at an accident in which a chauffeur-driven car hits a bicycle messenger. The passenger in the back seat of the car, Alaistair MacNeil (Stanley Holloway, a staple character in British comedy of the postwar years), is more shaken by the incident than the cyclist. A wealthy but eccentric alcoholic, Alaistair wants to travel with Gulliver to the South Seas as soon as his wife dies. The plan is expedited when Alaistair's wife runs off with his chauffeur, Parkes, and Alaistair's solicitors tell him that he gets all her property on grounds of desertion.

Gulliver is surprised to find himself overcome with concern when he sees Jennifer's car crashed, as he was sure that he didn't reciprocate her feelings for him. He is relieved to find that she is unhurt, and on the eve of his departure for his dream destination, he spends his last night in Dublin with her. As Gulliver and Alaistair drive off the next day to catch the boat and begin their exotic journey, a friend of Jennifer's named Yellow (Michael Medwin) accidentally crashes into their vehicle. Jennifer takes advantage of Gulliver's dazed condition to convince Yellow to go in his stead to Tahiti. When Gulliver recovers, he returns to his dull civil service job in the Custom House for the first time in a year and a half, and accepts his fate with Jennifer in Dublin.

Dublin-born actor Wilfred Brambell (better known as Steptoe Senior in *Steptoe and Son*, less so as Paul McCartney's crazy Irish grandfather in *A Hard Day's Night*), plays the solicitor Moore who handles MacNeil's affairs. *Another Shore* was a precursor of the quirky features that would proliferate from Ealing Studios under the aegis of producer Michael Balcon in the late-1940s and early-1950s. By the following year, Ealing comedies were in full swing, with *Whisky Galore, Kind Hearts and Coronets* and *Passport to Pimlico* all released in 1949, and *The Lavender Hill Mob* two years later. *Another Shore* was billed as a tragi-comedy on its release; the tragi-part may well refer to the attempt by its producers to pass off as a happy ending Gulliver's abandonment of his dream in favour of a banal domestic life.

DAUGHTER OF DARKNESS
(1948) UK b&w 91 mins

Production Team

Producer .... W Victor Hanbury
Director .... Lance Comfort
Screenplay .... Max Catto
Cinematography .... Stanley Pavey
Editor .... Leto Carruthers
Musical Score .... Clifton Parker

Cast

Síobhan McKenna .... Emmy Beaudine
Liam Redmond .... Father Corcoran
Maxwell Reed .... Dan
George Thorpe .... Mr Tallent
Grant Tyler .... Larry Tallent
Honor Blackman .... Julie Tallent
Anne Crawford .... Bess Stanforth
David Greene .... David Price
Arthur Hambling .... Jacob
George Merritt .... Constable
Barry Morse .... Robert Stanforth
Nora O'Mahoney .... Miss Hegarty
Ann Clery .... Miss Foley

DAUGHTER OF DARKNESS
(1948) UK b&w 91 mins

Based on the Max Catto play *They Walk Alone*, Lance Comfort's *Daughter of Darkness* gave renowned Irish stage actress Síobhan McKenna her first starring role on the big screen – she had debuted the previous year with a supporting role in *Hungry Hill*, and turned down the Bridie Quilty lead in *I See a Dark Stranger* (played instead by Deborah Kerr) the year before. In Comfort's grand guignol psychodrama, McKenna plays Emmy Baudine, an angelic young Irish girl who plays the church organ and works as a priest's housekeeper in a rural village. Despite these saintly credentials, the womenfolk of the locality find her unsettling – she has an indefinable quality that their men find irresistably attractive, and they send a delegation to the parochial house to suggest to the priest, Father Corcoran (Liam Redmond), that she be run out of town.

The problem gets out of hand when Emmy goes on a date with a boxer from a visiting English fairground called Battling Dan (Maxwell Reed). He wins prizes for her at the various attractions and they get sufficiently close for him to make physical advances. She responds by savagely lacerating his face with her fingernails. This doesn't go down well with her employer and Father Corcoran decides to solve the problem by exporting it, as was the custom at the time. He arranges employment for her with the Tallents, a wholesome farming family of his acquaintance in rural England. She settles in well with them and behaves herself at first, despite generating tensions among the women of the household with her innate attractiveness. Her old trouble soon comes back to haunt her when Battling Dan's nomadic troupe sets up camp at the village near the Tallent farm. The Tallent family and their in-laws are excited about the funfair, and they all go there in Larry Tallent's (Grant Tyler) car for an evening out, bringing the reluctant Emmy with them.

At the funfair she meets the scarred boxer Dan, who is still transfixed by her despite her penchant for disfigurement. He takes her to his caravan where his dog frightens her, but not as much as she frightens the dog. She runs away from him, taking refuge in a barn, and when he chases after her she screams psychotically. The next day Dan's dog goes searching for him, and when he comes upon Dan's body in the barn he howls loudly for his dead master. At the Tallent Farm, Mr Tallent announces that there's been a murder – a fairground gypsy has been found dead. Emmy runs in distress to the nearby seashore where she meets a charming, sensitive young man named David Price (David Greene). He makes advances at her and is never seen alive again.

One of the daughters of the Tallent house, Bess Stanforth, suspects that there is a connection between the murdered gypsy, the disappeared David and the highly strung Irish girl. When the Tallents' barn mysteriously catches fire during the night, Bess' suspicions intensify. Her brother Larry makes a horrific discovery – in the smouldering ruins of the barn he finds David Price's charred body. Bess screams hysterically and insists that Emmy must leave. She confronts Emmy with her forebodings about

DAUGHTER OF DARKNESS
(1948) UK b&w 91 mins

her rottenness and the feeling of horror that she inspires in her.

At a church service for David Price, the Tallent menfolk pass notes through the congregation like schoolboys, to let everyone know that they intend to catch the murderer that night. They convene later in the churchyard during a thunderstorm, and when they hear the organ playing, they dash into the church to apprehend the organist, assuming it is murderer. They catch a glimpse of a fleeing figure as they enter the organ loft.

At the Tallent house, Bess encounters a nervous Emmy coming in from outside, drenched to the skin. She demands that Emmy be gone by dawn. Emmy accuses her of heartlessness, and begins packing her bags. As she packs, a wicked look crosses her face and she decides to seduce Larry Tallent. The action cuts to the police station, where the officer on duty is organising road blocks and search parties following the murder of Larry. Bess knows where to find the perpetrator, and heads for the church. She confronts the hysterical Emmy, who makes a pitiful attempt to disclaim the terrible impulses that came over her when the men looked at her the way they did. She meekly asks Bess if she's going to die, and Bess thinks that she is. Bess lets her leave the safety of the church to face Dan's snarling, lupine hound, waiting outside to avenge the death of his master.

DAUGHTER OF DARKNESS
(1948) UK b&w 91 mins

Daughter of Darkness presents an early instance on screen of that rare villain, the female serial killer, and was daring for its time in its lurid portrayal of the psychotic side of sexual attraction. Catto's original play describes the Emmy character as a 'homicidal nymphomaniac', though the film role manifests more signs of aversion to sex than compulsion. Síobhan McKenna acquits herself well in her first lead role as the jittery murderer Emmy, but she remained very much a stage actress and her film appearances were rare in later years. She made a notable return to the screen in 1962 to play Pegeen Mike in Brian Desmond Hurst's *Playboy of the Western World,* when she was already much older than the ingenue type Synge had in mind for the role. In that same year, her *Daughter of Darkness* co-star and screen debutant Honor Blackman would trade in the English Rose persona of her Julie Tallent character to become leather-trousered martial arts expert Cathy Gale in the classic television series, *The Avengers.*

LUCK OF THE IRISH
(1948) US b&w 98 mins

Production Team

Producer .... Twentieth Century Fox/
                                      Fred Kohlmar
Director .... Henry Koster
Screenplay .... Philip Dunne
Cinematography .... Joseph La Shelle
Editor .... J Watson Webb Jr
Musical Score .... Cyril J Mockridge

Cast

Tyrone Power .... Stephen Fitzgerald
Cecil Kellaway .... Horace
Anne Baxter .... Nora
Lee J Cobb .... D C Augur
Jayne Meadows .... Frances Augur
James Todd .... Bill Clark
J M Kerrigan .... Taedy
Phil Brown .... Higginbotham
Charles Irwin .... Cornelius
Louise Lorimer .... Secretary
Tim Ryan .... Patrolman Clancy
Harry Antrim .... Senator Ransom
Margaret Wells .... Mrs Augur
John Goldsworthy .... Butler
Douglas Gerrard .... Receptionist
Tito Vuolo .... Greek vendor
William Swingley .... Terrance

LUCK OF THE IRISH
(1948) US b&w 98 mins

New York reporter Stephen Fitzgerald (Tyrone Power) meets a diminutive man mending shoes by a waterfall while looking for help after his car goes off the road. Stephen had been speeding to Shannon airport with fellow journalist Bill Clark (James Todd) to catch a flight back to the US. The shoemaker gives Stephen directions to a nearby village, and the journalists spend the night there at an inn with a view to flying out the next day. The innkeeper Taedy (J M Kerrigan) is surprised to hear of the encounter with the little man, who he claims is a leprechaun. Taedy leaves out some whiskey for him, despite Stephen's insistence that the wee folk drink milk. When the little man appears for a sup, Stephen catches him and makes him reveal where his crock of gold is hidden. Stephen refuses the treasure, and the leprechaun is extremely grateful. Stephen accepts just a single coin from the crock. Before Stephen leaves for the airport the next day, the innkeeper's daughter Nora (Anne Baxter) tells him that the waterfall where he met the shoemaker doesn't exist.

Stephen returns to New York to work as a scriptwriter for publisher and senatorial candidate D C Augur (Lee J Cobb), a job arranged by Augur's daughter Frances (Jayne Meadows), who fancies Stephen and wants to marry him. The little man shows up at Stephen's apartment, introduces himself as Horace (Cecil Kellaway) and offers his services gratis as butler. Stephen doesn't recognise him. Horace proves to be an incompetent and drunken servant, but Stephen can't bring himself to fire him. Horace dislikes Augur's policies and prevents Stephen from going by car to a political rally. When he takes the subway instead, Stephen meeets Nora, by an uncanny coincidence.

A rift develops between Stephen and his employer when his scripts are at odds with the candidate's viewpoint, but he hangs on in the hope of getting a top job after the election. Frances assures him he will soon be running the publishing house and they get engaged. Bill returns from Ireland and tempts Stephen with a job as foreign correspondent there. Torn between working for the corrupt Augur and following his heart to do something in which he believes, Stephen runs into further dilemmas when he meets Nora at a New York Irish wedding on the eve of her return to Ireland. Though his own wedding is weeks away, he realises that he really loves Nora. Then it finally dawns on him that the servant is the leprechaun he met in Ireland, and that Nora's appearance in New York is part of his scheme. Stephen decides his future lies with Nora and abandons his engagement and Augur's big job offer to return to Ireland and marry the girl.

Tyrone Power, son of a Broadway matinee idol of the same name, and great-grandson of the legendary Irish actor of the early-19th century, also Tyrone Power, returned to his roots with this piece of eccentric shamroguery. He had resumed his acting career after a stint in the marines in World War II, determined to broaden his range beyond the pretty-boy roles that made him Fox's biggest star in pre-war years. He would return to Ireland almost a decade later to narrate John Ford's *The Rising of the Moon*, one of his last films before his premature death from a heart attack at the age of 44.

SAINTS AND SINNERS
(1949) UK b&w 73 mins

Production Team

Producer .... London Films/British Lion
Productions/Leslie Arliss
Director .... Leslie Arliss
Screenplay .... Paul Vincent Carroll
and Leslie Arliss
(with additional dialogue
by Mabbie Poole)
Cinematography .... Osmond Borradaile
Editor .... David Newhouse
Musical Score .... Philip Green

Cast

Kieron Moore .... Michael Kissane
Christine Norden .... Blanche
Sheila Manahan .... Shelah Flaherty
Máire O'Neill .... Ma Murnaghan
Michael Dolan .... The Canon
Noel Purcell .... Flaherty
Liam Redmond .... Dan O'Driscoll
Pam Arliss .... Betty
Maureen Delany .... Postmistress
Tom Dillon .... J P O'Brien
Anita Bolster .... Julia Ann Dermody
Tony Quinn .... Berry
Eddie Byrne .... Norreys

SAINTS AND SINNERS
(1949) UK b&w 73 mins

Three years before *The Quiet Man* was released, Leslie Arliss produced, wrote and directed *Saints and Sinners*, a romantic comedy that stands as a dark, acerbic precursor to the John Ford epic. The film opens with a similar scenario – a young man returns to his native village by train, and is met at the station by an assortment of eccentric locals. Michael Kissane (Kieron Moore) has a great welcome for himself, but no one else does. The Kilwirra natives would rather fuss over a wealthy returned yank, J P O'Brien (Tom Dillon), and his glam moll, Blanche (Christine Norden) than give the time of day to Kissane. He is shunned as he walks down the village, and it becomes clear that he has just spent two years in jail, having been wrongly convicted of stealing the parish funds raised for a new church bell. Unlike John Wayne's Sean Thornton, who left a violent past behind him to find his utopia in Inisfree, Kissane knows that Kilwirra is a festering den of petty hypocrites, and that to clear his name he must not only find the real thief, but expose the misdeeds of his holier-than-thou neighbours.

The villagers are distracted from their shunning of Kissane by a hot racing tip – Dark Glory in the Grand National – spread around town by local gossip, clairvoyant and trickster, Ma Murnaghan (Máire O'Neill). Everyone bets on the horse, except the local priest (Michael Dolan), who takes a dim view of such forecasts. He insists that the future belongs to God alone, and forbids Ma to make any more predictions.

Kissane returns to the scene of the crime – Flaherty's Hotel, where the church bell fund was stolen while in his care. Looking for work, Kissane gets a flat refusal from Flaherty (Noel Purcell), but accepts a menial job, offered by his ex-girlfriend, Shelah Flaherty (Sheila Manahan), after a bitterly funny exchange in which he accuses her father of being crooked.

Kissane makes a little extra on the side as chauffeur and guide for the proto-Marilyn tourist Blanche, while the wealthy American O'Brien is getting hit up for church improvement funds by the Canon. This tour-guide role gives Kissane the chance to get stranded overnight in a ruin with the flirty voluptuary, during a rainstorm (much as John Wayne would do with Maureen O'Hara three years later).

Ma Murnaghan takes to her bed, declaring herself deathly ill, and makes a final prediction: that the world will end the following Tuesday evening, at the sound of the Angelus bell. Her success at picking horses gives credibility to her doomsday prophecy, and pious souls turn up in droves at the church to blurt their scams, swindles and acts of thievery to the Canon. Impending doom flushes out the real perpetrator of the crime for which Kissane served time and the Canon, horrified to find that all his saints are sinners, wonders is life worth living, as his flock waits in the churchyard under blackening skies for the world to end.

Arliss' dark comedy tears down the false facades of small-town life in Ireland, exposing the moral dry rot behind, where Ford's *The Quiet Man* adds a few coats of green paint and views them through a lens heavily trowelled with vaseline. A cynical doppelganger to the more famous rural idyll, *Saints and Sinners* is a hilarious and acetic antidote to Ford's cloying saccharine.

NO RESTING PLACE
(1951) UK b&w 77 mins

Production Team

Producer .... Colin Lesslie
Director ....Paul Rotha
Screenplay ...... Michael Orrom, Colin Lesslie
and Paul Rotha
from the book by Ian Niall;
dialogue in Irish by Gerard Healy
Cinematography .... Wolfgang Suschitsky
Editor .... Michael Orrom, Betty Orgar
Musical Score .... William Allwyn

Cast

Michael Gough .... Alec Kyle
Noel Purcell .... Guard Mannigan
Eithne Dunne .... Meg Kyle
Jack MacGowran .... Billy Kyle
Brian O'Higgins .... Tom Kyle
Maureen O'Sullivan .... Nan Kyle
Diana Campbell .... Mrs Mannigan
May Craig .... Farmer's Wife
Fred Johnson .... Ross
Robert Hennessy .... Police Superintendant
Christy Lawrence .... Paddy Kyle

NO RESTING PLACE
(1951) UK b&w 77 mins

Respected documentarian Paul Rotha brought to his fiction debut *No Resting Place* the same hard realist values that typified his earlier work on England's shipyards. He adapted Ian Neill's English-based novel to create a compelling, if downbeat, crime-and-retribution drama about travellers in Ireland, and their treatment at the hands of the police when one of them accidentally kills a man in an argument.

Alec Kyle (Michael Gough), his brothers, Billy (Jack MacGowran) and Tom (Brian O'Higgins), and their families travel the roads by horse and cart, scraping a living as farm labourers along the way. Their wandering kind meets with constant hostility from settled folk who don't want them around, and prefer them to keep moving.

A gamekeeper named Ross (Fred Johnson) accuses the travellers of poaching, and when they deny it, he fires a shotgun to frighten them. A ricochet strikes Alec's son (Christy Lawrence) and the volatile Alec loses his temper. He hits Ross with a rock, killing him instantly. The Kyles hide the body in a ditch, and hit the road in a hurry. They meet a policeman, Guard Mannigan (Noel Purcell), cycling towards them. Mannigan wants to know what's their hurry, and their unlikely story makes him suspicious. When Ross' body is found, Mannigan asks the Kyle brothers about it. All three are unco-operative, and Mannigan takes them into the barracks to make a statement. The Gardaí can't pin anything on them, and they are released after signing their statements with an 'x'. The Kyles repair to the local bar for a few whiskeys to celebrate their narrow escape from the law. When Mannigan comes in later for an off-duty pint, Alec, the worse for drink, berates him. A brawl breaks out and Alec crowns Mannigan with a bottle. The Kyles flee the bar and hit the road once again, scattering in different directions to make it harder for the Guards to catch them.

Laid up in bed with bandaged head, Mannigan recovers from the assault as his colleagues try to find Alec. The Super (Robert Hennessy) at the barracks advises him to take it easy on his return to duty for the short period left before he retires. But the knock on the head has hardened Mannigan's resolve to bring Alec Kyle to justice. He comes back to work transformed from diligent officer to pitiless, avenging automaton. He pursues Alec Kyle far beyond his jurisdiction, a terminator in bicycle clips determined to see the traveller hanged for murder before he leaves the force.

Rotha's film is an unflinching stare at the hardships faced by Ireland's nomads. The travellers are presented not as quaint gypsies with charming customs and colourful costumes, but as poor illiterates with limited skills, struggling to make a living, and with scant regard for the rules and regulations of a society that barely tolerates them. When a farmer orders the Kyles off his land without paying them for work they've done, the Kyle women and children retaliate by stealing everything that isn't nailed down – a scene that few directors would risk in more politically correct times.

Rotha returned to documentary film-making, making a history of the Abbey Theatre in 1958, titled *Cradle of Genius*. His cinematographer on *No Resting Place*, Wolfgang Suschitsky, shot another Irish-themed film, *The Oracle*, the same year, and would become director of photography on Joseph Strick's *Ulysses* in 1967.

THE QUIET MAN
(1952) US colour 129 mins

Production Team

Producer ....Republic/Argosy/
Ford/Merian C Cooper
Director.. John Ford
Screenplay .... Frank S Nugent,
from a story by Maurice Walsh
Cinematography .... Winton C Koch
Archie Stout
Editor .... Jack Murray
Musical Score............................ Victor Young

Cast

John Wayne .... Sean Thornton
Maureen O'Hara .... Mary Kate Danaher
Victor McLaglen .... Red Will Danaher
Barry Fitzgerald .... Michaleen Flynn
Ward Bond ....Father Peter Lonergan
Mildred Natwick .... Sarah Tillane
Francis Ford .... Dan Tobin
Eileen Crowe .... Mrs Elizabeth Playfair
May Craig .... The woman
at the railway station
Arthur Shields .... Reverend Cyril Playfair
Charles Fitzsimmons .... Forbes
James Lilburn ....Father Paul
Sean McClory .... Owen Glynn
Jack MacGowran .... Feeney
Joseph O'Dea ....Guard Maloney

THE QUIET MAN
(1952) US colour 129 mins

Love it or hate it, **The Quiet Man** is too big to ignore. John Ford's romantic comedy strides like a jolly green giant across the verdant sward of stage-Irish cinema, and is largely responsible for convincing the world that our rural villages have more than their fair share of idiots. Cherished by Irish people abroad for its unabashed sentimentality, this heart-warming drama is shunned in equal measure by Euro-sophisticates at home for perpetuating ludicrous stereotypes and spawning a host of shamrock-festooned imitations. The Academy was sufficiently charmed by the film to give **The Quiet Man** four Oscars, one for Best Picture.

Set in the west of Ireland, **The Quiet Man** centres on the tempestuous romance between Irish-American ex-boxer Sean Thornton, played by John Wayne, and bad-tempered local redhead Mary Kate Danaher (Maureen O'Hara). Thornton has returned from America to his mother's birthplace, burdened with a past he's trying to forget, and falls for the contrary lass when he sees her herding sheep across a meadow. She takes a shine to him too, but covertly, scurrying like a red squirrel in a headscarf and shawl to peek at him from behind hedgerows and gateposts. An awkward courtship ensues, chaperoned by thirsty leprechaun Michaleen Flynn (Barry Fitzgerald), and the pair travel about by jaunting car past beautiful scenery of both kinds, real and back-projected. Sub-plots include the courtship by Mary Kate's brother Red Will (Victor McLaglan) of the local wealthy widow (Mildred Natwick), and an ongoing dispute between Red Will and Mary Kate about her dowry. Red Will refuses to hand the money over, and Mary Kate refuses Sean his conjugals because this ancient custom has not been observed.

The film culmintates in a dragged-out pub brawl between Sean Thornton and Red Will, of the sort that Irish people in films seem to enjoy almost as much as they do drinking. The fight goes on for so long that the combatants have to stop periodically for refreshments while the entire population of the village wagers on the outcome. It holds the dubious distinction of being the longest fight scene in cinema history (McLaglan had been a professional boxer in real-life before he took up acting, and went the distance in a bout with heavyweight legend Jack Johnson; in a real slugfest with Wayne he probably would have decked the Duke in no time, even though the saddlesore cowboy was almost twenty years his junior).

Shot on location in the idyllic village of Cong, County Mayo, and on the grounds of Ashford Castle, Ford's lush melodrama unfolds over a lengthy two hours and more (it would have taken about 90 minutes if Wayne had delivered his lines at the same speed as his fellow actors) of Technicolor chlorophyll overkill, and is swathed in a soundtrack of Ireland's most pedestrian melodies. Watch it a few times and you'll never want to hear 'The Wild Colonial Boy' again. When it comes to shades of green, John Ford's verdant pastoral canvas far exceeds the accepted maximum of 40.

HAPPY EVER AFTER
(1954) UK colour 91 mins

Production Team

Producer .... Mario Zampi
Director .... Mario Zampi
Screenplay .... Jack Davies and Michael
Pertwee, with additional dialogue by
L A G Strong
Cinematography .... Stanley Pavey
Editor .... Kathleen Connors
Musical Score .... Stanley Black

Cast

David Niven ....Jasper O'Leary
Yvonne De Carlo ....Serena McGlusky
Barry Fitzgerald ....Thady O'Heggarty
George Cole .... Terence
A E Matthews .... General O'Leary
Noelle Middleton .... Kathy McGlusky
Robert Urquhart .... Doctor Michael Flynn
Michael Shepley .... Major McGlusky
Joseph Tomelty .... Dooley
Eddie Byrne .... Lannigan
James Mageean .... Divarsion
Patrick McAlinney .... O'Connor
Brian O'Higgins .... Milligan
Liam Redmond .... Regan
Patrick Westwood .... Murphy
Fred Johnson .... Father Cormac
Ronan O'Casey .... Reporter

HAPPY EVER AFTER
(1954) UK colour 91 mins

The success of John Ford's *The Quiet Man* in 1952 inevitably inspired lesser directors to try their hands at Irish tales of drink-addled buffoonery. Two years later, Mario Zampi, an English-based Italian emigré, plunged fearlessly into the genre with his ludicrous comedy *Happy Ever After*. Its theme had been used before but never for comedy value: disgruntled tenants plot to kill a greedy landlord who is trying to evict them. Shot in garish Technicolor, Zampi's film makes Ford's lavish precursor seem like a grim documentary of Irish life.

The fictitious village of Rathbarney is introduced as having local industries such as "hunting, shooting and drinking", and a population that includes "three leprechauns and a number of begorrahs". Irish rascally types also abound there, among them Barry Fitzgerald as Thady O'Heggarty, reprising his tippling factotum persona from *The Quiet Man* with an exuberance that makes his Michaeleen Flynn in that film look like a model of Anglo-Saxon propriety. To balance the scorecard, the Anglo gentry in the film are as much caricatures as the Irish peasantry: the squire, General O'Leary (A E Matthews), is a gruff old coot, fond of sherry and riding to hounds; his cousin Major McGlusky (Michael Shepley), a blustery idiot; and his nephew and successor, Jasper O'Leary, a conniving cad oozing all the oily charm that David Niven can muster.

The General, a doddery gent in his eighties, always buys his round and doesn't hold it against his tenants if they fall behind in their rent. But a nasty fall at the hunt proves fatal for the old boy and brings his benign rule to an end. His English nephew Jasper inherits his estate, and quickly establishes his boorish credentials by burning books from the library to keep warm. He extorts as much money as he can from his new property, calling in debts that his uncle had cancelled on his deathbed, demanding rent arrears, and evicting those who can't pay. He fires his retainers, disbands the hunt, and sells the trusty steeds for horse meat.

This roughshod gallop over local sensibilities causes the villagers to assemble in the pub with murder in mind. They each draw a piece of paper from a hat, the recipient of the one marked 'x' to do the dastardly deed. It falls to the delicate barman Terence (a very young George Cole) to kill Jasper, but the others doubt his murdering abilities. The poachers, the bookie, the bailiff and Thady all decide to give it a try themselves. Various methods are employed – bombing, decapitation, shooting and poisoning – to no avail. But the discovery by the village doctor (Robert Urquhart) that Jasper has a dicky heart gives them fresh hope, and they set about sending the bounder to an early grave by dressing up as the local ghost and frightening him severely.

Between *Happy Ever After*'s slapstick caricatures lurk some of the worst Irish accents on film – the ineffectual doctor, played by Scottish actor Robert Urquhart, is patently lost, and Yvonne De Carlo, Candian-born Hollywood exotic of *Slave Girl* and *Song of Scheherezade* fame, struggles hopelessly as a Celtic temptress, afflicted by a rigor mortis better suited to her later efforts on television as Lily Munster. As for scenery, if the village and surrounding countryside look suspiciously like Hertfordshire and not rural Ireland, this may have something to do with the fact that the entire farce was shot at Elstree Studios in England.

JACQUELINE
(1956) UK b&w 89 mins

Production Team

Producer ....George H Brown/
Rank Organisation
Director.. Roy Baker
Screenplay .... Patrick Kirwan and Liam
O'Flaherty from the Catherine Cookson
novel *A Grand Man*
Cinematography ....Geoffrey Unsworth
Editor .... John Guthridge
Musical Score................ Cedric Thorpe Davie

Cast

John Gregson .... Mike McNeil
Kathleen Ryan .... Elizabeth McNeil
Jacqueline Ryan ....Jacqueline McNeil
Noel Purcell .... Reverand Mr Owen
Cyril Cusack .... Mr Flanagan
Tony Wright .... Jack McBride
Maureen Swanson ....Maggie
Liam Redmond................................ Mr Lord
Maureen Delany ....Mrs McBride
Richard O'Sullivan .... Mike MacNeil Jr
Maire Kean ....Mrs Flanagan
Josephine Fitzgerald ....Mrs McMullen
Barry Keegan .... Bob Quinton
Rita Begley ....Sarah Flanagan
Harold Goldblatt................................. Teacher

Catherine Cookson's novel *A Grand Man* was brought to the screen as *Jacqueline*, a warm-hearted comedy-drama starring child actress Jacqueline Ryan in the title role. The transfer from the original English setting of the book to Belfast gave a rare opportunity to see that divided city on screen in a context free of violence and sectarian enmity. The story is set during the week of Queen Elizabeth's coronation in 1953, and the neighbourhoods of Belfast are decked out for street parties to celebrate the event. Behind the fanfare and buntings, the McNeil family is barely making ends meet, as the father, Mike McNeil (John Gregson), struggles to keep his job at the shipyards.

Mike's daughter Jacqueline, a mischievous and determined little girl, thinks her father is the grandest man in the world. No one else does. Her mother, Elizabeth (Kathleen Ryan), contemplates moving out if Mike doesn't stop drinking and falling behind with the rent. Jacqueline's grandmother, Mrs McMullen (Josephine Fitzgerald) wants Elizabeth to leave Mike and encourages an old suitor, wealthy, courteous Bob Quinton (Barry Keegan), to pursue her daughter again. Mike's boss, Mr Lord (Liam Redmond) wants to fire him because his drunken dizzy spells are a danger to his workmates. Even when he's not drinking, Mike is getting his hen-pecked neighbour (Cyril Cusack) in trouble with his shrewish wife (Maire Kean) at the Coronation Day party, by getting him drunk for the first time in twenty years. To compensate for these shortcomings, Jacqueline makes up outlandish stories about her dad's life to impress her schoolmates. But in private she worries about him. She prays to God in church that her dad will get a nice job on a farm, away from the city and the shipyards, promising, as her side of the bargain, to stop telling lies if her prayers are answered.

Jacqueline shares her anxieties with the local vicar, Reverend Mr Owen (Noel Purcell), who promises to have a word with the Lord on her behalf. Owen approaches the shipyard owner Mr Lord about a farm job for Mike. By a peculiar contrivance of the plot, Mr Lord happens to be a prosperous farmer as well as owning the shipyard. Mr Lord is most unsympathetic to Owen's request, having already seen at the dry dock what a liability Mike can be after a few whiskeys. But his heart is softened when Jacqueline brazenly visits him for breakfast at his mansion and he offers Mike a job, complete with country cottage, restoring harmony to the troubled family.

Jacqueline has all the hallmarks of the classic Cookson story – ordinary people muddling through life's difficulties to arrive at a moderately happy ending, with a combination of humour, pluck and a little luck. Newcomer Jacqueline Ryan's boisterous performance in the title role gives *Jacqueline* a chirpy momentum, mercifully free of the Shirley Temple tendencies that usually make this sort of film so appalling. She confidently holds her own among Abbey veterans with decades of film and stage experience behind them, including Maire Kean and Maureen Delany as her nosey neighbours, and Noel Purcell as that *rara avis* of Irish film narrative, the sympathetic, caring clergyman. Noel Purcell, Maire Kean and Liam Redmond were reunited with John Gregson two years later under the director George Pollock for another Hibernicised Cookson adaptation, *Rooney*.

THE RISING OF THE MOON
(1957) IRL b&w 81 mins

(Still reproduced courtesy of Lady Killanin)

Production Team

Producer .... John Ford/Lord Killanin/
                 Four Provinces Productions
Director .... John Ford
Screenplay .... Frank S Nugent
Cinematography .... Robert Krasker
Editor .... Michael Gordon
Musical Score .... Eamonn O'Gallagher

Cast

The Majesty of the Law

Cyril Cusack .... The Inspector
Noel Purcell .... The old man
Jack MacGowran .... Mickey J,
                  the poitín maker
John Cowley .... The gombeen man

A Minute's Wait

Jimmy O'Dea .... Porter
Tony Quinn .... Station master
Maureen Potter .... Barmaid
Michael Trubshawe .... Col Frobisher
Anita Sharp Bolster .... His wife

1921

Donal Donnelly .... The prisoner
Denis O'Dea .... Police sergeant
Eileen Crowe .... His wife
Frank Lawton .... British officer

THE RISING OF THE MOON
(1957) IRL b&w 81 mins

John Ford returned to Ireland five years after making *The Quiet Man* to co-produce and direct a screen trilogy based on Irish literary and dramatic sources from the early part of the 20th century. The trilogy was released as a feature entitled *The Rising of the Moon* in Ireland, and as *Three Leaves of a Shamrock* in America, the market at which it is clearly aimed. Tyrone Power acts as narrator of the three films: *The Majesty of the Law*, adapted from a Frank O'Connor story; *A Minute's Wait*, based on Martin J McHugh's 1914 Abbey comedy; and *1921*, based on Lady Gregory's play *The Rising of the Moon*.

In *The Majesty of the Law*, stubbornness masquerades as honour when a contrary old man (Noel Purcell) chooses to go to jail rather than pay a fine for assaulting the local gombeen man (John Cowley) for calling him a liar. The onerous duty of arresting the shillelagh-wielding O'Flaherty falls to his friend, Inspector Dillon (Cyril Cusack), who tries to persuade him to pay the fine. O'Flaherty won't budge, not even when the victim of his assault offers to pay the money for him, and he presents himself at the barracks to serve his time.

A Minute's Wait riffs on the relaxed approach of Ireland's private citizens and public institutions to the concept of punctuality. The steam-train at Dunfaill station halts for the time period specified in the title. In an elaborately choreographed series of passenger stampedes from the train to the refreshment room and back, delays occur because of a prize goat ("the champeen pucán of all Ireland"), lobsters for the bishop's jubilee dinner, and the Ballyscran hurling team, to the exasperation of the gentry in the first class compartment. The train finally departs with the hurling team on a flatbed car, the goat in first class, and the gentry left behind at the station. *A Minute's Wait* features one of the most romantic marriage proposals ever aired in an Irish film, when station porter Paddy Morrisey (Jimmy O'Dea) asks refreshment room waitress Pegeen Mallory (Maureen Potter), "How would you like to be buried with my people?"

1921 is set, as the title suggests, during the War of Independence, and features a daring rescue from jail of an Irish rebel on the eve of his hanging. The prisoner (Donal Donnelly) escapes with the help of IRA women dressed as nuns, and evades recapture thanks to a sympathetic RIC sergeant (Denis O'Dea). The peasantry of Ireland collectively resist and make fools of the British authority figures (which always plays well in Ireland), by pretending to be fools themselves (which doesn't). The film is shot with arty diagonal framing, popular in German Expressionist works of the time, in which the film is based.

Time has not been kind to these slices of overripe whimsy, and the comedy falls even flatter at the end of the century than it did in the middle. Scriptwriter Nugent, culpable for *The Quiet Man* screenplay as well as these adaptations, offers dialogue larded with "your honour" and "is it himself" phrasing that curdles in the non-American ear and negates solid effort by the Abbey players to raise a laugh from hopelessly clichéd material. *The Rising of the Moon* failed to capitalise on the commercial success of *The Quiet Man*, but it marked the start of a series of Irish-made features that launched a film industry, finally made possible by the creation of an indigenous film studio.

THE STORY OF ESTHER COSTELLO
(1957) UK b&w 103 mins

Production Team

Producer .... Jack Clayton/Romulus
Director .... David Miller
Screenplay .... Charles Kaufman
from the novel of the same name by
Nicholas Monsarrat
Cinematography .... Robert Krasker
Editor .... Ralph Kemplen
Musical Score .... Georges Auric

Cast

Joan Crawford .... Margaret Landi
Rossano Brazzi .... Carlo Landi
Heather Sears .... Esther Costello
Lee Patterson .... Harry Grant
Denis O'Dea .... Father Devlin
Ron Randell .... Wenzel
Fay Compton .... Mother Superior
John Loder .... Paul Marchant
Sidney James .... Ryan
Bessie Love .... Matron in the art gallery
Robert Ayres .... Mr Wilson
Maureen Delany .... Jennie Costello
Harry Hutchinson .... Irish publican
Tony Quinn .... Irish pub customer
Janina Faye .... Esther Costello (as a child)
Estelle Brody .... Tammy
Sheila Manahan .... Esther's mother

THE STORY OF ESTHER COSTELLO
(1957) UK b&w 103 mins

Camp films with an Irish accent almost invariably involve leprechauns, blarney and a crock of gold, but *The Story of Esther Costello* bypasses these celtic clichés and still manages to reach impressive standards of self-parody and grand guignol. In this lurid tale of embezzlement, treachery and revenge, durable Hollywood icon Joan Crawford revels in the role of a generous Irish socialite whose good deeds turn horribly wrong.

Crawford plays wealthy Margaret Landi, born in Ireland and resident of the US. While visiting her native village of Cloncraig, she is prevailed upon by the gently manipulative priest Father Devlin (Denis O'Dea) to bankroll a new stained-glass window for his church. During her visit she is horrified at the plight of teenager Esther Costello (Heather Sears), who lives in a wretched hovel with her cruel aunt Jennie (Maureen Delany). Esther has been deaf, dumb and blind since a childhood accident that killed her mother (Sheila Manahan), and Jennie has never forgiven her for causing it. Shown in a rain-drenched prologue, young Esther (Janina Faye) blows up her mother with a box of IRA grenades, and loses her sight and hearing from the trauma.

Margaret takes pity on Esther and brings her to America for treatment. She enrols her in a special school, but Esther's distress at being abandoned there prompts Margaret to try educating her herself. Esther's courage and determination in learning to read and write gains national attention, and foster-mommie dearest Margaret founds a charity with the saintly Irish lass as its figurehead.

The charity is tremendously successful, and its bursting coffers soon attract Margaret's estranged Italian husband, Carlo Landi (Rossano Brazzi). Carlo weasels his way back into her confidence and milks the Esther Costello Fund of millions, with the help of his corrupt associate Wenzel (Ron Randell). Jaded newspaper editor Joe Ryan (Sid James) smells a rat when charity organisers travel first class, and he sends eager young reporter Harry Grant (Lee Patterson), who fancies Esther, to investigate. Harry tracks Margaret, Carlo and Wenzel across Europe looking for improprieties, and falls in love with Esther in the process. Lecherous Carlo has taken a shine to her himself, and sneaks peeks at the blind girl undressing. He contrives to be alone with Esther while Margaret is away, and, in a morally deplorable plot development, he forces his manhood on the angelic orphan, causing her sight and hearing (and her lilting Irish accent) to return. After this shocking twist, the plot has nowhere else to go for resolution but a spectacular murder-suicide combo that gives Margaret revenge on her scoundrel husband.

Marketed with the much more fabulous title *The Golden Virgin* in America, Heather Sears positively radiates chastity in the title role, while Crawford indulges her full range of histrionics in a performance that she rated above her 1945 Oscar-winning work in *Mildred Pierce*. The high point of this kitsch Crawford vehicle is a lavishly choreographed fund-raiser in an Art Deco auditorium in Times Square. A choir of blind children sings hymns and a squadron of volunteer girls, shamrocks emblazoned on their tunic fronts, stands to attention, as the benighted Esther scrawls the word 'GIVE' in huge letters on a blackboard. The volunteers then pass their twizzle-handled collection baskets through an audience of the blind, the lame and the halt to amass a fortune for the charity hucksters to plunder, while the orchestra cranks away at 'The Rising of the Moon'.

ROONEY
(1958) UK b&w 88 mins

Production Team

Director .... George Pollock
Producer .... George H Brown
Screenplay .... Patrick Kirwan
 (from the novel of the same name
 by Catherine Cookson)
Cinematography .... Christopher G Challis
Editor .... Peter Bezencenet
Musical Score .... Philip Green

Cast

John Gregson .... James Ignatius Rooney
Muriel Pavlow .... Máire Hogan
Barry Fitzgerald .... Grandfather
Marie Kean .... Mrs O'Flynn
Noel Purcell .... Tim Hennessy
Jack MacGowran .... Joe O'Connor
Philip O'Flynn .... Paddy Ryan
Eddie Byrne .... Micky Hart
Irene Browne .... Mrs Manning-ffrench
Pauline Delaney .... Mrs Wall
Harold Goldblatt .... Police Inspector
Liam Redmond .... Mr Doolan
Godfrey Quigley .... Tom Reilly
Maureen Toal .... Kathleen O'Flynn
June Thorburn .... Doreen O'Flynn
Joan Phillips .... Sheila O'Flynn

ROONEY
(1958) UK b&w 88 mins

Charming dustbinman James Rooney (John Gregson) is a star player with the Sons of Erin hurling team, and an irresistible hearthrob to the landladies of Dublin. He constantly moves house to evade their lusty advances. After repelling Mrs Wall (Pauline Delaney) at his room near the Guinness Brewery, Rooney finds himself looking for new digs once more. A chat over pints with his jovial workmates Tim (Noel Purcell), Paddy (Philip O'Flynn), Joe (Jack MacGowran) and Micky (Eddie Byrne), leads to a tip from county hurling selector Mr Doolan (Liam Redmond) about a place in Rathmines. As a result Rooney moves into the house of the widow O'Flynn (Marie Kean).

The O'Flynn family keeps up an illusion of wealth and propriety, despite not owning their house, and having an eccentric grandfather (Barry Fitzgerald) upstairs who is rarely allowed down. The widow's orphaned niece Máire (Muriel Pavlow) also lives in the house and is treated as a maid by Mrs O'Flynn and her three daughters, Doreen (June Thorburn), affianced Sheila (Joan Philips) and Kathleen (Maureen Toal). The grandfather, however, is very fond of Máire. Rooney and the grandfather get on well, and the old boy warns the handsome binman about the wiles of women. Rooney also becomes friendly with Máire, and after she's mistreated at Sheila's wedding he gives her a gift of a necklace, which he found in the rubbish while at work.

Rooney's team makes it to the All-Ireland final, and he is chosen by the selectors to play in the big game. He celebrates in the pub with his pals, who regale him with a few verses of 'The Rooney-O', the film's theme song. Rooney arrives home drunk, making declarations of love as Márie puts him to bed. The nervous orphan retreats behind a curtain when Mrs O'Flynn shows up to investigate the fuss, and the widow mistakenly believes Rooney's declarations are meant for her, not Márie.

Tension mounts between Kathleen's husband Tom (Godfrey Quigley) and Rooney when Tom accuses him of giving money to Máire. Tom saw her entering a fancy hotel, and she arrived home later wearing a new outfit and bearing gifts for everybody – after receiving a letter, the contents of which she refused to disclose to Mrs O'Flynn. The next day Rooney has no recollection of his drunken ramblings. The grandfather dies, admitting before he goes that it was he who sent Máire the money. His funeral takes place the same day as the big match. In front of a huge crowd at Croke Park, Rooney scores the winning goal and the jubilant fans invade the pitch.

The police arrive at the O'Flynn's house to arrest Máire for stealing the necklace, which has been traced to a robbery at the Manning-ffrench residence. They arrive as the grandfather's will is being read, and the O'Flynns are shocked to find that the house has been left to Máire. Amidst scenes of antic comedy, in a police station packed with drunks, an exasperated seargent and a hurling-mad inspector (Harold Goldblatt), Rooney explains how Máire came by the jewels. The grandchildren of Mrs Manning-ffrench (Irene Brown) admit that they put the jewellery in the bin before the robbery happened, where it was discovered by Rooney. Tim tells Rooney that Máire loves him as she walks away, and the lovers finally kiss on the Ha'penny Bridge, to the rousing strains of 'The Rooney-O', one last time.

DARBY O'GILL AND THE LITTLE PEOPLE
(1959) US colour 93 mins

Production Team

Producer .... Walt Disney
Director .... Robert Stevenson
Screenplay .... Lawrence Edward Watkin,
adapted from the book of the
same name by H T Kavanagh
Cinematography .... Winton C Hoch
Editor .... Stanley Johnson
Musical Score .... Oliver G Wallace

Cast

Albert Sharpe .... Darby O'Gill
Janet Munro .... Katie
Sean Connery .... Michael McBride
Jimmy O'Dea .... King Brian
Kieron Moore .... Pony Sugrue
Estelle Winwood .... Sheelah
Walter Fitzgerald .... Lord Fitzpatrick
Denis O'Dea .... Father Murphy
J G Devlin .... Tom Kerrigan
Jack MacGowran .... Phadrig Oge
Farrell Pelly .... Paddy Scanlon
Nora O'Mahoney .... Molly Malloy

DARBY O'GILL AND THE LITTLE PEOPLE
(1959) US colour 93 mins

Walt Disney's *Darby O'Gill and the Little People* marked a return to form for his studio after the cloying schmaltz of *Old Yeller* two years earlier. Directed by Robert Stevenson, this children's comedy-drama is a ridiculous but entertaining romp through stage-Irish folklore, and a stellar example of Disney's special effects capabilities at the time.

Title character Darby O'Gill (Albert Sharpe) is the ageing caretaker of Lord Fitzpatrick's country estate, and spends more time in the pub recounting tales of King Brian, monarch of the leprechauns, than doing his job. Lord Fitzpatrick (Walter Fitzgerald) is concerned about Darby's age and his casual approach to his duties, and hires a replacement, Michael McBride (Sean Connery), from Dublin. He breaks the news to Darby, offering him a modest pension and a cottage. The crestfallen Darby hasn't the heart to tell his daughter Katie (Janet Munro) that he has lost his job and the gate lodge that goes with it.

While chasing his straying horse, Darby stumbles into the leprechaun kingdom and meets King Brian (Jimmy O'Dea) who shows him wonders and treasures that bring a greedy glint to his eye. Brian tells him that having entered this magical domain he must stay forever, but, through his fiddle-playing skills, Darby manages to escape. He later captures King Brian, by getting him drunk on poitín and keeping him in his house until daybreak. By leprechaun custom, the captured Brain must grant Darby three wishes. A battle of wits develops between them. The crafty rogue Darby's first wish is that Brian should stay a fortnight with him, to give him time to come up with two top-quality wishes, while trickster Brian tries to fool him into wasting them.

Meanwhile local bully Pony Sugrue (Kieron Moore) plots to usurp the caretaker's position and the gate lodge from Michael McBride. Things go awry for all parties involved when Darby enlists King Brian to bring Michael and Katie closer together, and Pony Sugrue, encouraged by his devious mother (Estelle Winwood), tries to discredit Michael in the eyes of Lord Fitzpatrick. Katie fights with Michael when an eviction notice arrives for Darby, and storms off to Knocknasheega where she is badly injured in a fall. A wailing Banshee appears, signifying her impending death. When the eerie Death Coach comes to collect her, Darby makes the ultimate sacrifice to save her with his last wish. But the capricious Brian has a heart of gold, as well as the proverbial crock. With his final trick he cheats Darby out of all his wishes for his own good, ensuring a happy ending.

Irish audiences may cringe at the Hollywood clichés, and folklore purists wonder what Disney's researchers did with all that information they gathered from Irish academics about leprechauns. But this boisterous kids' film remains eminently watchable decades after its release for its wonderful scenes of merriment and horseplay in the tiny kingdom of the leprechauns, as full-sized Darby regales them with tunes on the fiddle. Disney regulars Peter Ellenshaw and Eustace Lycett deserve credit for effects that still impress in an era of computer-generated images, and their scary Banshee can still stir nightmares in a sensitive five-year-old. Albert Sharpe and Jimmy O'Dea are well matched as the scheming adversaries Darby and Brian, and for curiosity value, the film features the bizarre sight of a pre-Bond Connery singing 'Pretty Irish Girl'.

HOME IS THE HERO
(1959) IRL b&w 82 mins

Production Team

Producer .... Emmet Dalton/
Robert S Baker/Monty Berman
Director .... J Fielder Cook
Screenplay .... Henry Keating,
from Walter Macken's
play of the same name
Cinematography .... Stanley Pavey
Editor .... John Ferris
Musical Score .... Bruce Montgomery

Cast

Walter Macken .... Paddo O'Reilly
Arthur Kennedy .... Willie O'Reilly
Eileen Crowe .... Daylia O'Reilly
Joan O'Hara .... Josie O'Reilly
Harry Brogan .... Dovetail
Eddie Golden .... Mr Shannon
Maire Keane .... Bid
Pat Layde .... Mr Green
Phillip O'Flynn .... Trapper
Geoffrey Golden .... O'Conner
Michael C Hennessy .... Manchester
Monaghan
John Hoey .... Finnegan
Mícheál O'Bríain .... 1st pub customer
Dermot Kelly .... 2nd pub customer
Máire O'Donnell .... Maura Green

HOME IS THE HERO
(1959) IRL b&w 82 mins

Irish novelist Walter Macken, who made his mark at mid-century with *Seek the Fair Land*, *The Silent People* and *The Scorching Wind*, had a parallel career as actor and playwright in the Irish theatre. He also made sporadic appearances in film, distinguishing himself in his lead debut in the 1959 adaptation of his own play *Home is the Hero*. The play premiered in the Abbey in 1952 and was brought to the screen seven years later, following on its success in London's West End, and failure on Broadway in 1954. *Home is the Hero* is a tough-minded drama produced by Emmet Dalton, his third in Ireland, that marked a departure from the lighter fare previously served by his production company, as it delves into the dark recesses of Irish family relationships.

In his screen debut, Macken plays Paddo O'Reilly, a brutal Galwayman who rules his family with an iron hand. Paddo becomes violent when he's had drink taken, and in a drunken brawl he accidentally kills a man from the neighbourhood, the father of his son's true love, Maura (Máire O'Donnell). He is sentenced to five years in jail for his crime, and his family undergoes many changes while he's inside. To make ends meet, his wife takes in boarders at the house, and becomes more financially independent than when Paddo ruled the roost. Paddo's son Willie (American actor Arthur Kennedy, best known for stage performances in the works of legendary playwright Arthur Miller), works as a cobbler at his own shoe repair business and is also much more well off. Free from her father's control, Paddo's daughter Josie (Joan O'Hara) goes out with the local bookie (Phillip O'Flynn), a romance that would be intolerable to the patriarch if he were around to notice it.

For Paddo, however, time stands still during his term behind bars, and when he emerges after serving his five-year sentence he expects to resume without question his former position of supremacy in the O'Reilly household. When he realises how much things have changed, he attempts to take charge again by physically threatening his family and the lodger, Dovetail (Harry Brogan). The barely restrained violence culminates in a showdown at knifepoint with the disabled Willie, who Paddo has never treated as a complete human being.

The claustrophobic atmosphere of this largely housebound drama fetters the film to its stage origins, and screenwriter Henry Keating's adaptation attempts little expansion of Macken's original Abbey version of seven years earlier. But it stands as a sobering counterpoint to the happy assessment of Irish life presented in *Mise Éire*, the government-sponsored and self-congratulatory documentary released the same year, and features a formidable central performance by Macken. The author went on to a second starring role in Arthur Dreifuss' film version of the Brendan Behan play, *The Quare Fellow*, three years later, playing the sympathetic prison warden Regan who gently brings his pro-capital punishment colleague Crimmin round to reconsidering his position. His novel *Flight of the Doves* was adapted in 1971 to make the children's film of the same name, starring Ron Moody and Jack Wild.

SHAKE HANDS WITH THE DEVIL
(1959) UK b&w 110 mins

Production Team

Producer .... Troy Films/Michael Anderson
Director .... Michael Anderson
Screenplay .... Ivan Goff and Ben Roberts
adaptation by Marian Thompson
from the novel of the same
name by Reardon Conner
Cinematography .... Erwin Hillier
Editor .... Gordon Pilkington
Musical Score .... William Alwyn

Cast

James Cagney .... Sean Lenihan
Don Murray .... Kerry O'Shea
Dana Wynter .... Jennifer Curtis
Glynis Johns .... Kitty Brady
Michael Redgrave .... The General
Sybil Thorndike .... Lady Fitzhugh
Cyril Cusack .... Chris Noonan
Marianne Benet .... Mary Madigan
John Breslin .... McGrath
Harry Brogan .... Cassidy
Rober Brown .... 1st Sgt, Black & Tans
Lewis Casson .... The judge
Noel Purcell .... O'Sullivan
Ray McAnally .... Paddy
Harry Corbett .... Clancy
Eileen Crowe .... Mrs Madigan
Richard Harris .... Terence O'Brien

SHAKE HANDS WITH THE DEVIL
(1959) UK b&w 110 mins

Even in the late-1950s, Ireland's War of Independence was still a recent enough memory to be regarded as a controversial subject for film-makers. Many of those involved were still alive, some in positions of prominence, and films about the turbulent early-1920s usually steered clear of facts to focus on fictitious characters of minor importance in that time. Michael Anderson's raw 1959 drama, *Shake Hands with the Devil*, showed some daring in presenting several protagonists that bear resemblances to actual leaders in the war. The film deals with the split caused by the Treaty with Britain, and its main charcters, played by James Cagney, Michael Redgrave and Sybil Thorndike, are a little too close for comfort to Eamon De Valera, Michael Collins and Countess Markievicz in an otherwise fictional plot.

Like De Valera, Cagney's character Sean Lenihan is a teacher, lecturing in medicine at the College of Surgeons by day. By night, he's a ruthless rebel commandant, leading a vicious street war against the British. Lenihan is determined to fight to the last man when his comrades are heading for a compromise solution with the enemy.

Among his students is Kerry O'Shea (Don Murray), raised in America after his father died, and returned to Ireland to study at his late father's college. As the war escalates, Kerry avoids getting involved. Having served in the Great War, he's seen enough killing. But an incident with the Tans on a Dublin street leaves his friend Paddy (Ray McAnally) dead and forces Kerry to go on the run. Lenihan arranges a passage to America for him, but first tries to get him to join his squad. O'Shea declines, but agrees to help rescue a rebel, O'Sullivan (Noel Purcell), who recently escaped from Dublin Castle with the help of the august Lady Fitzhugh (Sybil Thorndike). The rescue goes wrong, O'Sullivan is killed, and Lady Fitzhugh and O'Shea are arrested by the British. In a daring raid, Lenihan springs O'Shea from jail, and, cured of his pacifism by a brutal beating while in custody, he joins Lenihan's squad.

O'Shea's misgivings about using violence to win freedom resurface when he shoots a soldier during a hostage abduction. He soon realises that Lenihan is driven by psychotic tendencies stronger than his passion for the cause. Lenihan has no qualms about roughing up a woman (Glynis Johns) who flirts with his men (among them Richard Harris, in a brawny early performance) or shooting her when he suspects her of treachery. A treaty negotiated in London by a Collins-type leader known as 'The General' (Michael Redgrave, whose grand-daughter's husband, Liam Neeson, would play Collins in the 1996 Neil Jordan biopic), fragments morale among the rebels. When Lady Fitzhugh dies on hunger strike in prison, the volatile Lenihan is determined to shoot their British hostage (Dana Wynter) in reprisal, treaty or no. In a bitter showdown on a windy Wicklow hilltop, Lenihan's compulsion towards violence inevitably brings about his own end, at the hands of his former student.

In his penultimate film before retirement, Cagney still pulsates with violent energy as the ruthless psycho-Dev republican with puritanical ambitions for a free Ireland. Co-star Redgrave would play another pivotal figure from the same era, W B Yeats, in the Sean O'Casey biopic *Young Cassidy* six years later.

THIS OTHER EDEN
(1959) IRL b&w 80 mins

(Still courtesy of the Irish Film Archive of the Film Institute of Ireland)

Production Team

Producer ... Emmet Dalton/Alec C Snowden
Director.. Muriel Box
Screenplay .... Patrick Kirwan and Blanaid
Irvine from the play of the
same name by Louis D'Alton
Cinematography ....Gerald Gibbs
Editor ....Henry Richardson
Musical Score .... W Lambert Williamson

Cast

Audrey Dalton .... Máire McRoarty
Leslie Phillips .... Crispin Brown
Niall MacGinnis .... Brendan Devereux
Ria Mooney ....Mother Superior
Harry Brogan ....Clannery
Geoffrey Golden .... McRoarty
Edward Golden .... Sergeant Crilly
Philip O'Flynn .... The postman
Paul Farrell .... McNeely TD
Hilton Edwards .... The canon
Milo O'Shea .... Pat Tweedy
Derry Power ....Jarvey Hanrahan
Mícheál O'Bríain .... Patrick Layde
Norman Rodway .... Conor Heapy
Bill Foley .... McPherson

THIS OTHER EDEN
(1959) IRL b&w 80 mins

Emmet Dalton, veteran of the War of Independence and the Civil War that followed, had a second career as a film producer, using Abbey Theatre plays as source material. Prominent among them was *This Other Eden*, a caustic comedy about the manipulation of Ireland's recent history that resonates with echoes of Dalton's own experiences during the troubles. Directed by Muriel Box and adapted from Louis D'Alton's play, the film stars Audrey Dalton as Máire McRoarty, a strong-willed girl sent to school in England by her father, the village gombeen man. Old McRoarty (Geoffrey Golden), owner of Ballymorgan's newspaper, bar and hotel, sent her there to keep her apart from a suitor he deems unsuitable: Conor Heapy (Norman Rodway), a bitter young student of doubtful parentage.

Following a 1921 prologue in which IRA Commandant Carberry is killed in a British ambush from which his comrade Devereux (Niall MacGinnis), escapes unharmed, the action skips forward some twenty years. Máire and Conor are returning from their respective colleges to Ballymorgan. They arrive with eccentric Englishman Crispin Brown (Leslie Phillips), who they met on the train, to find the villagers excited over the imminent unveiling of a statue honouring Carberry's heroism. Further excitement occurs when Brown tries to buy Kilgarrig, a local mansion, and finds himself up against the nuns who also have designs on the place.

Local opinion is divided over the statue. The sardonic Devereux, now editor of the *Ballymorgan Eagle*, deplores the fuss, knowing Carberry would have hated it. As a survivor of the same ambush, he has also had to endure accusations of betraying his old comrade. McRoarty sees the statue as a lucrative tourist attraction, and doesn't care whether Carberry deserves it. Auctioneer and TD McNeely (Paul Farrell) uses the ceremony to display his admiration for Carberry, and by extension, his vote-winning love for Ireland. Other villagers see Carberry as an unsullied Irish hero and are keen to thump anyone who thinks otherwise. The statue is unveiled and the villagers are shocked to see a misshapen abstract sculpture. When a bomb destroys it, the villagers blame Brown, who had publicly denounced its ugliness. From a hotel balcony he calms an angry mob with an impassioned speech about his love for Ireland and offers to sponsor a new and better statue. The mercurial Englishman soon reveals that he has much in common with the ostracised Conor, and closer connections to Kilgarrig and Ballymorgan history than anybody could have guessed.

This Other Eden succeeds as a sharp satire of the anomalies of independent Ireland: that the Irish prefer martyrs to survivors, can define their love for Ireland solely in terms of hatred for Britain, and will do everything for Ireland but live in it. But its chief fascination lies in the parallels between producer Emmet Dalton's life, and the film's IRA characters, Carberry and Devereux. Dalton had been with Michael Collins when he was shot in 1922, and despite being Collins' right-hand man, was not deemed above suspicion in the national guessing-game of the killer's identity. Like most pro-Treaty veterans, Dalton was sidelined in the mid-1920s as the anti-Treaty faction won out in the national change of management. In Ballymorgan's exaltation of Carberry and denigration of Devereux, *This Other Eden* gave Dalton an opportunity to remind us that Ireland treats its dead heroes a lot better than its live ones.

A TERRIBLE BEAUTY
(1960) UK b&w 89 mins

Production Team

Producer .... DRM/Raymond Stross
Director .... Tay Garnett
Screenplay .... Robert Wright Campbell
from the book of the same name
by Arthur Roth
Cinematography .... Stephen Dade
Editor .... Peter Tanner
Musical Score .... Cedric Thorpe Davies

Cast

Robert Mitchum .... Dermot O'Neill
Anne Heywood .... Neeve
Dan O'Herlihy .... Don McGinnis
Cyril Cusack .... Jimmy Hannafin
Richard Harris .... Seán Reilly
Niall MacGinnis .... Ned O'Neill
Marianne Benet .... Bella O'Neill
Christopher Rhodes .... Malone
Harry Brogan .... Patrick O'Neill
Eileen Crowe .... Kathleen O'Neill
Geoffrey Golden .... Sergeant Crawley
Hilton Edwards .... Father McCrory
Wilfred Downing .... Quinn
Edward Golden .... Corrigan
Joe Lynch .... Tim
Noel Purcell .... Father Sheehy
Godfrey Quigley .... IRA man
TP McKenna .... IRA man

A TERRIBLE BEAUTY
(1960) UK b&w 89 mins

Before *The Story of GI Joe* earned him is first Oscar nomination and made him a bona fide star, Robert Mitchum played a minor role in a 1943 studio war film with an Irish setting called *Doughboys in Ireland*. In 1960, he took his rugged nonchalance over there in person to play the lead role in Tay Garnett's *A Terrible Beauty* as an IRA volunteer in rural County Derry during the Second World War. Playing somewhat against type, Mitchum's character is plagued with doubts about the IRA's struggle, a rebel with a cause supporting the principles more than the violent methods of the illegal organisation to which he belongs.

The film is set in 1941. The war generates an upsurge of nationalist activity as the IRA colludes with the Nazis to disrupt British control of Northern Ireland, with the help of German arms and military training. The action takes place in the village of Duncrana, where an IRA commandant from Belfast is recruiting volunteers. Don McGinnis (Dan O'Herlihy), a disabled shopkeeper, is appointed leader. Dermot O'Neill and his friend Seán Reilly (Richard Harris) are among the recruits. Dermot's father (Harry Brogan) approves of his involvement, but his mother (Eileen Crowe) and girlfriend Neeve (Anne Heywood) are against it. Dermot's romance with Neeve is jeopardised by his commitment to the cause, and she urges him to leave the hardships and violence of Ireland behind and travel with her to England, a course of action that he knows would cause his father to disown him.

McGinnis sends O'Neill and Reilly to raid a British munitions dump to boost their arsenal of weapons. The mission is successful, but results in condemnation of IRA activities by the parish priest, Father Sheehy (Noel Purcell), and enquiries from the RUC as to Dermot's whereabouts when the raid was carried out.

The next assignment goes wrong, and there are casualties on both sides. Seán is injured and Dermot takes him to a hospital across the border in the South. When Seán is captured on his return and McGinnis refuses to approve a raid to free him from jail, Dermot falls out with his commanding officer. For their next operation, McGinnis plans an attack on a barracks that will result in civilian casualties, and Dermot tries to leave the organisation in disgust. McGinnis warns him that nobody is allowed to leave, and Dermot threatens to warn the RUC about the impending raid. He is arrested by the IRA and beaten as an informer, but escapes before his court martial and inevitable execution. He informs on his comrades to the RUC, and he and Neeve flee to Belfast to catch the ferry to England.

IRA films tend to focus on the heroic deeds of the War of Independence and steer clear of the murky and unresolved issues of post-partition Ireland. *A Terrible Beauty* was the first film since *Odd Man Out* to even attempt to address the continuing grassroots-level struggle in Northern Ireland that percolated through the 1940s and 1950s before exploding into full fury again at the end of the 1960s. For its US release, the film was stripped of its original title (a quotation from W B Yeats' poem *Easter 1916*) and renamed more prosaically as *The Night Fighters*.

THE QUARE FELLOW
(1962) UK b&w 86 mins

Production Team

Producer .... Anthony Havelock-
Allen Productions
Director .... Arthur Dreifuss
Screenplay .... Arthur Dreifuss and
Jacqueline Sundstrom from the
play of the same name
by Brendan Behan
Cinematography .... Peter Hennessy
Editor .... Gitta Zadek
Musical Score .... Alexander Faris

Cast

Patrick McGoohan .... Crimmin
Sylvia Syms .... Kathleen
Walter Macken .... Regan
Dermot Kelly .... Donelly
Jack Cunningham .... Chief warder
Hilton Edwards .... Holy Healy
Philip O'Flynn .... Prison Governor
Leo McCabe .... Dr Flynn
Norman Rodway .... Lavery
Marie Kean .... Mrs O'Hara
Pauline Delaney .... Mickser's wife
Eddie Golden .... 1st customs officer
Eric Gorman .... Neighbour
Joe O'Donnell .... Poet
Aubrey Morris .... Silvertop
Iris Lawler .... Minna
Harry Brogan .... Dunlavin
Arthur O'Sullivan .... Himself (the hangman)

THE QUARE FELLOW
(1962) UK b&w 86 mins

Brendan Behan's prison play *The Quare Fellow*, a passionate polemic against the death penalty that premiered in Ireland in 1954 and established his name abroad two years later, was brought to the screen by German-born American director Arthur Dreifuss eight years after its Dublin launch. Directing from his own screenplay, Dreifuss shot the film in stark black and white almost entirely on location inside Dublin's historic Kilmainham Gaol. Some of the exterior scenes were shot around Mountjoy Prison, where Behan's play was set. Dreyfuss' adaptation of the Behan text is a fillet of the original that tones down much of the playwright's famously salty dialogue, and shifts the balance of the ensemble acting to focus on two of the prison staff – a naïve young warder new to the job, and a senior warder who has seen it all and had enough.

Patrick McGoohan stars as the young officer Crimmin, in his second Irish screen role (he played a brawling Irish lorry-driver five years earlier in C Raker Endfield's gritty *Hell Drivers*). Crimmin arrives in Dublin from Inishbofin to begin his new job in the city prison, at a time when two executions are imminent. Crimmin quickly impresses the prison governor (Philip O'Flynn) and appals senior warder Regan (actor/writer Walter Macken, gloomily carrying the moral weight of the film) with his enthusiasm for capital punishment, but soon reconsiders his position when faced with the realities of taking a man's life in retribution for murder.

Crimmin is influenced by the religious Regan, who has witnessed fourteen hangings during his years in the prison service and is vehementy opposed to the death penalty. Regan's disdain for the brutal mechanisms of counterweight, trapdoor and rope, the tools of the trade required to end the life of a healthy human being, deeply affect Crimmin, as does his humane concern for the welfare of the prisoners. The junior warder's simplistic view of law and order is occluded further by encounters with Kathleen (Sylvia Syms), the boozy, unfaithful wife of the condemned fratricidal murderer known to prisoners and staff alike as 'the Quare Fellow'; Silvertop (Aubrey Morris), a highly strung condemned man who gets a reprieve from the rope, only to commit suicide the same day by hanging himself because he can't face the endless years in jail; and the hangman (Arthur O'Sullivan), a disagreeable drunkard who approaches his grisly work with a disconcerting callousness.

The background status to which the prisoners are relegated prevents the film from ever becoming the uninhibited romp that theatre-goers often witnessed on stage. But the prominence of the warders, the governor, and the addition of characters outside the prison walls allows Dreifuss to focus on the central moral issue and make the original anti-hanging argument more forcefully. Enough vestiges of lively Behan wit remain to add levity to the protracted deathwatch – two old lags, Neighbour (Eric Gorman) and Dunlavin (Harry Brogan), swig meths from the bottle behind Crimmin's back, as the warder administers a leg-rub to ease their rheumatism, and the crew on grave-digging detail start betting the bacon from the following Sunday's lunch on whether the Quare Fellow will get a reprieve or not. But the overall tone of the film remains relentlessly downbeat, despite strong performances from Macken and McGoohan, and solid back-up from the all-Irish supporting cast.

DEMENTIA 13
(1963) US/IRL b&w 75 mins

Production Team

Producer .... Roger Corman/Robert Wright
           Campbell/Charles Hannawalt
Director .... Francis Coppolla
Screenplay .... Francis Coppolla
Cinematography .... Charles Hannawalt
Editor .... Mort Tubor, Stewart O'Brien
Musical Score .... Ronald Stein

Cast

Luana Anders .... Louise Haloran
William Campbell .... Richard Haloran
Ethne Dunne .... Lady Haloran
Patrick Magee .... Justin Caleb
Mary Mitchell .... Kane
Bart Patton .... Billy Haloran
Peter Reed .... John Haloran
Karl Schanzer .... Simon
Perry Arthur .... Ron
Derry O'Donovan .... Lilian

DEMENTIA 13
(1963) US/IRL b&w 75 mins

The Irish mastery of terror in literature, ranging from Lord Dunsany and Bram Stoker to Kitty the Hare, has rarely been reflected on screen, despite the popularity of US and British horror films with Irish audiences. Cut-price Hollywood legend Roger Corman produced a rare example of this genre in Ireland in 1963, directed by his protegé Francis Ford Coppolla. The future director of *The Godfather* and *Apocalypse Now* had begun his career shooting nudie shorts in California, and graduated to assistant director with Corman by the early-1960s. At the age of 34, he was given the chance to make his feature debut directing *Dementia 13*, using the cameras and equipment from a film that Corman was shooting in Europe at the time.

This creepy horror movie is set in Castle Haloran, home of widowed matriarch Lady Haloran (Eithne Dunne, misspelt in the credits) who hasn't been the same since her daughter Kathleen drowned in the castle pond seven years earlier. Her three sons are at home for the annual memorial ceremony for the dead Kathleen, at which Lady H invariably takes a funny turn and collapses. Her eldest son John (Peter Reed) takes a funny turn himself a few days before the ceremony while rowing on the pond with his blonde gold-digger wife Louise (Luana Anders), and has a fatal heart attack. Louise, realising that she'll be cut out of the Haloran fortune if he's dead, dumps his body overboard and fakes a letter to his mother saying that he had to leave suddenly for the US on urgent business. Trying to ingratiate herself with her looney mother-in-law by claiming a psychic connection to Kathleen's spirit, Louise plays tricks on Lady Haloran's mind, arranging for the dead girl's dolls to float up from the depths of the pond in which she drowned. But Louise's interference in Lady Haloran's 'relationship' with Kathleen precipitates her death at the hands of a deranged axe murderer, who then conceals her body, giving the impression that she left the house in a hurry just like her husband. Lady Haloran herself is attacked by the axe-wielding madman soon after, but she narrowly escapes.

The family doctor, Justin Caleb (Patrick Magee, the renowned stage actor for whom Beckett wrote *Krapp's Last Tape*) decides to get to the bottom of the mystery. He persuades the groundsman Arthur to drain the pond, yielding a clue that would seem to implicate Richard Haloran (William Campbell), the sculptor of the family. More shrink than physician, given the demented clan he's dealing with, Dr Caleb probes his suspects and sets a trap at the wedding of Richard and his fiancée Kane (Mary Mitchell) that will flush the murderer out in the open.

Billed as Francis Coppolla in the credits, the fledgling director shows little portent of the future Hollywood epics that would make him a legend. *Dementia 13* bears the stamp of its producer more than its director in its sustained mood of eerie eccentricity and tension, and relies on Ronald Stein's score to do most of the work in maintaining the suspense. Visually, the film has a sinister, murky atmosphere, with night sky and pondwater black as squid ink, an effect that may well be due to Cormanesque frugality of light-bulb wattage as much as the talents of the lighting designer.

GIRL WITH GREEN EYES
(1963) UK b&w 92 mins

Production Team

Producer .... Oscar Lewenstein/
Woodfall F P
Director .... Desmond Davis
Screenplay .... Edna O'Brien
from her book The Lonely Girl
Cinematography .... Manny Wynn
Editor .... Brian Smedley-Aston
Composer .... John Addison

Cast

Peter Finch .... Eugene Gaillard
Rita Tushingham .... Kate Brady
Lynn Redgrave .... Baba Brennan
Maire Kean .... Josie Hannigan
Arthur O'Sullivan .... Mr Brady
Julian Glover .... Malachi Sullivan
T P McKenna .... Priest
Lislott Gottinger .... Joanna
Patrick Laffan .... Bertie Counihan
Eileen Crowe .... Mrs Byrne
May Craig .... Aunt
Joe Lynch .... Andy Devlin
Yolande Turner .... Mary
Harry Brogan .... Jack Holland
Michael Hennessy .... Davey
Joe O'Donnell .... Patrick Devlin
Mícheál O'Bríain .... Lodger
Dave Kelly .... Ticket collector

GIRL WITH GREEN EYES
(1963) UK b&w 92 mins

Writer Edna O'Brien caused a sensation in 1962 with her autobiographical novel *The Lonely Girl*, a frank chronicle of a country girl's transition to womanhood in 1950s Dublin. She adapted it for the screen as *Girl with Green Eyes*, a romantic drama directed by Desmond Davis and shot on location in the city.

Shy, sensitive Kate Brady (Rita Tushingham) shares digs with boisterous Baba Brennan (Lynn Redgrave). The girls go everywhere together, dancing at the Four Provinces in Harcourt Street and going to the pictures, always looking for romance. Baba is very much available in this department, but Kate is more particular and finds the chit-chat of boys their own age dull and shallow. Fate takes a hand when they drive with Baba's friend Bertie (Pat Laffan) to the Dublin mountains to deliver a pup to an English writer, Eugene Gaillard (Peter Finch). Kate is curious about the suave, middle-aged Eugene. Much to her delight, she bumps into him in a Dublin bookshop soon afterwards. Precocious Baba invites him to join them for tea. At Bewley's Cafe, Eugene is charmed by Kate's innocence. Kate notices that Eugene wears no wedding ring and assumes that he is single.

Kate takes the initiative for their next encounter, inviting Eugene into town to meet her. She is shocked to discover from Eugene's college friend Malachi (Julian Glover) that Eugene is married, and runs away from him. He apologises to her by phone some days later for his negligence in mentioning it and invites her to his house. She stays overnight and chastely stays in the guest room; but the next time she visits, she makes bold advances and they sleep together for the first time. Kate likes this racy new side of herself, as does Eugene.

Kate's father gets wind of her relationship with this married foreigner and hauls her back to County Clare. Kate is disgusted at her father's vulgarity in the bar on the train home, having grown used to Eugene's urbane manner. At home, the parish priest (T P McKenna) gives her a stern talking-to about her sinful ways and forbids her to see Eugene again, but Kate flees the dismal farm and returns to Dublin. She resumes her affair, despite an attempt by her father and an angry mob of Claremen to take her back by force from Eugene's house. Eugene's cantankerous housekeeper Josie (the inestimable Maire Kean) calms them down with a blast of her shotgun, and sends them on their way. Kate moves in with Eugene and suffers feelings of inadequacy caused by his sophisticated but cynical friends. The relationship remains unequal, and despite the commitment implied when he buys her a ring, Kate realises that they have no future together. She bows out gracefully from the romance in a Dublin hotel. When Baba emigrates to London, Kate decides to go with her and make a fresh start, sad but wiser – a woman with a past.

Liverpudlian actress Rita Tushingham plays convent girl Kate as a rustic version of the gawky ingenue that made her famous in *A Taste of Honey* three years earlier. Peter Finch is engaging as the worldly older man, bruised by the failure of his marriage, and fearful of emotional commitment to her. The entire film is shot on location in Dublin and its environs, and features wonderful footage of the Liffey Quays, the Wellington Monument and the now-demolished Royal Hibernian Hotel.

YOUNG CASSIDY
(1965) UK colour 110 mins

Production Team

Producer .... John Ford/Sextant Films/
Robert Emmett Ginna
Director .... John Ford, Jack Cardiff
Screenplay .... John Whiting based on Sean
O'Casey's autobiography
Mirror In My House
Cinematography .... Ted Scaife
Editor .... Anne V Coates
Musical Score .... Seán O'Riada,
Marcus Dods

Cast

Rod Taylor .... John Cassidy
Maggie Smith .... Nora
Julie Christie .... Daisy Battles
Flora Robson .... Mrs Cassidy
Jack MacGowran .... Archie Cassidy
T P McKenna .... Tom Cassidy
Siân Phillips .... Ella
Julie Ross .... Sara
Robin Sumner .... Michael
Phillip O'Flynn .... Mick Mullen
Pauline Delaney .... Bessie Ballynoy
Edith Evans .... Lady Gregory
Michael Redgrave .... William Butler Yeats
Donal Donnelly .... Undertaker
Arthur O'Sullivan .... Foreman
Joe Lynch .... Hurler
Vincent Dowling .... Hurler

YOUNG CASSIDY
(1965) UK colour 110 mins

Jack Cardiff's colourful drama *Young Cassidy* is a highly fictional bio of Sean O'Casey's early life, charting his ascent from working-class origins to international renown as a playwright. The script is based on O'Casey's autobiography *Mirror in my House*, but sets out on a tangent to reality by renaming its subject 'Johnny Cassidy'. Cassidy (Rod Taylor) is a bookish labourer with literary ambitions, outwardly cheerful, but disturbed by the poverty that keeps his mother (Flora Robson) and sister (Siân Phillips) in a constant state of worry. His friend, Mick Mullen (Phillip O'Flynn) shares his concern and they work together planning a general strike. Their protest turns violent when strikers assault a scab driving a delivery cart under police protection, and toss him into the River Liffey. While old and infirm protesters are clubbed and trampled all around him, Cassidy gallantly rescues a blonde chorus girl, Daisy Battles (Julie Christie), from the fray. His gallantry is rewarded with a night in her bed.

Cassidy joins the nationalist cause and drills with the Volunteers in the Wicklow hills. He quits in disgust when his comrades squabble over the colour of uniforms (O'Casey resigned over Countess Markiewicz's appointment as officer in the Citizen's Army, which could hardly be played for laughs like the fashion dispute in this film) and decides to attack injustice with a pen instead. When the 1916 Rising comes, however, Cassidy is not found hiding in the library but joins the fight for Ireland's freedom.

Cassidy keeps up his reading by stealing books. When he's caught red-handed, he charms prim shop girl Nora (Maggie Smith) with his literary knowledge and she lets him have the books on the never-never. They begin a warm romance despite their contrasting temperaments. Following his mother's death, Cassidy moves in with Mullen and tries writing plays for the Abbey Theatre. After initial rejection, he is championed by an imperious W B Yeats (Michael Redgrave) and a kindly Lady Gregory (Edith Evans). Nora encourages the rising theatre star, but his yearning for fame and fortune in London and beyond frightens the staid bookseller, so she leaves him. His friendship with Mick ends when the earnest socialist denounces him for betraying his class and caricaturing him on stage. Cassidy realises that he can only fulfil his theatre ambitions by leaving his past behind. Fortified by success in Dublin, he takes the boat to England to conquer the London stage, a prosperous but solitary man.

Burly Australian Rod Taylor is an unlikely choice to play the cerebral playwright, and looks like he'd rather be tearing up telephone books with his bare hands than leafing pensively through slim volumes of poetry. His Irish accent alternates between a passable rural lilt, incongruous in the mouth of a Dublin navvy, and a Berlitz tape 'speak-Leprechaun-in-seven-days-or-your-money-back' brogue that renders risible any attempt to take his performance seriously. John Ford began shooting *Young Cassidy* in Dublin, but fell ill and was replaced by Jack Cardiff, acclaimed colour cinematographer on *Black Narcissus* and *The African Queen*. Cardiff's use of Technicolor in *Young Cassidy* makes Dublin look like Havana, an appealing artifice after years of monochrome images of the city. The film features great footage of lost Dublin, including the long-since demolished Georgian architecture of the city quays.

ULYSSES
(1967) UK b&w 127 mins

Production Team

Producer .... Ulysses FP/Joseph Strick/
Walter Reade Jr
Director .... Joseph Strick
Screenplay .... Joseph Strick, Fred Haines
from the book of the same
name by James Joyce
Cinematography .... Wolfgang Suschitsky
Editor .... Reginald Mills
Musical Score .... Stanley Myers

Cast

Milo O'Shea .... Leopold Bloom
Barbara Jefford .... Molly Bloom
Maurice Roëves .... Stephen Dedalus
T P McKenna .... Buck Mulligan
Anna Manahan .... Bella Cohen
Martin Dempsey .... Simon Dedalus
Chris Curran .... Myles Crawford
Fionnuala Flanagan .... Gerty McDowell
Geoffrey Golden .... Citizen
Eddie Golden .... Martin Cunningham
Máire Hastings .... Mary Driscoll
David Kelly .... Garrett Deasy
Graham Lines .... Haines
Des Perry .... Bantam Lyons
Rosaleen Linehan .... Nurse Callan
Joe Lynch .... Blazes Boylan
Maureen Potter .... Josie Breen

ULYSSES
(1967) UK b&w 127 mins

A sporadic twenty-year movie career that yielded a documentary, a docudrama, and a bizarre screen version of Jean Genet's *The Balcony* scarcely qualified American director Joseph Strick to film one of the superlative novels of the 20th century, but he did it anyway. Working with writer Fred Haines, Strick managed to piledrive the complex, multi-stylar narrative of James Joyce's *Ulysses* into a truncated two-hour screenplay that omits more than it includes of the original work. Shot in Panavision to no particular advantage, and in black and white to some, Strick's film moves briskly through a day in the life of Joyce's three renowned Dublin characters, Jewish ad canvasser Leopold Bloom (Milo O'Shea), his libidinous soprano wife Molly (Barbara Jefford), and the young poet and teacher Stephen Dedalus (Maurice Roëves). From the opening scene in the early morning at the Martello Tower in Sandycove, to the closing scene at the Bloom residence in Eccles Street at dawn, 24 hours later, Strick skims the surface of the day's events, while disregarding the specifics of Joyce's chosen date of 16 June 1904, by ample use of anachronisms vehicular, sartorial and technological.

Cruelly dismissed by critic Pauline Kael as "an act of homage in the form of readings from the book, with illustrated slides", Strick's *Ulysses* may be a failed attempt at filming a work of fiction that stubbornly resists transfer from paper to celluloid, but credit is due to the director for even attempting such an impossible task. Flawed though his results may be, Strick's Joyce reduction retains value as a synopsis for people who are too busy, too lazy, or too impatient to finish the book (a lot more copies of the daunting paperback are bought than read), and as a visual aid for those who have read and enjoyed it, but have never made the Joyce pilgrimage to Dublin. The film gives them an opportunity to see on the big screen at least a few of the diverse locations described so vividly by the exiled author, as his rambing protagonist Bloom travels around the city. Strick depicts Bloom's voyeuristic encounter with Gerty McDowell (Fionnuala Flanagan) at Sandymount Strand, Dedalus' breakfast with Buck Mulligan (T P McKenna) in Sandycove, and the journey of Paddy Dignam's funeral cortege from Sandymount to Glasnevin cemetery, while giving us extensive location footage in between of Joyce's Georgian milieu.

Expediency, budget constraints and the erosion of Joyce's Dublin inevitably result in omissions and substitutions – Davy Byrne's doesn't get a mention, and the pub scene at Barney Kiernan's of Little Britain Street, in which the mood shifts from the genial banter of the customers to anti-semitic invective directed at Bloom by the one-eyed citizen (Geoffrey Golden), was filmed in the bar of the old Dolphin Hotel in Temple Bar (with Murty Leonard, late of Leonard's of Dame Street, dispensing pints to the thirsty actors from behind the counter). The famous nighttown scenes, set in a red-light district that was already disappearing by the time Joyce's book was published, were all filmed on sets. To the detriment of the film, these scenes depicting Bloom's outlandish fantasies of self-aggrandisement and self-abasement at the hands of the judiciary, and of the women he has offended, are reduced to cheap theatrical absurdities by Strick's bargain-basement production values. By the time the avuncular Bloom and the drunken Dedalus leave nighttown to walk to Bloom's house in Eccles Street, Strick, hardly the most visually inventive of directors, gives up all pretense of aspiring to cinematic art. All on-screen dialogue ceases, cinema surrenders to literature, and *Ulysses* runs to its conclusion with voiceovers, initially in didactic Q & A format by Bloom and Dedalus, followed by almost half an hour of salacious highlights from Molly's notorious soliloquy.

Much as Joyce's book had done almost a half century earlier, the film ran afoul of the censors on account of its risqué language. Even though it was 1967, not 1922, and the 1960s were about as swinging as they were ever going to get in Ireland, Strick's *Ulysses* was banned by the Irish Film Censor upon its release. The ban was upheld when it came up for review again in 1974. In the US, the Academy looked more favourably on Strick's foray into Irish letters and nominated *Ulysses* for an Oscar in the Best Adapted Screenplay category. In a year of tough competition that included *Cool Hand Luke*, *The Graduate* and *In Cold Blood*, Strick's adaptation lost out to Stirling Silliphant's script for *In the Heat of the Night*.

Though the actors in *Ulysses* may have been overlooked when it came to awards and nominations, the film features some notable portrayals of Joyce's characters. Milo O'Shea gives a full-contact performance as the meandering cuckold Bloom, engaging the role as thoroughly as Strick's limited script allows him. By turns obsequious, testy, and reflective, O'Shea energetically delivers a well-rounded incarnation of the put-upon Poldy that transcends the parsimonious budget and does justice to the author's best-known creation. Flashes of brilliance by established Irish stage actors illuminate the minor roles: T P McKenna enjoys himself immensely as the gregarious, hedonistic medic Buck Mulligan, master of the bawdy song and the well-turned phrase, and Martin Dempsey shines as the irascible spendthrift Simon Dedalus, father of Stephen. David Kelly, in the small role of Dedalus' superior, Garrett Deasy, captures in a few lines the essence of that character's anglophile snobbery, pedagogic condescension and shameless anti-semitism. By contrast, Maurice Roëves is less successful as the contrarian introspector and Joyce alter-ego Stephen Dedalus. An actor from the north of England with paltry Irish credentials (amounting to little more than a minor role in Disney's *The Fighting Prince of Donegal* a year earlier), Roëves struggles with the Dublin cadences so important to Joyce's ear, and the results, like the meteorological analysis of Dedalus pére, are as uncertain as a child's bottom. The sibilant sounds of his Sunderland accent seep through his attempts at urban Irish locution and, coupled with the limited dialogue given to him by the writers – apart from spitting out the odd contentious aphorism, he spends most of the film walking, pondering or passing out – render ineffective his performance as the iconoclastic Dubliner.

Barbara Jefford fares little better as Molly. She fails to project the raw sensuality and the formidable womanly presence that made her an object of fascination for feminists and onanists alike in Joyce's book. Strick's over-reliance on voiceover effectively prevents her from raising her performance above the level of miming to a soundtrack of herself reading extracts from Joyce's text. Fionnuala Flanagan, who plays Gerty in Strick's *Ulysses*, showed how to do Molly Bloom properly eighteen years later in Michel Pearce's 1985 docudrama *James Joyce's Women*, a film in which she also played Nora Barnacle and Joyce's publisher Sylvia Beach, as well as reprising the exhibitionist Gerty. Strick's other female roles in his *Ulysses* are reduced to inconsequential status, but, given that the film is based on a naughty Joyce novel, almost all of the women in the cast end up in their underwear at some point, while few of the men do.

Undeterred by the scant praise and scathing comments that *Ulysses* drew from critics, and its indifferent performance at the box office, Strick persevered with his mission to bring the works of Ireland's most renowned writer to the screen. A decade later he would revisit the Joyce canon with more than half a dozen of the same actors, to film the author's earlier and more overtly autobiographical novel, *Portrait of the Artist as a Young Man*.

PADDY
(1969) IRL colour 88 mins

Production Team

Producer .... Allied Artists/
                                 Tamara Asseyev
Director .... Daniel Haller
Screenplay .... Lee Dunne from his book
                             Goodbye to the Hill
Cinematography .... Daniel Lacambre
Editor .... Christopher Holmes
Musical Score .... John Rubinstein

Cast

Des Cave .... Paddy Maguire
Milo O'Shea .... Harry Redmond
Dearbhla Molloy .... Maureen Murphy
Maureen Toal .... Claire
Marie O'Donnell .... Ma
Peggy Cass .... Irenee
John Molloy .... Watchbox Dawson
Ita Darcy .... Josie
Clive Geraghty .... Tony Deugan
Desmond Perry .... Mr Cahill
Pat Layde .... Mr Hayes
John Kavanagh .... Willie Egan
Judy Cornwell .... Breeda
Donal LaBlanc .... Larry

PADDY
(1969) IRL colour 88 mins

Writer Lee Dunne, king of Ireland's radio soaps, came to prominence in the 1960s with tales of Dublin working-class life that broke the prevailing rules on sexual frankness. His notorious account of his youth in Ranelagh's Mountpleasant flats, *Goodbye to the Hill*, was hugely successful on stage, and was adapted for the screen, by the author himself, as *Paddy*. Abbey actor Des Cave plays the title character Paddy Maguire, an Irish Alfie who dreams of rising above his station, but squanders his time carousing.

Paddy lives with his fretful mother (Marie O'Donnell), nagging sister (Ita Darcy) and two brothers in a dilapidated house in the inner city. He wangles a menial job in an insurance firm and studies at the Tech at night to improve himself, and escapes from his dreary home life as often as he can into the arms of a succession of women.

Among Paddy's paramours are a well-heeled widow, Claire (Maureen Toal) who gives him money and flashy new clothing, a blonde English masochist (Judy Cornwell) who gets him into a threesome with a chap (Clive Geraghty) from work, and Maureen (Dearbhla Molloy), a nice girl who loves him and makes him feel something similar. Paddy has a reprobate mentor in the form of Harry Redmond (Milo O'Shea), a workshy drink-cadger and seducer of American tourists, who provides the film's scarce comic relief. Whenever his sister nags him about his lifstyle, Paddy meets Harry for pints (mostly in Mulligan's on Poolbeg Street), to listen to his theories on the terrors of work and women.

Dunne's screenplay mercifully spares us the image of the tortured artist chafing at the nine-to-five grind as the poetry blossoms in his heart, presenting Paddy instead as a shallow hedonist and a selfish bowsie. Attempts are made to make him seem like he's not all bad – he saves his sickly brother Larry (Donal LeBlanc) from bullies, and dives in the canal in his best flared slacks to rescue a dog belonging to a drinking companion, Watchbox Dawson (John Molloy) – but he remains a charmless Casanova nonetheless.

Like Strick's *Ulysses*, *Paddy* was banned in Ireland. The censor's decision may have had less to do with sexual content than Paddy's evasion of comeuppance at the film's end. Director Haller, better known as Roger Corman's art director during his cheaply cobwebbed Edgar Allen Poe phase, manages to show a lot of promiscuity with almost no nudity in a film that wouldn't warrant an 'R' rating nowadays. However, the portrait of a young Dubliner who ignores his worried mother as she begs him to mend his ways, and cheerfully abandons his pregnant girlfriend to a loveless marriage with a duped suitor (John Kavanagh) who thinks the child is his own, sent out a message that was deemed unsuitable for late-1960s Ireland. A nasty end for the remorseless rake might have provided the requisite retribution for his sins, and allowed the people of Ireland to see this film when it came out.

The lead role could have been essayed with a bit of devil-may-care swagger, but Des Cave plays Paddy as though he had a moral objection to playing an amoral lecher, holding back on the full thrust the role needs to make the film take off. Paddy ends up looking like a joyless *Carry-On* film, replete with naughty bits and double entendres, but none of the laughs.

QUACKSER FORTUNE HAS A COUSIN IN THE BRONX
(1970) US colour 90 mins

Production Crew

Producer .... UMC Pictures/Sidney Glazier
Director .... Waris Hussein
Screenplay .... Gabriel Walsh
Cinematography .... Gilbert Taylor
Editor .... Bill Blunden
Musical Score .... Michael Dress

Cast

Gene Wilder .... Quackser Fortune
Margot Kidder .... Zazel
May Ollis .... Mrs Fortune
Seamus Forde .... Mr Fortune
Liz Davis .... Kathleen Fortune
Caroline Tully .... Vera Fortune
Eileen Colgan .... Betsy Bourke
David Kelly .... Maguire
Danny Cummins .... Donal
Tony Doyle .... Mike
Paul Murphy .... Damien
Brendan Matthews ..... Milk depot attendant
David Hogarty .... David

QUACKSER FORTUNE HAS A COUSIN IN THE BRONX
(1970) US colour 90 mins

Laconic Dubliner Quackser Fortune (Gene Wilder) resists parental pressure to follow in the footsteps of his father (Seamus Forde) and get a job in the local foundry. He prefers to make his living by following the city's horse-drawn delivery carts around and scooping the manure the horses leave behind, to sell to housewives for window-box fertiliser. His door-to-door sales method offers him the odd casual tryst with the likes of Betsy Bourke (Eileen Colgan), with no strings attached. But when he meets an attractive Trinity College student from Connecticut named Zazel (Margot Kidder), he is truly smitten. Quackser's bewildered demeanour and unusual occupation charm the bohemian Zazel in turn, and the mis-matched pair begin a quirky romance. Quackser quickly finds himself out of his depth. Her intellectual take on historic Dublin, the city of Swift and Handel's *Messiah*, means nothing to him, and her libertine ways make him nervous. Zazel has a casual approach to dating, and is cavalier about showing up on time or at all, leaving the perplexed Quackser standing in the street wondering where she is.

Further trouble ensues for Quackser when his livelihood is taken away by a government ordinance. The city bans horse-drawn deliveries in favour of motorised trucks, leaving him with no poop to scoop. To his horror, Quackser's beloved horses are despatched unceremoniously to the knackers' yard for conversion to glue. In an inspired moment of madness, after a disastrous night on the town with Zazel during which he was given the bumps by posh Pav types at Trinity Boat Club, Quackser impulsively decides to rescue the doomed animals. He runs to the knackers' yard at Spencer Dock in white tie and tails, opens the gate, and stampedes the horses through the streets of the city to save them from their adhesive fate.

Deprived of his metier by the scarcity of horses, Quackser contemplates heading for America to the New York borough of the film's title, rather than work in the foundry like his dad. But as he's about to leave he squanders his travel money in the pub (in a wacky grotesque scene shot with a fisheye lens). The sudden death of his American cousin further alters the plan. The cousin leaves him enough money in his will to start his own business, and Quackser becomes a tour guide, armed with the knowledge of Dublin's history that he learned from Zazel.

Casual and loopy as its title, *Quackser Fortune has a Cousin in the Bronx* rambles in no particlular hurry to its idiosyncratic conclusion. Renamed more generically as *Fun Loving* for its US release, the film finds the young Gene Wilder at his eccentric best, a year before *Willy Wonka and the Chocolate Factory* made him famous, and long before eccentricity became a rote affectation for the actor. This off-beat comedy was shot entirely on location during a bell-bottomed, sideburned summer in Dublin as the swinging 1960s were drawing to a close. The film features great footage of the city as the camera follows Quackser on his rounds, including several scenes in the legendary gravediggers' bar, Kavanagh's in Prospect Square, at the back gate of Glasnevin cemetery.

RYAN'S DAUGHTER
(1970) UK colour 206 mins

Production Team

Producer .... MGM/Faraway/Anthony Havelock Allen
Director .... David Lean
Screenplay .... Robert Bolt
Cinematography .... Frederick A Young
Editor .... Norman Savage
Musical Score .... Maurice Jarre

Cast

Robert Mitchum .... Charles Shaughnessy
Trevor Howard .... Father Collins
Sarah Miles .... Rosy
Christopher Jones .... Randolph Doryan
John Mills .... Michael
Leo McKern .... Tom Ryan
Barry Foster .... Tim O'Leary
Owen O'Sullivan .... Peter
Marie Kean .... Mrs McCardle
Evin Crowley .... Moureen
Barry Jackson .... Corporal
Douglas Sheldon .... Driver
Ed O'Callaghan .... Bernard
Philip O'Flynn .... Paddy
Niall O'Brien .... Joseph
Niall Toibin .... O'Keefe
Emmet Bergin .... Sean

RYAN'S DAUGHTER
(1970) UK colour 206 mins

Ryan's Daughter, the most ambitious motion picture production in Ireland since *The Quiet Man*, is remembered by international audiences more as a glorious failure in the otherwise illustrious career of its director David Lean than as an artistic triumph. Lean had made the transition from intimately scaled and highly acclaimed features *Blithe Spirit* and *Brief Encounter*, to even greater success with the lavish dramas *Bridge on the River Kwai*, *Lawrence of Arabia* and *Doctor Zhivago* and *Ryan's Daughter* was expected to match the scale and Oscar-winning success of those epics. But Lean's painstaking methods and impossibly long shooting schedule (twelve months in total) yielded an unwieldy love story that failed to impress critics and enjoyed only modest success at the box office.

The film was a big hit at local level in County Kerry where it was made. The filmmakers generated sizeable revenue and the celebrity sightings provided a great source of fascination for the people of Dunquin where the film was shot, prompting observer Mícheál Ó Mórdha to write an account of the whole proceedings called "The Best Government We Ever Had" (a title based on a local woman's assessment of the impact that the film-makers had on their community).

The film is set in the fictitious village of Kirrary on the south west coast of Ireland in 1916. A young woman named Rosy (Sarah Miles), daughter of local pub owner Tom Ryan (Leo McKern), yearns for more excitement than life in the area can offer. She is attracted to a shy older man, Charles Shaughnessy (Robert Mitchum), the tweedy village school teacher. Charles is a cultured gentleman, a keen flower arranger and Beethoven enthusiast, clearly more interested in the life of the mind than 'the satisfaction of the flesh' that fascinates Rosy and deeply concerns her priest Father Collins (Trevor Howard). She boldly declares her interest in Charles, which he considers infatuation. Her persistence convinces him that she's serious about him and he asks her to be his wife. She consents, to the dismay of her most persistent suitor, Michael (John Mills), the village idiot.

The wedding night is an awkward conjunction that disappoints Rosy and sends her to Father Collins for advice. He tries to impress upon her the value of a steady marriage to a man like Charles, and hopes that the relationship will tame her wilful ways. These hopes are soon dashed when she meets the highly strung Major Doryan (Christopher Jones), a shell-shocked British Army officer, sent to this quiet part of Ireland to recover from his harrowing experiences in World War I. Rosy first meets Doryan in her father's pub. The grinning fool Michael precipitates a battle flashback in the Major's mind by drumming loudly with his feet against a wood panel in the bar. Michael runs in panic when he sees Doryan's trauma, leaving Rosy alone with the distressed officer. Her attempts at comforting him turn quickly to an intimacy she finds exciting. Soon they're having an affair that is not entirely secret. The ubiquitous idiot Michael, who has a keener knowledge of what goes on in the village than might first be suspected, mimics Doryan in front of the villagers and makes it perfectly clear

RYAN'S DAUGHTER
(1970) UK colour 206 mins

to those present that Rosy and Doryan have been more than just horse-riding partners. Shaughnessy's suspicions about his wife's affair are confirmed when he confronts her directly about it, and he disappears for two days to struggle quietly with his despair. He tries to maintain his dignity, hoping that his young wife will soon tire of the British soldier.

The 1916 Rising in faraway Dublin begins to effect Kirrary when fugitive rebel leader Tim O'Leary (Barry Foster) organises the landing of a shipment of German guns and ammunition on the nearby strand. The plan goes awry due to the unpredictability of Atlantic gales, and the Fenians prevail upon Tom Ryan, Rosy's buffoon of a father, to get some local men to save the weapons before the sea takes them. The entire population of the village descends upon the beach to help, showing their sympathy for the rebellion against the British. They are successful in saving most of the shipment, but the rebels are intercepted by the British soldiers before they can make their escape. Because of her known association with Doryan, Rosy is immediately suspected of betraying the Fenians, and the villagers exact their revenge by stripping her and cropping her hair in front of her father and husband. Doryan, already deeply disturbed, reacts to this humiliating punishment of his lover by detonating some of the explosives which Michael had recovered from the sea to take his own life. Rosy and Charles decide to leave the town whose inhabitants have cast them out, and board a bus to Dublin where they can make a new start.

As the shy, sensitive Shaughnessy, Mitchum gives a performance of remarkable restraint, acting against every type he had previously portrayed in a quarter century of knocking heads, driving fast, and firing guns on the big screen. Mitchum didn't stay in character off-camera however, and passed the tedious hours between takes swigging whiskey and sorting out local lads who fancied themselves taking a swipe at a Hollywood tough guy. For a lengthy period while they were making the film, close-ups of the mild-mannered teacher Charles were ruled out by a black eye administered to Mitchum's craggy face by a local bruiser in a pub brawl.

Sarah Miles, then wife of the playwright Robert Bolt who wrote the script for the film, recounts in her autobiography *Serves Me Right* some of the difficulties the cast and crew had to endure to meet Lean's exacting standards during the shoot. Storm scenes were filmed up close by cameramen wearing wetsuits and using cameras chained to rocks, and the actors were imperilled by shooting and re-shooting the scenes where they tried to retrieve the German arms at the shore in rough waters. In one particular incident, Leo McKern was almost swept out to sea, but managed to stagger ashore with the help of extras who recoiled in horror when they saw sand and saltwater gushing from his empty eye socket. They were previously unaware that he had a glass eye, and he hadn't yet realised in his dazed state that he had lost the prosthetic while being buffeted by the waves.

The picturesque village of Kirrary seen in the film is not only fictitious, it is also an

RYAN'S DAUGHTER
(1970) UK colour 206 mins

architectural artifice, constructed especially for the film. The existing Kerry villages just weren't quaint enough, and production designer Stephen Grimes built the facades for the school, shops and houses near the real village of Carhoo in Kerry to create the street scenes in the film. Most of the beach scenes in *Ryan's Daughter* were shot at Inch Strand, east of Dingle, and Coumeenoole Strand, near Dunquin. Towards the end of the shooting schedule, as the Irish winter approached and the light became more and more pallid, Lean had trouble matching the brightness and colour of the beach scenes shot months earlier, and had to take cameras, crew, and actors to South Africa for six weeks to match the relevant shots. Down there, the light was right, but the rocks were wrong, and had to be painted a darker colour to replicate the limestone crags of the Irish coastline.

Lean's three previous films were nominated by the Academy for Best Picture, Best Director, Best Cinematography and Best Screenplay, and racked up nine Oscars in these major categories. Though *Ryan's Daughter* received four nominations, the Oscar cupboard was bare for Lean himself that year. Actors John Mills and Sarah Miles were both nominated for their performances, with Mills winning his first and only statuette for Best Supporting Actor. Long-time Lean collaborator Freddie Young scooped his third Oscar with the director for his lush cinematography. Young's lens caresses the Kerry coastline to create arguably the most beautiful portrayal of Irish landscape ever filmed – a sumptuous pastoral idyll in 70 millimetre Panavision that makes the scenery the real star of the film, and ultimately dwarfs the painful love story at the heart of *Ryan's Daughter*.

IMAGES
(1972) IRL/US colour 101 mins

Production Team

Producer .... Lion's Gate/
                                                      Tommy Thompson
Director .... Robert Altman
Screenplay .... Robert Altman
Cinematography .... Vilmos Zsigmond
Editor .... Graeme Clifford
Musical Score .... John Williams

Cast

Susannah York .... Cathryn
René Auberjonois .... Hugh
Marcel Bozzuffi .... René
Hugh Millais .... Marcel
Cathryn Harrison .... Susannah
                                                      (the daughter)
John Morley .... Old man

IMAGES
(1972) IRL/US colour 101 mins

Two years after US director Robert Altman came to international prominence with M*A*S*H, he travelled to Ireland to make *Images*, starring Susannah York and René Auberjonois. This unsettling psychodrama slots in between *McCabe and Mrs Miller* and *The Long Goodbye* in the Altman oeuvre, and is a sparsely populated film of modest scale compared to his later sprawling, overcrowded works. *Images* runs counter to the director's tendency to grimly satirise or reinvent existing film genres, as he often did in his better-known (and often overpraised) later features. In this underrated film, Altman explores the theme of mental disintegration without irony or cynical detachment. He reunited with *McCabe and Mrs Miller* cinematographer Vilmos Zsigmond to shoot the spectacular landscapes of County Wicklow as a metaphor for the main female character's dizzying descent into madness. Zsigmond had also worked with John Boorman on *Deliverance*, providing the connection that brought Altman to Ireland.

Cathryn (Susannah York), a highly strung writer of children's books, lives in a luxurious city apartment with her husband Hugh (René Auberjonois), a self-absorbed photographer. While he's away, she works on her book 'In Search of the Unicorn', and is interrupted by an anonymous phone caller claiming that her husband is having an affair. When Hugh returns, Cathryn starts to confuse his identity with that of René, (Marcel Bozzuffi) a lover from her past who has been dead for several years. The experience terrifies her. Hugh takes her to Green Cove, their country house (a mansion on the Powerscourt estate in County Wicklow), to calm her down. Her hallucinations continue at the house and become more outlandish. Hugh doesn't help by inviting to dinner another of her former lovers, Marcel (Hugh Millais), who gets drunk and gropes her aggressively. She confuses him with her husband and becomes hysterical. Soon she sees recurring images of herself and of her former lovers, and calmly resolves to get rid of them by violent means. She attacks one lover with a kitchen knife and shoots the other with Hugh's gun. Far from achieving peace of mind by dispelling these images, she panics again, convinced that the murdered illusions may actually be real.

The final scenes of this difficult, intriguing drama are tantalisingly unresolved, leaving the viewer unsure as to what is real and what is imagined. As if the plot isn't bewildering enough already, Altman perversely adds to the confusion by giving each character the first name of a cast member other than the one playing that role.

Vilmos Zsigmond, later an Oscar winner for *Close Encouters of the Third Kind*, shoots *Images* largely from Cathryn's warped viewpoint, switching abruptly from intense close-ups of the actress to vertigo-inducing shots of Powerscourt waterfall and Lough Bray, to convey her disorientated take on reality. John Williams' soundtrack maintains the taut domestic atmosphere with shrill flute stylings and sonic effects from Red Buddha theatre experimentalist Stomu Yamash'ta that sound a lot like piles of saucepans tipping over onto a tiled floor. Williams was nominated for an Oscar for his score.

The Academy that had lauded M*A*S*H so highly in 1970 wasn't as impressed by Altman's work this time round, and the film received no other nominations. The jury at Cannes liked *Images* better, giving the Best Actress Award to Susannah York for her performance as the schizophrenic Cathryn.

THE MACKINTOSH MAN
(1973) UK colour 90 mins

Production Team

Producer .... John Foreman
Director .... John Huston
Screenplay .... Walter Hill from the book
The Freedom Trap by Desmond Bagley
Cinematography .... Oswald Morris
Editor .... Russell Lloyd
Musical Score .... Maurice Jarre

Cast

Paul Newman .... Rearden
Dominique Sanda .... Mrs Smith
James Mason .... Sir George Wheeler
Harry Andrews .... Angus Mackintosh
Ian Bannen .... Slade
Michael Hordern .... Brown
Nigel Patrick .... Soames-Trevelyn
Peter Vaughan .... Brunskill
Roland Culver .... Judge
Percy Herbert .... Taafe
Robert Lang .... Jack Summers
Donal McCann .... Local
John MacDarby .... Old man
Hugh Manning .... Prosecutor
Wolfe Morris ..... Malta Police Commissioner
Noel Purcell .... O'Donovan
Donald Webster .... Jervis

THE MACKINTOSH MAN
(1973) UK colour 90 mins

Director John Huston, a long-time resident of the west of Ireland, shot sizeable portions of the cryptic thriller *The Mackintosh Man* in the rocky terrain around his Connemara home. Adapted from Desmond Bagley's bestseller *The Freedom Trap*, the film stars Paul Newman as a British intelligence officer who goes undercover to infiltrate a gang of jail breakers known as 'the Scarperers'. He is assigned the fake identity of Australian thief Joseph Rearden by Angus Mackintosh (Harry Andrews), a senior MI5 figure. Mackintosh and his secretary, the oddly Gallic Mrs Smith (Dominique Sanda) set him up to carry out a jewel heist that goes wrong, landing him in Chelmsford prison (actually shot in Dublin's Kilmainham Gaol) for twenty years and into the clutches of the Scarperers.

In exchange for a cut from the jewel robbery, the Scarperers arrange to have Rearden sprung from jail, along with a communist spy named Slade (Ian Bannen). Both of them are liberated, sedated and sequestered in a remote mansion in the countryside (neither of them knows where, though Rearden guesses Yugoslavia or Greece) until the balance of the escape fee is paid.

Back in London, Mackintosh leaks information to sinister MP Sir George Wheeler (James Mason) that he has an agent inside the Scarperers' operation. Wheeler tips off Brown (Michael Hordern), top Scarperer at the mansion, who sets his dog and his henchmen on Rearden to make him talk. Rearden escapes thanks to some clever spy tricks, setting the place on fire on his way out, and heads off across the wild countryside. He meets an old man (John MacDarby) who speaks Irish to him, and finally realises where he is. After a drink in a pub in Roundstone, County Galway, he contacts Mrs Smith in London from the call box on the pier. She blurts that Mackintosh, the only one who can verify his identity, is in a coma from a hit-and-run which she believes is no accident.

Sir George arrives at Roundstone harbour in his yacht, ostensibly for a fishing holiday but actually to retrieve Slade. He ingratiates himself locally by promising to buy rounds in the pub – to the disgust of one local (Donal McCann), that his countrymen's affection can be bought so easily. Mrs Smith flies in to meet Rearden, and between them they divine Wheeler's role in Slade's destiny, and his plan to bring the communist spy by sea to Malta. Rearden borrows a battered Ford Transit to take them to the airport. The henchmen spot them and give chase, hurtling at high speed down narrow Connemara roads, and clattering into drystone walls and turf-ricks (instead of cardboard boxes, as usually seen in urban car chases). The chase ends on a surreal note as the pursuing white Mercedes goes off the road and over the cliffs of Moher, dropping hundreds of feet to the sea. Free to continue, Rearden and Smith head for Malta to solve this mystery and bring the film to its bloody, unlikely conclusion.

Huston had enjoyed working with Newman two years earlier on *The Life and Times of Judge Roy Bean* and shot *The Mackintosh Man* both as a paying gig and an opportunity to work with the actor again. The tepid thriller provided menial spailpín work for a formidable line-up of Irish actors, most of whom didn't bother to attempt a Galway accent, giving the impression that the bar in Roundstone is packed with farmers and fishermen from Dublin.

ZARDOZ
(1974) IRL colour 104 mins

Production Team

Producer ....John Boorman
Director.....................................John Boorman
Screenplay ....John Boorman
Cinematography ....Geoffrey Unsworth
Musical Score....................... David Munrow

Cast

Sean Connery .... Zed
Charlotte Rampling .... Consuella
Sara Kestelman .... May
Sally Anne Newton .... Avalow
Niall Buggy .... Arthur Frayn
Bosco Hogan .... George Saden
Reginald Jannan .... Death
Bairbre Dowling .... Star
John Alderton .... Friend
Christopher Casson .... Old scientist
Jessica Swift .... Apathetic

ZARDOZ
(1974) IRL colour 104 mins

Ireland is used as a location for historical dramas more often than futuristic fantasies, but director John Boorman saw the potential for post-apocalyptic dystopia in the Wicklow hills and shot his only sci-fi feature there. *Zardoz* is set in the year 2293, and the survivors of an unspecified cataclysm live in the Outlands and the Vortex, zones separated by an invisible force-field. Vortex-dwellers the Eternals control both zones. Their Outland serfs, the Brutals, are subjugated by a deity, Zardoz – devised by an Eternal (Niall Buggy) to keep order and maintain crop quotas – and his hitmen, the Exterminators. The only connection between the effete Vortex and the harsh Outlands is a flying stone head that Brutals worship as Zardoz. The giant head spits firearms and aphorisms ("the gun is good; the penis is evil" – a tacit tenet of the fledgling Irish Free State) at the Exterminators, among them, Zed (Sean Connery).

If size counts, Zed comes up short – the hirsute thug gets only a revolver from Zardoz' weapons-spew, while his mates all get rifles. He makes up for this in cunning. To find the truth about the flying head, he conceals himself inside it and flies to the Vortex. The Eternals he meets there are fascinated and frightened by his musky sensuality – having achieved immortality, they have lost the will to procreate and want to know how he does it. Some Eternals, led by Consuella (Charlotte Rampling), want to kill Zed. Others, led by scientist May (Sara Kestelman), want him alive for genetic analysis and possible copulation. Zed is allowed to live and soon becomes the catalyst for the destruction of their sterile society.

A prologue delivered by Zardoz promises a tale "rich in irony and most satirical". He's lying of course – Boorman is far too serious about the dangers of religious governance to entertain such levity. But this trippy film buckles under the weight of his intellectual aspirations, and the plot trajectory defies explanation without the aid of pie charts, glove puppets and a glossary of Zardozian lingo. The Wicklow hills may not look arable in the film, but they must surely yield abundant crops of magic mushrooms.

Zardoz marked a change of pace for Connery, charging round the Sally Gap and Luggala in orange drawers, thigh-high boots and mariachi moustache after half a dozen outings as sardonic spy 007. Cinematographer Geoffrey Unsworth, who shot Connery before in *Hell Drivers*, struggles to make art of a film with the production values of *The Prisoner*. Boorman may have made a million-and-a-half of his investors' dollars look like a million-and-three-quarters, but his visual ambitions for *Zardoz* are still beyond the scope of the budget. Despite *Zardoz'* narrative chaos and resulting audience bewilderment, Boorman deserves credit for sheer daring, in making an anti-religious film in a country whose president had tried to make a theocracy of the place 36 years previously (with a Constitution vetted by the Vatican!). Boorman may not have been in Ireland long enough to realise the value of proper colour-coding of opposing sides (Eternals and Exterminators both wear orange) but he knew a spiritual flim-flam when he saw one. The nudity may never again be so flagrant or gratuitous in a film made in Ireland's damp climate, and for this alone *Zardoz* deserves its enduring cult status, if not any kind of serious respect.

CAOINEADH AIRT UÍ LAOIRE
(1975) IRL colour 52 mins

(Still courtesy of the Irish Film Archive of the Film Institute of Ireland reproduced courtesy of Bob Quinn)

Production Team

Producer .... Bob Quinn/Cinegael
Director .... Bob Quinn
Screenplay .... Bob Quinn,
based on the lament of the
same name by Eibhlín
Dhubh Ní Chonaill
Cinematography .... Joe Comerford
Editor .... Máirtín Mac Donnacha
Musical Score .... Mickey Finn/Máirtín Ó
Fáthartha/Gearóid Ó hAinle/
Michael Sweeney

Cast

Seán Bán Breathnach .... Art Uí Laoire
John Arden .... Director
Caitlín Ní Dhonnchú .... Eibhlín
Tomás Mac Lochlan ....
Síobhan Ní Shúilleabháin ....
Máire Ní Dhrisceoil ....
Joe Clancy ....

grúpa aisteoirí:

Bernadette Ní
 Fhlatharta
Máirtín Davy .
Bairbre Ní Balustrum
Colm R Ó Finneadha
Máirtín
 MacFhlannchada
Síobhán Dhabharáin
Padraic Bradley

Sarah McKenzie-Bary
Máirtín Ó Colaí
Tommy Healy
Gurney Campbell
Margaretta D'Arcy
Pascal Finnan
Seán Mac Iomhair
Coilín Tuathail
Julie Cummins
Kieran Lawton

CAOINEADH AIRT UÍ LAOIRE
(1975) IRL colour 52 mins

The Irish film industry was virtually dormant during the mid-1970s, but there were signs of vitality in the west of Ireland in the form of Bob Quinn, a pioneering director in the Irish language and virtually a one-man industry in Connemara at the time. Quinn had learned his trade at Raidio Teilifís Éireann in the 1960s before starting his own independent company, Cinegael, in Galway. He made his feature debut with the historic drama *Caoineadh Airt Uí Laoire*, a play-within-a-film shot on a minuscule budget with acting talent from the Galway stage. The subject matter is political and emotive, addressing the circumstances leading to the murder of an Irish nobleman by an English sherriff in Ireland in 1773, with pointed references to the hostility that still lingers between Irish and English people two centuries later.

Art Uí Laoire had lived in Austria and served as an officer in the Hungarian Hussars with all the rights and privileges accorded to a man of high social standing. On his return home to Macroom, County Cork, however, he found his own people subjugated by penal laws which denied even basic rights to Catholics. Art caused quite a stir with his confident demeanour and his refusal to bend to English rule. The cocky nobleman courted a young widow, Eibhlín Dhubh Ní Chonaill, married her against the wishes of her parents, and started a family. An English sherriff named Morris coveted Art's fine horse and offered him £5 for it. A rarely enforced penal law forbade Catholics to own a horse worth more than this sum, and when he refused the offer, Art was deemed to have broken the law. Morris mercilessly harassed the boisterous Uí Laoire, who cheerfully defied his attempts to subdue him. Finally, in an argument, Uí Laoire assaulted the Englishman, and later threatened to kill him – a far more serious offence than owning a quality horse. Morris despatched soldiers to arrest Uí Laoire. They shot him dead, though he was unarmed at the time. Morris was later tried and convicted of his murder.

Art Uí Laoire is played by Seán Bán Breathnach, Galway native and later (more ríabhach than bán) a major figure on Teilifís na Gaeilge, the Irish language television station. In Quinn's film, Breathnach's character is rehearsing an Irish play about Art Uí Laoire's death, under the direction of a pompous, exasperated Englishman (John Arden) with some understanding of Gaeilge, though he doesn't bother speaking it. Breathnach's brash character resists the director's orders throughout the film, mirroring Uí Laoire's vigorous resistance to Sherriff Morris' authority more than 200 earlier. The parallel between history and the current story is reinforced by the director playing Morris in the stage drama. Segments of the heartrending lament of Art's widow are interspersed through the narrative, lending a sombre tone that contrasts with the lively jousting between director and cast in rehearsal, and the sherriff and the nobleman in the play. This lament, traditionally believed to have been composed over Art's fallen body by his distraught wife Eibhlín Dhubh Ní Chonaill, provides the departure point for Quinn's screenplay. In his debut – the first fiction film in Ireland's native language – Quinn proved that it was possible to make an Irish feature without major government finance. However, making a film is one thing, finding an appreciative audience for it is another, and despite Quinn's daring narrative style, *Caoineadh Airt Uí Laoire* remains an underrated work in the Irish cinema canon.

PORTRAIT OF THE ARTIST AS A YOUNG MAN
(1977) UK/IRL colour 92 mins

Production Team

Producer .... Ulysses FP/Hanseat/
RTÉ/Joseph Strick
Director .... Joseph Strick
Screenplay .... Judith Rascoe
Cinematography .... Stuart Hetherington
Editor .... Leslie Walker
Musical Score .... Stanley Myers

Cast

Bosco Hogan .... Stephen Dedalus
T P McKenna .... Simon Dedalus
John Gielgud .... The preacher
Rosaleen Linehan .... Mrs Dedalus
Maureen Potter .... Dante
Niall Buggy .... Davin
Brian Murray .... Lynch
Desmond Cave .... Cranly
Leslie Lalor .... Milly
Desmond Perry .... Mr Casey
Susan Fitzgerald .... Emma
Luke Johnston .... Stephen, age 10
Danny Figgis .... Wells
Cecil Sheehan .... Uncle Charles
Edward Golden .... Father Conmee
Emmet Bergin .... Father Dolan
Bill Foley .... Confessor
David Kelly .... Dean of studies

PORTRAIT OF THE ARTIST AS A YOUNG MAN
(1977) UK/IRL colour 92 mins

Ten years after his flawed screen homage to James Joyce's **Ulysses**, director Joseph Strick turned his attention to the author's more approachable debut novel *A Portrait of the Artist as a Young Man*. The straighforward narrative of this earlier book presented fewer problems for Strick than the meandering 1922 epic, and yielded a visual précis truer to its source than the previous film had done. Strick adhered closely to the late-Victorian setting of the author's youth, avoiding the anachronisms that marred his first Joyce adaptation, and delivered a faithful, if pedestrian, account of the life of a young Dublin intellectual growing up in late-19th century Ireland.

Framed as the coming-of-age of Joyce's alter ego Stephen Dedalus, *Portrait of the Artist as a Young Man* faithfully chronicles the title character's passage from shy, serious schoolboy to university student and tentative blasphemer, elucidating the notable incidents of youth and adolescence that shaped the 20th century's most renowned author. Judith Rascoe's screenplay begins in 1885, when young Stephen was a three-year-old bedwetter and Ireland was striving to achieve Home Rule under the leadership of Parnell. The story moves on to Stephen's humiliations and small triumphs as a ten-year-old Clongowes Wood schoolboy (Luke Johnston), winning respect from a bully (Danny Figgis) for keeping his mouth shut when the bigger boy pushed him in a stream, and from his classmates for disputing with the school rector (Edward Golden) an undeserved beating from a sadistic priest (Emmet Bergin) during Latin class. The impressionable Stephen is exposed to lively arguments against the Church during Christmas dinner at home, by his father Simon (T P McKenna), and a guest, Casey (Desmond Perry), die-hard Parnellites both, even after the Home Ruler's popularity declined when his relationship with a married woman was made public; and a staunch defence of the Catholic hierarchy by another guest (Maureen Potter) who fears for Stephen's moral welfare in such an impious household.

Financial difficulties leave Stephen's father unable to pay the 40 guineas a year required to keep Stephen in boarding school at Clongowes. He is enrolled instead as a day boy in Belvedere College, back in Dublin. The money problems of the Dedalus family continue, thanks to the business ineptitude of the downwardly mobile dad, and they are forced to move to humble digs. Simon Dedalus is declared bankrupt, and an auction of his goods and property fails to raise enough money to pay off his debts. Simon maintains an outward appearance of hollow bravado despite this defeat, pompously declaring over pints in the pub afterwards that he's a better man than his son will ever be.

Despite his unstable home environment, the teenage Stephen (Bosco Hogan) excels at his studies in Belvedere, and wins a national essay competition. He also develops an interest in worldly pleasures, consorting with prostitutes and ogling pictures of naked women, until he hears a fiery preacher (John Gielgud) describe the horrors of hell so vividly that he fears for his corrupted soul. Confession gives him some relief and he resolves to abstain from gratification of the flesh and devote himself to a life of prayer. His reform is so exemplary that the Dean of Studies (David Kelly) considers him a likely candidate for the priesthood, and discusses the prospect over afternoon tea. Dedalus piously considers this holy life, and takes a stroll by the sea-shore to think about it, carrying with him a prayer for a vocation given to him by the Dean. The sight of a comely maiden perriwinkling in the waves makes him realise that he could never endure celibacy, and he casts to the wind the paper on which the prayer is written, and with it the last vestige of his commitment to the Catholic Church.

The callow Dedalus becomes more confident of his iconoclastic opinions when he enters university (shot on the Trinity College campus, though Joyce was a UCD man), and he strives to outdo Aristotle and Aquinas in his philosophising about pity, terror and beauty. He pontificates to his fellow students, who he clearly considers intellectually inferior, about religion, history and nationalism, and wilfully opposes the causes with which his contemporaries align themselves. Only on the issue of religion does he encounter a serious challenge, when his friend Cranly (Desmond Cave) makes him realise that his nervousness about committing blasphemy (by receiving communion at Easter to make his mother happy, even though he's a non-believer) implies some residual fear on his part, and thus belief, in the religion that he so vigorously rejects.

Uncomfortable with the strictures of Church, family, and academia, and chafing against the conservative mores of Irish society, Dedalus soon decides to leave Ireland. He goes abroad in search of the freedom to create, through his writing, the synthesis of carnal pleasure and intellectual discourse that preoccupies him so much at home; or as Joyce would describe it through his stand-in Stephen, "to forge in the smithy of my soul the uncreated conscience of my race". As he had done in *Ulysses*, Strick abandons any attempt at further cinematic development when the student Dedalus turns introspective, and hands the film back to the book once more. *Portrait of the Artist as a Young Man* ends with long passages from Dedalus' diary, read by Bosco Hogan, over footage of his encounters with friends, family and acquaintances, as he makes up his mind to abandon all and head for Europe.

Admirers of Joyce's work and fans of literate film will find that Strick's second attempt at the Joyce canon is as fascinating and unsatisfying as the first. The dialogue stays close to the spirit of the book, but is let down by the stilted visuals (mostly walking and talking in Victorian garb). While the film is competently directed it has a flat quality that resists leavening despite the efforts of a fine cast of notable Irish actors of the time. In the lead role, Bosco Hogan fares considerably better as Dedalus than Maurice Roëves had done in *Ulysses*, and T P McKenna, Strick's erstwhile Buck Mulligan, gives a spirited performance as Simon Dedalus, self-deluding paterfamilias and incorrigible rogue. Desmond Cave and Brian Murray provide capable foils to the contentious young Dedalus as Cranly and Lynch, his fellow students and intellectual sparring partners.

PORTRAIT OF THE ARTIST AS A YOUNG MAN
(1977) UK/IRL colour 92 mins

The costume department strives to create a convincing historic accuracy in the outfits worn by the actors, but runs into the problem of contemporary hair. There is a prevailing blowdried look among the extras that makes it hard to accept them as youths from the slicked-back fin-de-siecle era in which the film is set – an inevitable consequence of making the film during that brief interlude in the 1970s when Irish men used hairdryers.

The high point of the film, as in the book, is the nightmarish description of hell witnessed by Stephen and his classmates during a retreat at Belvedere College. John Geilgud, as the preacher, describes in breathy tones an inferno of gelatinous putresecence, rank stench, and fetid carcasses massed together in the reeking darkness, petrifying the young scholars and sending the sinful Stephen straight to the confession box. The veteran actor Gielgud rises magnificently to the occasion to strike a chord that resonates deeply in Dedalus and makes him realise that, deny the faith as he may, he can never shake himself completely free from his dread of eternal damnation.

POITÍN
(1978) IRL colour 60 mins

(Still courtesy of the Irish Film Archive of the Film Institute of Ireland reproduced courtesy of Bob Quinn)

Production Team

Producer .... Bob Quinn/Cinegael
Director .... Bob Quinn
Screenplay ...... Bob Quinn and Colm Bairéad
Cinematography .... Séamus Deasy
Editor .... Bob Quinn

Cast

Cyril Cusack .... Michil
Donal Mac Cann .... Labhcás
Niall Tóibín .... Sleamhnán
Mairead Ní Chonghaile .... Máire
Tomás Ó Flatharta .... Marcus
Macdara Ó Fátharta .... Garda
Micheál Ó Maollalaí .... Sergeant
Seán Ó Coisdealbha .... Publican
Tomás MacEoin .... Singer
Bairbre Ní Dhonncha .... Woman at fair
Colm Bairéad .... Farmer

POITÍN
(1978) IRL colour 60 mins

Bob Quinn continued to plough the lonely furrow he had started three years earlier with his second Irish-language feature film, *Poitín*. The film is set in the heart of the Connemara Gaeltacht and shot in a blunt realist style that rejects the heroic grandeur of Robert Flaherty's *Man of Aran* and shreds the sentimental blueprint of John Ford's *The Quiet Man*. Quinn reveals instead a bleak rural existence of criminal chicanery, in a harsh landscape that sets people against each other more than it unites them. Quinn's protagonists are neither ennobled by a heroic struggle with the sea nor assembled at the local shebeen for the amusement of tourists. They are engaged instead in the illegal business of making and distributing poitín, the potent potato alcohol distilled in rural Ireland since time immemorial.

Grizzled poitín maker Michil (Cyril Cusack) works his still at his house beside a lake. His daughter Máire (Mairead Ní Chonghaile) helps him by keeping an eye out for the local Garda patrol car, and when the coast is clear he prepares a batch of the distillate for his distributors Sleamhnán (Niall Tóibín) and Labhcás (Donal Mac Cann). The two boys are spotted and chased by Gardaí when they leave with the poitín but they evade their pursuers and stash the contraband by the sea. The Gardaí suspect that they're up to no good and question them, to no avail, when they collect their dole. A local man named Marcus (Tomás Ó Flatharta) helps the Gardaí with their enquires and lets them know where the poitín is hidden. The Gardaí confiscate the booze and celebrate by having a few shots themselves.

Marcus visits Michil and Máire and tells them that the Gardaí found the poitín, without explaining how. That night Sleamhnán and Labhcás go to the police station and find the Gardaí passed out from drinking. They take back the poitín and sell it surreptitiously at a market the next day. Pleased with their scheme, they celebrate in the pub that night.

Labhcás' dog worries Michil's sheep, vexing the old man, and when he hears from Marcus that Sleamhnán and Labhcás were seen selling poitín at the fair, he angrily kills the dog. Sleamhnán and Labhcás arrive at Michil's house looking for more booze, claiming that the Gardaí still have the previous batch in custody. Michil pretends to believe them and goes outside, apparently to get more for them. While waiting in Michil's house for the poitín, giddy from their ruse and the previous night's drinking, Sleamhnán and Labhcás have a mock fight, throwing potatoes at each other. They find a bottle of poitín and aggressively demand more when Michil returns. He tells them it's hidden in the middle of the lake, and offers them his boat to fetch it. Knowing that neither Sleamhnán and Labhcás can swim, Michil has removed the bung from his boat to get them back for their treachery. Greedy for more poitín, they hurriedly row far from the lakeshore, and as the boat fills with water they sink to their doom.

Quinn's film is a salutary retort to its pastoral Irish antecedents and boldly makes the point that struggling with stony ground and bad weather, far from fortifying the people, can make them callous and vindictive. This modestly scaled story is helped tremendously by a strong cast of skilled and experienced actors, and the rugged Connemara landscape that needs no cinematographic artifice to impress.

MAEVE
(1981) UK colour 110 mins

(Still courtesy of the Irish Film Archive of the Film Insititue of Ireland reproduced courtesy of Pat Murphy)

Production Team

Producer .... BFI/Kate McManus/Alastair
Herron/John Davies/Robert Smith
Director .... Pat Murphy, John Davies
Screenplay .... Pat Murphy
Cinematography .... Robert Smith,
David Barker
Editor .... John Davies
Musical Score.............. Molly Brambeld *et al.*

Cast

Mary Jackson .... Maeve Sweeney
Mark Mulholland .... Martin Sweeney
Bríd Brennan .... Róisín Sweeney
Trudy Kelly .... Ellen
John Keegan .... Liam Doyle
Nuala McCann .... Young Maeve
George Shane .... Causeway man
Aingeal Grehan .... Joan O'Neill
Carmel Grehan .... Carmel Noonan
Mel Austin .... Joe Sweeney
Justin Duff .... Colm Sweeney
Billy Kane .... Frank Doyle
Lucie Jamison .... Woman in hospital
Sheila Graham .... Mrs McIlroy
Hugh McCarthy .... Airport security
Mike Vernon .... Seeker of lost knowledge

MAEVE
(1981) UK colour 110 mins

The republican ideology of Northern Ireland's nationalist community is almost invariably presented on screen from the male standpoint. Women are depicted in peripheral roles as nurturers, worried lovers and camp followers relegated to the background while decision-making and action are men's prerogatives. Director and screenwriter Pat Murphy explores this anomaly in her feature debut, *Maeve*, which she co-directed with John Davies (also the editor of the film, and not to be confused with Northern Ireland's maverick documentary film-maker John T Davis). Dublin-born Murphy spent some of her teenage years in Belfast when her family moved there in the 1960s shortly before the Troubles began, and her film is informed by detailed autobiographical knowledge of the city. This provocative drama evaluates republican ideology from a feminist angle, through the eyes of a young Belfast woman who has returned to her native city from England.

Maeve stars Mary Jackson in the title role as Maeve Sweeney, a native of a nationalist housing estate in inner-city Belfast who has been living in London for several years. She comes back to visit her family and friends and finds that little has changed – the neighbourhood is disrupted by a bomb threat on the night of her arrival. Through a series of encounters with family members and people from her past, and reminiscences shown in flashback, she comes to realise that her innate nationalism has changed radically from her previous acceptance of the prevailing orthodoxy. She is compelled to question the lack of clear definition of the woman's role in a united Ireland, should that objective be achieved. Her evaluation of her past and the formative events that moulded her adult consciousness is unsentimental and highly critical. She recalls her childhood relationship with her father (Mark Mulholland), when she used to travel in his van making deliveries around the Province. He passed the journeys telling rambling stories from Irish folk memory about the surrounding landscape, fostering a folkloric cultural nationalism in his young daughter.

Maeve reminisces about her first love, Liam (John Keegan), a committed republican, with whom she used to make love in his flat over the headquarters of a religious cult. She meets with Liam and finds that his political thinking has remained unchanged since she left. In a frank exchange of views she contends that men's relationship to women resembles England's relationship to Ireland. The changes Liam sees in her are troubling for him and he regards her feminism and her revised attitude to nationalism as a betrayal of the cause in which they had both believed wholeheartedly when they were going out together. Disappointed with the menfolk from her earlier life, Maeve finds solidarity in the company of her mother and her sister Róisín (Bríd Brennan) with whom she visits the basaltic outcrop of the Giant's Causeway on the Antrim coast.

Murphy's wordy and intelligent script challenges audience preconceptions of the social and personal politics behind Northern Ireland's big issues and demands close attention from the viewer. This confrontational and formally innovative film is shot entirely on location in Belfast and surrounding countryside, including the historically significant Cave Hill overlooking the city, where United Irishmen pledged to subvert the authority of England over their island in 1798.

TRAVELLER
(1981) IRL colour 81 mins

(Still courtesy of the Irish Film Archive of the Film Insititue of Ireland reproduced courtesy of Joe Comerford)

Production Team

Producer .... Joe Comerford/Margaret
Williams/RTÉ/
Arts Council of Ireland
Director .... Joe Comerford
Screenplay .... Neil Jordan
Cinematography .... Thaddeus O'Sullivan
Editor .... Joe Comerford
Musical Score .... Davy Spillane

Cast

Judy Donovan .... Angela Devine
Davy Spillane .... Michael Connors
Alan Devlin .... Clicky
Johnny Choil Mhaidhc .... Devine
Paddy Donovan .... Mr Connors
Joe Pilkington .... Traveller man
Nora Donovan .... Traveller's wife
Christy Howley .... Priest
Róisín O'Hehir .... Post Office woman
Mick Tully .... Arcade man
Tiffy Moylan .... Hotel woman
Agnes O'Donnell .... Singer
Marian Richardson .... Angela's voiceover

TRAVELLER
(1981) IRL colour 81 mins

The travellers, Ireland's nomadic community, featured previously in Paul Rotha's film *No Resting Place*, a grim drama about life on the road. Thirty years on, Joe Comerford's film *Travellers* illustrates that little has changed for those who resist social pressure to settle in conventional housing. They continue to live in a parallel society with customs and codes different from those of the settled majority, in a relationship of mutual hostility with the authorities. Comerford's film centres on the travails of reluctant newlyweds, quiet Michael Connors, (uilleann piper Davy Spillane), and silent Angela Devine (Judy Donovan). Their marriage is arranged by their fathers, after cagey haggling about the young bride's dowry. Mr Connors (Paddy Donovan) settles for a horse from Devine (Johnny Choil Mhaidhc) and the wedding goes ahead. The reception afterwards is spoiled by a row between the guests.

Angela's father puts Michael to work, sending him across the border into Northern Ireland with a bankroll to buy electronics from a traveller named Tom Devoy, then smuggle them back into the Republic. Michael takes Angela with him in Connors' van, and gives a lift to a guy named Clicky (Alan Devlin), a gregarious republican. They reach their destination at a halting site in Strabane after an edgy encounter with a British army patrol, and Michael buys hi-fi equipment from Devoy. They return to the South after entertaining the crowd in a republican bar, Clicky tap dancing and Michael playing a low whistle. On the return journey, Michael crashes the van. While Michael steals a horse and gallops to a nearby village for help, Angela tells Clicky that she had been locked up years before for hitting her father with a bottle after he molested her. Michael arrives at a post office, and impulsively robs the elderly post-mistress.

Michael and Angela spend the night in a derelict house, but are kicked out in the morning by cops. On the run from the law, they proceed to Galway and Clare on a dismal post office-sponsored honeymoon. In a frank exchange with Michael in a hotel, Angela tells him that she doesn't want him or his children. He admits he doesn't want her either. Angela blurts the story of her assault on her father after he interfered with her, and angrily smashes a window. They scarper on foot when the hotel owner (Tiffy Moylan) hears the commotion. They soon encounter Clicky, who gives them a lift to a seaport where they plan to take a boat abroad. Before they leave, Michael borrows Clicky's revolver and heads to his father-in-law's caravan to settle the score over Devine's molestation of Angela.

Seminal cinema talents converged on this film with mixed results. Neil Jordan's screenplay shows glimmers of the stuff that would fascinate him later in his own career as a director – intimacies thwarted by prior parental interference, characters who express themselves better with music than words, and the tawdry attractions of Ireland's seaside resorts. Cinematographer Thaddeus O'Sullivan records the depressing fate of the travellers on a budget that can ill-afford the beauty of his later work, and maverick director Joe Comerford consolidated a track record of giving the foreground to characters who are rarely given exposure on-screen. *Travellers* is marred by poor sound (excessive use of voiceover distances both characters and audience from the plot), leaden pacing and stunted acting, and is of interest mostly as a study of the early efforts of its production team.

ANGEL
(1982) IRL colour 92 mins

(Still courtesy of Star Stills)

Production Team

Producer ... Barry Blackmore/Motion Picture
Co of Ireland/IFB
Director .... Neil Jordan
Screenplay .... Neil Jordan
Cinematography .... Chris Menges
Editor .... J Patrick Duffner
Musical Score .... Paddy Meegan

Cast

Veronica Quilligan .... Annie
Stephen Rea .... Danny
Alan Devlin .... Bill
Peter Caffrey .... Ray
Honor Heffernan .... Deirdre
Lise-Anne McLoughlin .... Bride
Ian McElhinney .... Groom
Derek Lord .... Best man
Ray McAnally .... Bloom
Donal McCann .... Bonner
Marie Kean .... Mae
Don Foley .... Bouncer
Gerard McSorley .... Assistant
Liz Bono .... Female assistant
Tom Collins .... Photographer
Tony Rohr .... George
Anita Reeves .... Beth

158

ANGEL
(1982) IRL colour 92 mins

Acclaimed author Neil Jordan combined a formidable writing talent with burgeoning directorial ambition to make his first feature *Angel*, a meditation on the culture of violence that dominated Northern Ireland in the 1970s and 1980s, framed as a taut thriller and set in rural Ulster. The rural setting takes the narrative away from the more crowded tribal stand-offs of Belfast and Derry and allows Jordan to present violence in the raw, without nationalist ideology or loyalist rhetoric to hide behind. The forces of law and order are ineffectual or absent – the army checkpoints, Land Rovers and metal detectors ubiquitous in urban Ulster at the time are nowhere to be seen. Control of the border areas in which the film is located (known as 'bandit country') is divided between rival paramilitary groups who extort cash in return for dubious protection from the other crowd.

The film centres on a double murder resulting from failure to pay the right thugs, and stars Stephen Rea as Danny, a casual, flirtatious tenor sax player, transformed by that act of violence into a ruthless killer. A showband musician known to his bandmates as the 'Stan Getz of South Armagh' (a compliment), Danny fancies their lead singer Di (Honor Heffernan) but lingers with a taciturn young girl named Annie (Veronica Quilligan) outside the Dreamland ballroom before their gig starts. When the show is over, he spends time with a silent girl in a construction pipe facing the ballroom entrance, and realises she is a deaf mute. Two cars arrive, and their occupants argue with his manager Ray (Peter Caffrey) over protection money. They shoot him dead. When Annie emerges from the shadows she too is gunned down. A bomb destroys the ballroom, and a traumatised Danny survives with minor injuries. Questioned by policemen Bloom (Ray McAnally) and Bonner (Donal McCann) in hospital, he remembers nothing of the masked gunmen, only the orthopaedic footwear that one of them wore. This clue starts him on his mission to avenge the death of an innocent girl he barely knew. He tracks down the gunmen one by one and kills them, consumed by a ferocious rage that he no longer understands and is unable to control.

Jordan's screenplay remains tantalisingly oblique about a key issue of Northern Ireland life: the need to identify which side people are on. Knowing a person's family name is usually sufficient to gauge a person's religion; sometimes knowing the first name is enough. Jordan gives his characters Annie, Danny, Ray, Mae and Di neutral names that could belong to either side, and only discloses slowly through hints and casual comments what their religious and, by implication, political affinities might be. The assumption that the Ulster police are all Protestant is subverted by borrowing a name from Joyce (Bloom) for the investigating officer (that he should belong to a third religion in a province divided between two is untenable to Danny, and he asks Bloom sarcastically if he's "a Catholic Jew or a Protestant Jew"). The point is well made; it doesn't matter which side they belong to, the violence ceases to be an instrument of the ideology of those who use it, but becomes instead a monstrous force, bigger than them and beyond their control. A stylish first outing rich in symbol and metaphor, *Angel*'s cryptic depiction of the Ulster divide broke new ground in its genre and gave promise of greater films to come. The film was re-titled ***Danny Boy*** for US distribution.

BALLROOM OF ROMANCE
(1982) UK/IRL colour 52 mins

(Still courtesy of RTE)

Production Team

Producer .... Kenith Trodd/BBC TV
Director .... Pat O'Connor
Screenplay .... William Trevor,
based on his short story
Cinematography .... Nat Crosby
Editor .... Maurice Healy
Musical Score .... Tony Chambers
and Martin Murray

Cast

Brenda Fricker .... Bridie
John Kavanagh .... Bowser Egan
Michael Lally .... Dano Ryan
Bríd Brennan .... Patty Byrne
Ingrid Craigie .... Eenie Mackie
Niall Toibín .... Eyes Horgan
Joe Pilkington .... Tim Daly
Cyril Cusack .... Mr Dwyer
Pat Leavy .... Madge Dowding
Bob Carrickford .... Fogarty
May Ollis .... Mrs Dwyer
Anita Reeves .... Cat Bolger
Brendan Conroy .... Dan
Sonny McNulty .... Bridie's father
Pat Gallagher .... Man with long arms

BALLROOM OF ROMANCE
(1982) IRL/UK colour 52 mins

Based on the short story of the same name by William Trevor, Pat O'Connor's television film debut is set in the west of Ireland in the 1950s and was shot on location in the beautiful but desolate County Mayo landscape at Ballycroy, near Blacksod Bay. This deeply affecting drama addresses the search for love in a poor farming community depleted by emigration, where emotions are held in check not by the usual joyless dictates of the Catholic Church (attributable, perhaps, to the fact that scriptwriter Trevor is a noted observer of rural Protestant mores) but more by neighbours' close scrutiny of each other's business. O'Connor's sensitive handling of his subject matter and Trevor's astute writing create a sad vignette of rural life, suffused with delicate emotive nuances that resonate long after the final credits roll.

In the lead role, Brenda Fricker gives a performance that is at least the equal of her Oscar-winning work in *My Left Foot* seven years later. She plays an unmarried farmer's daughter named Bridie, who is no longer young and lives with her widowed father (Sonny McNulty). She's been going year after year to the local ballroom, and still holds out faint hope of finding love or at least the makings of a marriage from the courtship rituals in the desolate shed. Bridie's past is revealed through her conversations with local girls Eenie Mackey (Ingrid Craigie) and Patty Byrne (Bríd Brennan), a newcomer to the ballroom scene whose spirit has not yet been crushed by waiting endlessly to be asked to dance by the awkward bachelors on parade. Bridie has a soft spot for Dano (Michael Lally), the drummer in the ballroom band and mothers him between sets, gently urging him to get a cure for an eye ailment he has. Her loneliness is underlined by his failure to see how she cares for him and by references to a lost love who emigrated to England promising to return to her but who never did.

The only people who seem to be enjoying themselves in this grim environment are the three town wastrels, Bowser Egan (John Kavanagh), Eyes Horgan (Niall Tóibín), and Tim Daly (Joe Pilkington). They spend the earlier part of the evening in the local pub, getting fortified for the dance later on and deluding themselves that they are prize catches for the women of the area.

Bowser has a thing for Bridie, based more on the imminent likelihood of her inheriting the family farm than her dainty footwork on the dance floor. He makes vague promises to her of a shared future together. The evening ends with Bridie feeling resigned to the fact that she's too old for this shuffling courtship, and realising that she must face a future alone or settle for the best of a bad lot in the form of the drunken Bowser.

Director Pat O'Connor, who later went on to international success with *Cal* and *Circle of Friends* used remembered details from his own rural background to lend authenticity to *Ballroom of Romance*, right down to the dark line along the walls from the Brylcreem in the men's hair. Even the 'Happy Homes for Ireland and for God' banner seen in the hall was remade for the film from recollections of O'Connor's dancing days of his youth in his native County Waterford.

ANNE DEVLIN
(1984) IRL colour 121 mins

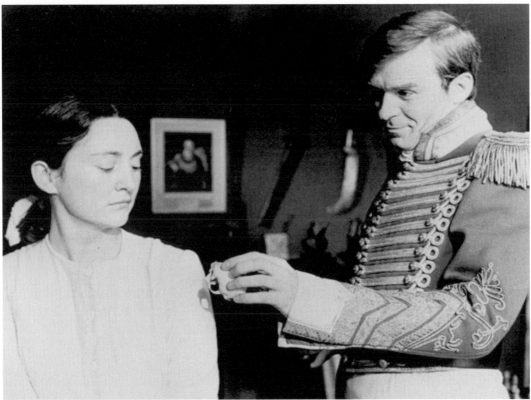

(Still courtesy of the Irish Film Archive of the Film Insititue of Ireland reproduced courtesy of Pat Murphy)

Production Team

Producer .... Aeon Films/IFB/
Pat Murphy/Tom Hayes
Director .... Pat Murphy
Screenplay .... Pat Murphy,
adapted from *The Prison
Journal of Anne Devlin*
Cinematography .... Thaddeus O'Sullivan
Editor .... Arthur Keating
Musical Score .... Robert Boyle

Cast

Bríd Brennan .... Anne Devlin
Bosco Hogan .... Robert Emmet
Des McAleer .... James Hope
Gillian Hackett .... Rose Hope
David Kelly .... Doctor Trevor
Ian McElhinney .... Major Sirr
Chris O'Neill .... Thomas Russell
Pat Leavy .... Mrs Devlin
Marie Conmee .... Mrs Darby
John Cowley .... Mr Devlin
Bernie Downes .... Julia Devlin
Niall O'Brien .... Michael Dwyer
Eamonn Hunt .... Arthur Devlin
Martin Dempsey .... The magistrate
Noel O'Donovan .... Tom Halpin
Vinnie Murphy .... Michael Quigley
Liam Halligan .... John Fleming

ANNE DEVLIN
(1984) IRL colour 121 mins

Pat Murphy continued her exploration of the role of women in the cause of Irish nationalism with her second feature, *Anne Devlin*, a historic drama set in 1798 and based on the diaries of the title character. An associate of Robert Emmet, Anne Devlin had previously featured in Walter MacNamara's *Ireland a Nation*, in which she was threatened with hanging by British soldiers in 1803 to get her to reveal the whereabouts of the fugitive rebel. The real-life Anne Devlin survived this ordeal and subsequent imprisonment, and was given her freedom in 1806. Her account of these events was written down by a contemporary clergyman, the Carmelite Brother Luke Cullen, during her lifetime. She died in poverty in Dublin in 1851.

The film opens in the aftermath of the failed rising of 1798. Anne Devlin (Bríd Brennan) lives in Rathdrum, County Wicklow, with her staunchly nationalist family. Rebel leader Michael Dwyer (Niall O'Brien) is her cousin and her father (John Cowley) has been jailed without trial for alleged rebel activities on the evidence of a dubious informer. The father's incarceration causes hardship for the family and the Devlins are unable to pay the rent, forcing Anne and her mother to plead with their landlady (Marie Conmee) for an extension on the arrears. Anne's father is finally freed after a trial in which the magistrate (Martin Dempsey) discounts the evidence of informer Tom Halpin (Noel O'Donovan). The Devlins move to Dublin, and the father starts a business hiring out horses.

In 1803 her father is approached for help by a cousin, Arthur Devlin (Eamonn Hunt), an ally of Robert Emmet (Bosco Hogan). Emmet's rebels have rented a house in Butterfield Lane and need someone to act as housekeeper there to give the place the appearance of normality. The politically aware Anne volunteers for the job, though her mother protests that none of her family has ever worked in service. Some of the men in the house treat Anne like a servant because of her gender, ordering her to do menial domestic chores for them, which incenses the headstrong young woman. She spends her time reading the revolutionary writings of Paine and running errands for Emmet. Anne's commitment to the cause remains clear and unwavering when the men in the household prevaricate and squabble over issues of class and religion.

When Emmet's rising fails, Anne is arrested and jailed in Kilmainham. She is threatened, tortured and manipulated by the yeomen, the infamous Major Sirr (Ian McElhinney), and a sadistic doctor named Trevor (David Kelly). Anne stoically endures her maltreatment and refuses to disclose any information about the rebel leaders. She is eventually released, haggard from her ordeal, but still defiant.

This beautiful, slow-moving drama features an extraordinary central performance by Bríd Brennan, manifesting all the compassion and unshakeable belief of this forgotten figure from Irish history. The camera lingers endlessly on the actress' wan, impassive face as she quietly embodies courage and strength greater than that of the men whose lives she saves by her silence. Shot on location in Strokestown Park, Dublin Castle and Kilmainham Gaol, Thaddeus O'Sullivan's stately cinematography and Consolata Boyle's exquisite costumes give the interiors the spare beauty of Vermeer paintings, and the exteriors a pastoral splendour to rival that of Kubrick's *Barry Lyndon*.

CAL
(1984) UK colour 102 mins

(Still reproduced courtesy of Goldcrest Films International)

Production Team

Producer .... Enigma/Goldcrest/
Warner Brothers/David Puttnam/
Stuart Craig
Director .... Pat O'Connor
Screenplay .... Bernard MacLaverty
from his own book
Cinematography .... Jerzy Zielinski
Editor .... Michael Bradsell
Musical Score .... Mark Knopfler

Cast

Helen Mirren .... Marcella
John Lynch .... Cal
Donal McCann .... Shamie
John Kavanagh .... Skeffington
Ray McAnally .... Cyril Dunlop
Stevan Rimkus .... Crilly
Catherine Gibson .... Mrs Morton
Louis Rolston .... Dermot Ryan
Gerard Mannix Flynn .... Arty
Seamus Ford .... Old Mr Morton
Edward Byrne .... Skeffington Senior
J J Murphy .... Man in library
Audrey Johnston .... Lucy
Brian Munn .... Robert Morton
Daragh O'Malley .... Scar-faced policeman
George Shane .... 2nd policeman
Julia Dearden .... Shop assistant

CAL
(1984) UK colour 102 mins

Pat O'Connor's second feature film gave Irish actor John Lynch the title role in *Cal*, Bernard MacLaverty's moral tale of doomed love between the older widow of a murdered RUC man, and a motherless Catholic boy whose IRA activities helped cause her husband's death.

Cal McCluskey (John Lynch) lives with his father Shamie (Donal McCann) on a Protestant estate in Belfast and occasionally works as a driver for the IRA under his local brigade commander, Skeffington (John Kavanagh). On one such mission Cal drives a gunman, Crilly (Stevan Rimkus), to an isolated farmhouse, home of an RUC man named Morton, his wife and his elderly parents. Crilly shoots the unarmed Morton (Brian Munn), who falls mortally wounded gurgling his wife's name: Marcella. Months later, Cal sees Marcella (Helen Mirren) in the local library and is attracted to her. He enquires about her and learns that she is the widow of the man targetted in his last IRA job. Cal is filled with remorse for his part in her loss, and he develops an aversion to IRA operations matched by a growing fascination with the widowed librarian.

Cal tries to meet with Marcella at the scene of the crime when he impulsively drives up to her house with a vanload of firewood he's selling. Old Mrs Morton buys the lot, and to Cal's delight, offers him a job on the farm when she sees how hard he works splitting the firewood. Cal begins work under a supervisor named Dunlop (Ray McAnally), a bigot who "has nothing against Catholics but hates their religion".

As the marching season draws near, loyalist thugs burn down the McCluskeys' house. With nowhere to go, Cal breaks into an abandoned cottage on the Morton farm. The police try to arrest him for burglary, but Marcella's mother-in-law allows him to live there when she learns that he's homeless.

Cal is happy to be so close to Marcella, and soon becomes her confidant. She confesses her misery at living under her mother-in-law's rule, and that she was unhappily married. When old Mr Morton's health declines and his wife takes him to hospital, the way is clear for Cal and Marcella to get closer still, and they tentatively begin an affair. Cal's pleasure in their romance is tempered by inner turmoil caused by his part in making a widow of her.

On a shopping trip to buy Marcella a gift, Cal meets his IRA comrade Crilly who persuades him to join him and Skeffington on a mission. En route they are stopped at an army roadblock. The driver panics and speeds off, crashing the car in a hail of rifle fire. Skeffington and the driver are killed and Crilly arrested, but Cal escapes and runs all night, wounded and bloody, to Marcella's house to unburden himself of his guilt and face his retribution.

Pat O'Connor drew an impressive performance from John Lynch in his first lead role, as the passive teen who surrenders to all the conflicting forces that assail him, knowing disaster looms but unable to do anything about it. He plays the frail Cal with delicacy and understatement, rendering unnecessary the intrusive flashbacks overutilised in the film to convey the troubles in his mind. His co-star Helen Mirren impressed the judges at Cannes Film Festival, where she won the Best Actress Award in 1984.

FOUR DAYS IN JULY
(1984) UK colour 96 mins

Production Team

Producer	Kenith Trodd
Director	Mike Leigh
Screenplay	Mike Leigh
Cinematography	Remi Adefarasin
Editor	Robin Sales
Musical Score	Rachel Portman

Cast

Bríd Brennan	Collette
Des McAleer	Eugene
Paula Hamilton	Lorraine
Charles Lawson	Billy
Brian Hogg	Big Billy
Adrian Gordon	Little Billy
Shane Connaughton	Brendan
Eileen Pollock	Carmel
Stephen Rea	Dixie
David Coyle	Mickey
John Keegan	McCoy
John Hewitt	Mr Roper
Ann Hasson	Midwife

FOUR DAYS IN JULY
(1984) UK colour 96 mins

Before *Secrets and Lies* earned him Oscar nominations, director Mike Leigh had already been developing his renowned work method in a series of films for the BBC since the 1970s. From months of character development with actors, he generated scripts and storylines featuring sympathetic working-class people and less flattering portraits of British nouveau riche that seemed a lot like real life. In 1983, he shifted his underdog sympathies to Northern Ireland to make *Four Days in July* for BBCTV. Leigh spent months studying the conflicts of daily life in the Province to create a more focused narrative than usual, concentrating on two couples on either side of Belfast's sectarian divide just before the births of their first-born babies. The timeframe of the film is one of the most volatile on the calendar in Northern Ireland: the build-up to the 12th of July, when Protestants commemorate King William's 1690 victory over James II at the Battle of the Boyne. The bonfires and all-night parties on the eve of the 12th often stir up trouble, and British television audiences were already familiar with horrific Belfast news footage when sectarian enmity boiled over into full-scale riots. Leigh's film features no bombs or gunfire, presenting instead Belfast's daily simmer, on which the British authorities vainly try to keep the lid.

When Leigh deals a hand of cards to the respective couples, Protestants Billy (Charles Lawson) and Lorraine (Paula Hamilton), have the deck stacked against them. Billy is a macho Ulster Defence Regiment soldier, insensitive to his wife's discomfort as childbirth looms. He is presented as a barbarian in a lagered-up story told by a fellow soldier about Billy's service on border patrol – bored and hungry on night duty, he chases a bullock with his bayonet, naked to avoid getting his uniform bloody, and slaughters it for steaks.

Catholics Eugene (Des McAleer) and Colette (Bríd Brennan) are portrayed more sympathetically. He's unemployed, and disabled from a stray British army bullet intended for joyriders; she's warm-hearted and easygoing. Their conversations with casual visitors Brendan (Shane Connaughton), a plumber, and Dixie (Stephen Rea), a window cleaner, unfold at a relaxed pace, in contrast with the terse exchanges in the Protestant household. Dixie and Brendan tell of antics in Long Kesh prison, where Brendan rigged up a poitín still in the toilet cistern, a tale of resourceful mischief compared to Billy's exploits.

The two couples finally intersect at the hospital; a neutral venue where the working-class from both sides might meet in a province otherwise segregated from infancy to cemetery. While the wives are in labour, genial Eugene becomes testy in the waiting room at the complaints of a Mr Roper (John Hewitt). Aggressive Billy advises Roper to emigrate. In the ward after the delivery, Colette and Lorraine chat warmly about their labours, but a frost descends when each realises, from the name that the other chose for her newborn, that they are of different religions. They have nothing more to say to each other.

Despite its overt bias, Leigh's film goes a long way to explaining to British and US audiences the daily tensions that cause the flashpoints on television news, and features fine performances from top Irish actors Stephen Rea, Bríd Brennan and Des McAleer.

PIGS
(1984) IRL colour 78 mins

(Still courtesy of the Irish Film Archive of the Film Insititue of Ireland reproduced courtesy of Cathal Black)

Production Team

Producer .... David Collins
Director..Cathal Black
Screenplay .... Jimmy Brennan
Cinematography .... Thaddeus O'Sullivan
Editor ....Sé Merry
Musical Score............................. Roger Doyle

Cast

Jimmy Brennan .... Jimmy
George Shane .... George
Maurice O'Donoghue .... Tom
Liam Halligan .... Ronnie
Kwesi Kay .... Orwell
Joan Harpur .... Mary
Bernie Downes .... Welfare girl
Máire Noone .... Survey woman
Johnny Murphy .... Detective
Pat Laffan .... Detective
Gerry Walsh .... Site foreman
Charles Roberts .... Labourer
Frank Roche .... Labourer
Robert Byrne .... Ronnie's friend
Anto Nolan .... Ronnie's friend
Larry Nolan .... Ronnie's friend
Enda Williams .... Ronnie's friend

PIGS
(1984) IRL colour 78 mins

Cathal Black's fiction feature debut *Pigs* marked a radical departure from standard picturesque portrayals of Irish life, by shooting entirely on location in an inner-city world of squats, glue-sniffing and burning cars. Black concerns himself more with detailed character studies of misfits in a squat than forward momentum in the plot in this portrayal of uneventful lives spent waiting for dole day. The film's central character, Jimmy Gibbons (Jimmy Brennan), is a morose Dubliner with a jail record and nowhere to live. He breaks into a derelict Georgian house, hooks up electricity, and makes himself at home. Dubious characters soon arrive on his doorstep and Jimmy passively allows them to move in. First comes George (George Shane), a compulsive liar from Northern Ireland who wears a suit every day and pretends to go to work. Next comes Ronnie (Liam Halligan), a small-time drug dealer. Ronnie brings in a mismatched couple, Mary (Joan Harpur), a prostitute, and her pimp, Orwell (Kwesi Kay), a would-be musician from Jamaica. The household is completed by Tom (Maurice O'Donoghue), a chronic paranoiac from Munster who lives on Complan and Mogadon.

Cautious friendships and bitter hostilities develop over the next few months, as the squatters scrape a living outside the house and share booze, cigarettes and pizza at home. Despite his depression and passivity, Jimmy finds work on a building site while signing on the dole for himself and his absent wife, who left him to go to Scotland. Confused about his sexuality, he makes a hapless attempt at getting picked up in a gay bar only to have his tryst interrupted by menacing thugs before it even starts. The same thugs find out where he lives through their association with Ronnie, and break in to give him a savage beating. The squat breaks up after Ronnie squeals to the police about Jimmy's dole scam and leaves before Jimmy finds out. George gets a corporation flat, Tom surrenders to pyschiatric care, and Orwell and Mary leave, too. Left alone in the house, Jimmy is arrested by detectives (Johnny Murphy and Pat Laffan) who manipulate him into admitting his welfare fraud in a comical good cop/ bad cop routine. The police, no strangers to porcine comparisons themselves, give the film its title when they disdain the skanky hygiene standards of the squatters.

Pigs exposes a side of Irish life that is rarely confronted and never so effectively presented on screen. Black's direction is masterfully spare and succinct, drawing strong performances from the actors, particularly George Shane as the lying Ulsterman and screenwriter Brennan as the lugubrious lead. In a smart, lean script, Brennan treats his characters sympathetically and neither passes judgement nor patronisingly tries to ennoble these luckless strugglers. *Pigs* avoids the pathos of contrast with the city's 'haves', a recurring flaw of similarly themed films by the likes of Mike Leigh and Ken Loach. The squatters are unlikely to meet anyone prosperous or in authority besides police and civil servants, and *Pigs* implies by this omission that a better life is beyond reach for these people. The hard urban context of the film is relieved by the elegance and fluidity of Thaddeus O'Sullivan's camerawork and the creative use of light and colour throughout the film. O'Sullivan, the most talented cinematographer of his generation in Ireland, would earn international recognition as a director in his own right with *December Bride* six years later.

LAMB
(1985) UK colour 110 mins

Production Team

Producer ..... Flicker Productions/Limehouse Pictures/Channel 4/Neil Zeiger
Director .... Colin Gregg
Screenplay .... Bernard Maclaverty, based on his novel *Lamb*
Cinematography .... Mike Garfath
Editor .... Peter Delfgou
Musical Score .... Van Morrison

Cast

Liam Neeson .... Michael Lamb
Harry Towb .... Priest
Hugh O'Conor .... Owen Kane
Frances Tomelty .... Mrs Kane
Ian Bannen .... Brother Benedict
Ronan Wilmot .... Brother Fintan
Denis Carey .... Mr Lamb
Eileen Kennally .... Neighbour Woman
David Gorry .... O'Donnell
Andrew Pickering .... Murphy
Stuart O'Connor .... O'Halloran
Ian McElhinney .... Maguire
Bernadette McKenna .... Jewellers' assistant
Jessica Saunders .... Bank teller on boat
Robert Hamilton .... Stranger at Holyhead
Roger Booth .... Farmer on train
Marjie Wallace .... Department store assistant

Eight years before *Schindler's List* made Liam Neeson a worldwide star, and fourteen before *Star Wars: The Phantom Menace* made him an inter-galactic entity, the Ballymena-born actor had his first lead role in Colin Gregg's moving drama *Lamb*. Neeson plays title character Michael Lamb, an idealistic young man who belongs to a religious brotherhood and teaches troubled boys in a reform school in the west of Ireland. The boys who live at St Kiaran's lead a tough life, working outdoors on the school farm in freezing weather, and suffering beatings if they disobey the rules.

Lamb develops a particular attachment to one boy, Owen Kane (Hugh O'Conor), an epileptic thief whose mother (Frances Tomelty) left him in the care of the Brothers. Lamb becomes protective of Owen, taking his side against bullies who menace him, and sorting him out for cigarettes. When Owen is beaten for something he didn't do, Lamb takes his superior, Brother Benedict (Ian Bannen), to task for this injustice. The hard pragmatist Benedict explains that as long as some boy is punished, the others will be kept in line, too frightened to misbehave. The casual cruelty and cynicism of Brother Benedict's viewpoint – he sees St Kiaran's as a "finishing school for the idle poor", where they teach boys "a little of God, and a lot of fear" – precipitates a crisis of faith in Lamb. His misgivings deepen when he realises that Brother Benedict has designs on the money raised from the sale of Lamb's late father's farm. When Lamb phones his father's solicitor to get an advance on this money, he finds that Benedict has already been in contact with him.

Lamb decides to take the advance and run away from St Kiaran's with the boy. Taking ferry and train, they travel to London. He pretends to be the boy's father, and buys Owen gifts for the first time in his life. The naïve Lamb spends his money foolishly and loses at a three-card trick, rapidly depleting their funds. Owen's epilepsy worsens and as his medication runs out, Lamb is unable to renew the prescription. Lamb hears on the radio news that the authorities are treating their disappeance as a kidnapping, and that Brother Benedict has reported him for misappropriation of funds earmarked for the school. With time and money running out for the ailing child, Lamb decides to fulfil some of the boy's dreams by taking him on a plane, and teaching him to swim. They fly to Ireland and head west to an isolated beach, where Lamb faces the agonising ordeal of ending the boy's suffering.

Scandals in recent years in Ireland about the abuse of children in the care of religious orders would have made the subject of this film too sensitive by far to get financial backing after the mid-1980s. The relationship of the naïve Lamb and the hard street kid Owen is intimate, without explicit sexual contact, but runs close enough to imply it. O'Conor, who would impress the world as the young Christy Brown in *My Left Foot* four years later, gives a heart-rending performance as the foul-mouthed young chain-smoker, and Neeson is solid as the righteous Brother. The reform school scenes are filmed in the suitably creepy Cornwall hotel known as King Arthur's Castle, at Tintagel – previously used as Dracula's Castle in a hammer horror film.

BUDAWANNY
(1987) IRL colour/b&w 79 mins

(Still provided and reproduced courtesy of Bob Quinn)

Production Team

Producer .... Arts Council/Channel 4/
Cinegael/Irish Film Board
Director... Bob Quinn
Screenplay .... Bob Quinn, based on
the novel *Súil Le Breith*
by Pádraig Standún
Cinematographer .... Séamus Deasy
Editor .... Martin Duffy
Musical Score.............................. Roger Doyle

Cast

Donal McCann .... Priest
Peadar Lamb.. Bishop
Maggie Fegan .... Marian
Martin O'Malley .... Boatman
Jonathan Ryan .... Secretary
Tomás Ó Flaithearta .... Sacristan
Seán Ó Coisdealbha .... Publican
Susan O'Flaherty .... Girl
Mary Winters.. Sister
Mary McCabe ....Wife
Anna Gill .... Mother of girl
Patrick O'Toole ....Husband
Freda Gillen .... Old woman
Oliver O'Malley .... Bearded man
Áine O'Malley .... Pregnant woman
Dominick O'Malley .... Boy
Chris O'Grady .... Doctor

BUDAWANNY
(1987) IRL colour/b&w 79 mins

Cinegael director Bob Quinn managed to produce provocative features from his Galway base with budget constraints that sometimes made even sound recording too expensive. In his controversial drama *Budawanny*, the lyric island scenes (shot on Clare Island, County Mayo) are silent and in black-and-white, while the mainland scenes feature both sound and colour.

The film opens with a bishop (Peader Lamb) receiving a review copy of a new book, *Budawanny: A Bishop's Tale*. The book tells of a young curate on an island off the west coast who falls for his housekeeper and fathers a child with her. The story is a little too familiar for the bishop and rouses his indignation. With the help of his secretary (Jonathan Ryan), he composes a high-minded letter to the author about the responsibility of the clergy to obey the rules in the face of doubt and human frailty. Their discussion is inter-cut with flashbacks of events described in the book.

A woman named Marian (Maggie Fegan) travels by boat to Clare Island, County Mayo and arrives soaked and bedraggled on the shore. The boatmen are unsure whether she fell or jumped from the boat, but the dip in the water leaves her feeling poorly and she is brought to the priest's house to recover. The priest (Donal McCann) looks after her, and it becomes apparent that they have met before. While saying mass, he recalls a visit to the Wellington Monument with her (in civvies, presumably prior to his ordination), in the Phoenix Park in Dublin. The priest is not domestically adept, and the woman offers her services as housekeeper.

Soon they are living like a long-married couple, he sitting by the fire, she darning socks. He enjoys a few pints in the pub with Marian by his side, a situation which the locals reluctantly tolerate. Priest and housekeeper become close but not intimate, until one night a wild storm terrifies her and she runs in her nightie to his bedroom for comfort and reassurance. Their intimacy grows, and before long the priest has an announcement to make from the pulpit: his parishioners will have another reason to call him father. He naïvely imagines that the bishop will endorse his plan to live with the woman and look after their child, and still continue with his parish duties. The bishop soon hears about this development from an irate parishioner, and calls the priest to order at his house on the mainland. When he returns to the island, the priest finds the pregnant housekeeper waiting at the harbour for the boat to take her away, knowing their love has no future.

The bishop concludes his letter, then deems it wiser not to send it as he has been rather more frank in his comments than he had intended. He decides instead to forward a generic acknowledgement of receipt of the book.

It is a testament to Bob Quinn's tenacity that he returned to *Budawanny* (named after a stubby crag on Clare Island that translates as 'monk's penis') to complete the film with sound and dialogue six years later. By that time the real-life story of Eamonn Casey, bishop of Galway, and his fecund affair with a young American woman had become public, giving the controversial *Budawanny* a prophetic quality that the upgraded later version (re-titled *The Bishop's Story*) lacks.

173

THE DEAD
(1987) UK/US colour 83 mins

Production Team

Producer .... Liffey Films/Vestron/
Wieland Schulz-Keil & Chris
Sievernich/Zenith Productions
Director .... John Huston
Screenplay .... Anthony Huston,
from the story of the same
name by James Joyce, in the 1914
collection *Dubliners*
Cinematography .... Fred Murphy
Editor .... Roberto Silvi
Musical Score .... Alex North

Cast

Anjelica Huston .... Gretta Conroy
Donal McCann .... Gabriel Conroy
Donal Donnelly .... Freddy Malins
Marie Kean .... Mrs Malins
Cathleen Delany .... Aunt Julia Morkan
Helena Carroll .... Aunt Kate Morkan
Dan O'Herlihy .... Mr Brown
Maria McDermottroe .... Molly Ivors
Ingrid Craigie .... Mary Jane
Cormac O'Herlihy .... Mr Kerrigan
Colm Meaney .... Mr Bergin
Rachael Dowling .... Lily
Frank Patterson .... Bartell D'Arcy
Sean McClory .... Mr Grace
Katherine O'Toole .... Miss Furlong
Maria Hayden .... Miss O'Callaghan

THE DEAD
(1987) UK/US colour 83 mins

In spite of James Joyce's overt interest in the cinema, both as a commercial proposition (he opened Ireland's first picture-house in 1909 in partnership with some bicycle merchants from Trieste) and an artistic medium (in Paris in the 1920s, he discussed with Eisenstein the suitability of film to convey his literary ideas to a mass audience) his words defied attempts by several film-makers to transpose them successfully to the big screen. Joseph Strick's adaptations of **Ulysses** and **Portrait of the Artist as a Young Man** are worth watching more as pictorial introductions to Joyce's characters and places than as cinematic fulfilment of his artistic intent. Mary Ellen Bute's **Passages from James Joyce's 'Finnegan's Wake'** is at best a quixotic attempt at visualising a book that is impossible to read, never mind film. Fionnuala Flanagan came closer to succeeding with Michel Pearce's **James Joyce's Women**, a feature based on Joyce's life that samples from several of his books and from writings about him, rather than adapting from one source.

It wasn't until 46 years after the author's death that a film director of the necessary stature undertook a piece from the Joyce oeuvre and honoured the spirit and tone of his language and imagination. John Huston, director of **The Maltese Falcon**, **Treasure of the Sierra Madre** and **The African Queen**, an Irish citizen and a Hollywood legend with a film career stretching back to the silent era when Joyce was still living in Paris, chose as his final film project Joyce's short story **The Dead**. Working from a screenplay adapted by his son Tony, John Huston created a modestly scaled and perfectly balanced masterpiece that resonates as a chamber music composition of the rarest delicacy in contrast to the robust symphonic structures of his earlier works.

The Dead is a meditation on the relationship between the living and those who have gone before, and the continuing influence that the past exerts on the present. Set on the feast of the Epiphany in 1904, a self-absorbed husband and man of letters has a painful epiphany of his own at a formal dinner party at his aunts' house. The soirée is an annual event with a sumptuous feast and entertainment, hosted by the Misses Morken, Kate and Julia, retired music teachers both. The majority of their guests are perennial attendees, and they settle in for an evening of social harmonies and minor discords of the sort that they have come to expect from previous years, much as they would anticipate the familiar notes of a favourite melody.

As the film opens, Kate and Julia (Helena Carroll and Cathleen Delany) are greeting their first arrivals, and fretting about two particular latecomers – their nephew Gabriel Conroy (Donal McCann), to whom they entrust the carving of the goose and the after-dinner speech, and Freddy Malins (Donal Donnelly), a tippler who is expected to arrive 'stewed' and difficult to manage. They are reassured a little about the latter by a charming guest named Brown (Dan O'Herlihy), who tells them that Freddy took the pledge on New Year's Eve.

Gabriel arrives with his wife Gretta (Anjelica Huston), blaming her for their lateness, and feeling tense about his speech. His composure is further ruffled by a frank

175

ouburst from the maid (Rachael Dowling) about the low quality of men nowadays, and later by Molly Ivors (Maria McDermottroe), an outspoken nationalist with whom he dances. Molly accuses the goloshes-wearing Europhile Gabriel of denying his own country and language, and challenges him to take his wife to the west of Ireland to join her friends on a holiday. Between these unsettling exchanges, Gabriel attends to Freddy who arrives, as expected, the worse for drink, and then distracts his mother, Mrs Malins (Marie Kean), with small talk while Freddy freshens up in the bathroom.

Musical interludes follow, and hostess Aunt Julia is prevailed upon to sing. She struggles to reach the high notes in Bellini's 'Arrayed for the Bridal' but the guests compliment her voice and insist that she never sounded better.

The company is seated, and Gabriel carves and serves the goose. The table-talk turns to great singers of the past and how poorly the current crop compares with them. The drunken Freddy misses the point of the conversation and becomes a target for gentle ribbing from Mr Brown. He turns testy when he realises that amusement is being had at his expense, generating an awkward shift in mood at the table.

At the end of the meal Gabriel delivers his speech to the assembled guests. He praises the hospitality of their hosts, with words that he knows are hollow and devoid of real feeling, despite the trouble he has taken over them. His aunts are moved to tears nonetheless by his compliments, and all the guests join in a hearty toast to Kate and Julia. Relieved to have carried out his evening's duties satisfactorily, Gabriel organises cabs for the guests, and prepares to leave for the Gresham Hotel where he and his wife are staying. After installing the hapless Freddy and his contrary mother in a cab, he goes back inside the house to look for Gretta. From upstairs he hears the strains of the unctuous tenor Bartell D'Arcy (Frank Patterson), who had refused earlier requests to sing, regaling the few remaining guests with his rendition of 'The Lass of Aughrim'. As Gretta comes down the stairs, wrapped against the outside cold in her overcoat and scarf, she hears Bartell's voice and stands transfixed against the stained-glass window of the landing. Gabriel stands silent, motionless, watching her intently from the bottom of the stairs. Gretta is visibly overcome with emotion as she listens to the song, her eyes closed. Gabriel is fascinated and perplexed, having no idea why the song moved her so.

In the cab to the hotel, as they go down Henrietta Street and pass along the quays, Gretta looks out the window, distracted. Gabriel takes hold of her hand and kisses it, and she barely notices. He tries to win her attention with an amusing story about his grandfather, and she smiles mechanically in response for a moment before returning to her dark reverie, causing him to sulk.

In their hotel bedroom, Gabriel probes to find the cause of her mood change. She tells him that a boy named Michael Furey used to sing 'The Lass of Aughrim' to her when she lived in Galway as a young girl. She evades Gabriel's direct questioning as to whether she loved this boy, and he accuses her of wanting to go to Galway to see

THE DEAD
(1987) UK/US colour 83 mins

him. She explains in tears that he is dead, and that she thinks he died because of her. On a wet night when he was forbidden to leave the house because of ill-health, he came to see her just before she was due to leave for a convent in Dublin. Soaked to the skin, he refused to go home and was dead within the week.

Gabriel is stunned to find that his wife has kept locked in her heart secrets he could never have imagined from long before he knew her. He realises as she drifts into tearful sleep that he has played a poor role in her life, and that he himself has never felt so strongly for anyone as that boy had for Gretta. As he gazes out the window at the falling snow outside, he realises that the boy was better off leaving this world in the full glory of that passion than to slowly flicker out and join the grey world of the dead. Casting his mind back on the events of the evening, he knows that his haggard Aunt Julia will soon enter that same grey world and become a shade like his grandfather. The other guests, himself included, are just as transient, as their solid reality dissolves and fades and they move on to rejoin those who have left them behind.

All the exteriors for this elegiac finale to Huston's career were filmed in Dublin, and in the midlands and west of Ireland. The interior scenes were shot in California, as the ailing director was unfit to travel to Dubin to film *The Dead* in its original setting, as he would have preferred. Though he was confined to a wheelchair for the entire shoot, Huston drew perfomances of remarkable subtlety from his cast, both from his daughter Anjelica and Donal McCann in the lead roles, and the talented ensemble of Irish and Irish-American actors supporting them. Cathleen Delany and Helena Carroll are wondrous as the flustered hostesses Julia and Kate, and veteran Dan O'Herlihy (an Oscar nominee in 1954 for his performance in the title role of Bunuel's *Robinson Crusoe*) is a delight as the urbane, silver-haired Mr Brown, the gallant charmer who turns cranky as fatigue and whiskey erode his bonhomie. Marie Kean is note-perfect as Mrs Malins, sweet and kind in public, but a vituperative harridan to her unfortunate son Freddy. The actors' sensitivity to their characters, and Huston's control of the pace and nuances of the screenplay, combine to create a cinematic tribute to Joyce that is unlikely to be bettered. *The Dead* was nominated for two Academy Awards, for Tony Huston's script and Dorothy Jeakins' costume design. John Huston's health continued to deteriorate when the shooting schedule finished, and he succumbed to cancer before the film was released.

CLASH OF THE ASH
(1987) IRL colour 50 mins

(Still courtesy of the Irish Film Archive of the Film Insititue of Ireland reproduced courtesy of Jane Gogan)

Production Team

Producer .... Jane Gogan/Circus Films
Director .... Fergus Tighe
Screenplay .... Fergus Tighe
Cinematography .... Declan Quinn
Editor .... Jim Duggan
Musical Score .... Stephen Cooney

Cast

William Heffernan .... Phil Kelly
Gina Moxley .... Mary Hartnett
Vincent Murphy .... Martin Hogan
Myles Breen .... Willy
Marian Dowley .... Rosie
Alan Devlin .... Mick Barry
Michael McAuliffe .... Mr Kelly
Kay Rae Malone .... Mrs Kelly
Donnacha Crowley .... Priest
Jim Queally .... Garda
Frank Duggan .... Barman
Michael Twomey .... Barman
Maura Young .... Mrs O'Brien
Charles Ruxton .... Paddy Murphy
Jimmy Dennigan .... Referee
Mary McCarthy .... Woman in cafe
Colette Egan .... Murphy's girlfriend

CLASH OF THE ASH
(1987) IRL colour 50 mins

Director Fergus Tighe shot his first film, about a teenage boy struggling with pressures from parents and teachers as the Leaving Certificate exams approach, in his home town of Fermoy, County Cork. A talented but unmotivated athlete on St Finbar's hurling team, Phil Kelly (William Heffernan) is pushed relentlessly by the coach, Mick Barry (Alan Devlin), to improve his performance on the pitch. Off the pitch, he endures constant criticism from his teachers and his mother (Kay Rae Malone) about his poor results in preliminary exams. His father (Michael McAuliffe), a hen-pecked, bumbling beekeeper, is more resigned to Phil's shortcomings and encourages him to take a dead-end job in the local garage.

To escape these pressures, Phil mopes around the town with his friends, trying to look hard by smoking cigarettes, drinking pints and playing pool. His best friend Martin (Vincent Murphy) has dropped out of school and drowns vague rock musician dreams in the local pub. Phil is fascinated by Martin's bohemian girlfriend Mary (Gina Moxley), who has returned from London exuding a worldly confidence which is otherwise absent in their provincial town. Her tales of life in the city are exotic and exciting for Phil.

Phil's commitment to his sport, if not his studies, is given a boost when the hurling coach finds Phil in the pub and delivers the time-honoured speech about the Gaelic Athletic Association "looking after its own". He tells Phil he can sail into a job in the bank with good GAA connections and bad exam results, and imagines him making a victory speech at Croke Park as he collects the championship cup. Mick's earnest conviction that they can beat their rivals, Mitchelstown, in a forthcoming cup match stirs Phil's enthusiasm for the game, and he begins to train aggressively for that match. Phil plays his heart out on the big day. After a hard tackle, Paddy Murphy (Charles Ruxton), a Mitchelstown player with a grudge against Phil, whacks him with his camán, causing Phil's suppressed frustrations to explode. In a blind rage, he chases after Murphy and strikes him viciously on the head. Sent off by the ref, he smashes his camán against the gate on the way out and decides to quit the whole scene – exams, sport and parents, and make a start in London with Mary's help.

Tighe's semi-autobiographical work presents an unflattering yet sympathetic portrayal of provincial life in Ireland that succeeds without the big themes – the Church, the nation, and the land – that had hitherto seemed indispensable in exurban Irish cinema. While the acting is variable, the narrative is firmly grounded by Tighe's spot-on dialogue and his knowledge of the social scene in small Irish towns. Tighe has an impeccable ear for clichés that pass as wisdom in this environment. He presents Phil's ineffectual dad spouting platitudes of the 'let-the-spade-do-the-work' variety, widening the chasm between the sullen teenager and himself, but deftly switches to sympathy for his character when the father covers for Phil while he's in the loo doing the other kind of hurling after too much stout. Stealing other people's pints, dodging Sunday mass, stealing dad's car to see a band in the next town, and other activities of the teenage small-town male in Ireland are faithfully depicted with a freshness and truth that heralded a new directorial talent at work and made viable a new realism in Irish cinema.

REEFER AND THE MODEL
(1988) IRL colour 93 mins

(Still courtesy of the Irish Film Archive of the Film Insititue of Ireland reproduced courtesy of Joe Comerford)

Production Team

Producer .... Berber Films/Irish Film Board
Director .... Joe Comerford
Screenplay .... Joe Comerford
Cinematography .... Breffini Byrne
Editor .... Sé Merry Doyle
Musical Score .... Johnny Duhan

Cast

Ian McElhinney .... Reefer
Carol Scanlan .... The Model
Eve Watkinson .... Mother
Sean Lawlor .... Spider
Ray McBride .... Badger
Birdy Sweeney .... Photographer
John Lillis .... Porter
Henry Comerford .... Waiter
Sabina Higgins .... Woman in restaurant
Henry Waters .... Pub musician
Pádraic Breathnach .... Quayside fisherman
Máire Chinsealach .... Island woman
Dave Duffy .... Sergeant
Rosena Browne .... The blonde
Little John Nee .... Boy soldier
Seán Ó Coisdealbha .... Rossaveal Captain
Noel Spain .... Boatman

REEFER AND THE MODEL
(1988) IRL colour 93 mins

Reefer and the Model continues the mission its director Joe Comerford began in the 1970s to subvert the standard character types of Irish film, and bring to the screen the unlovely and unloved from the margins of society. Working from his own script, his second feature is set and shot in the west of Ireland, and stars Ian McElhinney as Reefer, a former active republican from the North who works a trawler out of Galway harbour. While driving with his elderly mother in Connemara, Reefer gives a woman hitchhiker (Carol Scanlan) a lift. Reefer's mother (Eve Watkinson) is quite taken with her, dubbing her 'the Model' because she considers her striking enough to be one. She's a lot more disparaging about her son, and regards his abandonment of the republican cause as a betrayal of her own strongly held beliefs.

Reefer is curious about the Model, and learns that she has returned home from England to escape bad company she kept over there, and because she is pregnant. He takes her to dinner at an exclusive club restaurant, and during the meal phones the Dublin police, pretending to be a local officer, to get a background check on her. He discovers that she has been involved in prostitution in London, and has a heroin problem. Undeterred by this news, he invites her to join him on his trawler which he shares with Spider (Sean Lawlor) and Badger (Ray McBride). She joins their crew and has a slight softening effect on the strained atmosphere aboard the decrepit boat.

They bring goods and passengers to the Aran Islands, and that night go for drinks in a crowded pub. Badger takes a fancy to a soldier he meets there, and asks him to dance. When they kiss on the dance floor, the soldier's incensed sergeant hits Badger. Reefer breaks up the fight that follows. To get back at Reefer, the sergeant confronts him at the trawler and tries to stab him, but Reefer beats him unconscious and tosses him into the sea. They return in haste to the mainland. The trawler has engine trouble on the way back. Low on funds to make the necessary repairs, Reefer decides to carry out a fundraiser at that peculiar rural Irish institution, the mobile bank. Tooled up with guns and wearing disguises, they make the transition from living on the edge of the law to living outside it with disastrous results, as the robbery goes wrong and they become fugitives from the police.

With *Reefer and the Model*, Comerford maintains his fascination with society's underbelly, and fleshes out a cast of dubious characters impressively different from those we usually see in Irish films. Neither frustrated idealists nor rebellious youths, they band together out of necessity rather than fondness for each other's company, and co-exist in mutually parasitic relationships. Without declaring any particular gripes against the usual pillars of society, Comerford's misfits manifest a blanket contempt for all of them. As title character Reefer, Ian McElhinney consolidates his claim as first choice for roles requiring a cruel, menacing Northern Irish man. As his crewman Badger, Ray McBride stirred some controversy with the bar scene involving the soldier, an exchange that featured Irish cinema's first gay screen kiss. While Comerford deserves credit for his uncompromising exploration of dark themes like drugs, crime and rejection of traditional social mores, the lack of mainstream marketability for his ugly characters inevitably makes his output rather sporadic.

DA
(1988) US colour 102 mins

Production Team:

Producer .... FilmDallas Pictures/
Julie Corman
Director .... Matt Clark
Screenplay .... Hugh Leonard,
adapted from his play **Da** and his book
Home Before Night
Cinematography .... Alar Kivilo
Editor .... Nancy Nuttall Beyda
Musical Score .... Elmer Bernstein

Cast

Barnard Hughes .... Da
Martin Sheen .... Charlie
William Hickey .... Mr Drumm
Karl Hayden .... Young Charlie
Doreen Hepburn .... Ma
Hugh O'Conor .... Boy Charlie
Ingrid Craigie .... Polly
Joan O'Hara .... Mrs Prynne
Jill Doyle .... Mary 'the Yellow Peril'
Peter Hanly .... Young Oliver
Maurice O'Donoghue .... Older Oliver
Amiee Clark .... Danielle
Frank McDonald .... 'Cat' McDonald
Marie Conmee .... Nurse
Ronan Wilmot .... Taxi Driver
Kathy Greenblatt .... Sara
Martin Dempsey .... Barman

DA
(1988) US colour 102 mins

The work of Irish dramatist Hugh Leonard was first adapted to film in 1959, when scriptwriters Patrick Kirwan and Blanaid Irvine turned his play *The Big Birthday* into a Barry Fitzgerald vehicle, with Barry playing a rascally Irish villager claiming to be the oldest man in the world. Leonard's next screen airing, *Da*, was adapted by the playwright himself from his enormously successful play of the same name and his book *Home Before Night*, and features a curmudgeon closer to home. Using Leonard's best and most personal work as source material, the film takes a hard yet sentimental look at his exasperating relationship with his adopted father.

Martin Sheen plays Leonard's screen alter-ego Charlie Tynan, an Irish playwright living in New York. Immersed in rehearsals for a Broadway play, he is dragged back to reality by a phone call from Ireland: his aged father has died. He drops everything and heads home for the funeral. After the ceremony, he finds his attempts at grieving are thwarted by the contrary old coot's refusal to lie down in Dean's Grange where they buried him. Da (Barnard Hughes) reappears to Charlie in the family house (in his mind's eye, this isn't a ghost story), as irascible as he had been when he was alive and in his prime. In humourous and angry flashbacks, Charlie examines the pivotal incidents from his youth and early manhood that shaped his relationship with his Da, and recalls the old man's effortless ability to embarrass, upset and humiliate him at the worst possible moments. When young Charlie (Karl Hayden) was making head-way on a park bench with local fast girl 'the Yellow Peril' (Jill Doyle), Da happened along, interrupted them, and demystified the girl by letting Charlie know that he knew her Da and all belonging to her. Charlie's first job interview, with anglo-advo-cate Mr Drumm (William Hickey), was almost ruined by Da's tactless anti-British ranting, and Ma (Doreen Hepburn) didn't help by blurting to his prospective em-ployer that young Charlie was adopted, after his real mother took poison unsuccess-fully to rid herself of the unwanted pregnancy.

Leonard may be a tough critic of his Da's foibles, but he's no easier on himself, and some of the funniest exchanges in the film occur when playwright Charlie, young Charlie, and Da go for pints in The Arches in Dalkey, and the two Charlies carp on about what a disappointment they are to each other. This use of characters overlap-ping in time and space works as a theatrical conceit transferred intact from the play, but the film suffers elsewhere from a lack of cinematic ideas on the part of beginner-director Matt Clark and television cameraman Alar Kivilo. The play gains most in its transfer to screen from the walkabouts in Leonard's native Dalkey, a fishing village turned affluent Dublin suburb, and the exterior scenes of high drama that can only be hinted at on stage (such as Da's attempt to drown Charlie's beloved dog in Colliemore Harbour because he was chasing nuns). The film is fortified by having Barnard Hughes, a Tony Award winner with *Da* on Broadway, reprising the role he made his own on stage. Sheen is sincere and credible as the troubled Charlie, and William Hickey, an Oscar nominee two years earlier for *Prizzi's Honor*, excels in his role as young Charlie's creaky-voiced authoritarian boss Mr Drumm.

HUSH-A-BYE-BABY
(1989) IRL/UK colour 80 mins

(Still courtesy of the Irish Film Archive of the Film Insititue of Ireland reproduced courtesy of Margo Harkin)

Production Team

Producer .... Tom Collins/Derry Film
                     & Video Workshop
Director .... Margo Harkin
Screenplay .... Margo Harkin and
                     Stephanie English
Cinematography .... Breffini Byrne
Editor .... Martin Duffy
Musical Score .... Sinéad O'Connor

Cast

Emer McCourt	Goretti Friel
Michael Liebman	Ciarán
Cathy Casey	Dinky
Julie Rogers	Majella
Sinéad O'Connor	Sinéad
Rosina Brown	Mrs Friel
Seamus Ball	Mr Friel
Julie McDonald	Fidelma
Marie Jones	Mrs McGuigan
Alan Howley	Lenny
David Coyle	Father Devine
Brenda Winter	Schoolteacher
Sean Doherty	Irish-speaking soldier
Brendan MacGabhann	Irish teacher
Irene Bates	Bean A Tí
Maureen Dow	Sister Consilio
Declan McLaughlin	Patrick McGuigan

HUSH-A-BYE-BABY
(1989) IRL/UK colour 80 mins

Director Margo Harkin shot her debut feature *Hush-A-Bye-Baby*, a teenage slice-of-life addressing serious issues for Catholic schoolgirls, in her native city of Derry. Unplanned pregnancy is her central theme, in the mid-1980s context of the supergrass trials in the North of Ireland and an abortion referendum in the South.

After an aerobics workout (to Cindy Lauper tunes – the year is 1984), fifteen-year-old Goretti Friel (Emer McCourt) spots Ciarán McGuigan (Michael Liebman) at the local gym, and makes enquiries about him. Ciarán notices her too, and gets the low-down on her from lad-about-town Lenny (Alan Howley), who claims to have snogged her and all her friends as well. Lively character development follows before the pair finally meet. Ciarán, the responsible eldest of a widowed mother's eight boys, gets drunk instead of asking Goretti to dance at the local disco. Goretti's friends – naïve Sinéad (Sinéad O'Connor), ribald Dinky (Cathy Casey) and boisterous Majella (Julie Rogers) – all fail to find romance, resulting in a slagging match in the taxi on the way home. Goretti is learning Irish at night and bumps into Ciarán at one of her classes. He asks her in Irish to join him for a Coke and the pair get on well. Soon Goretti is babysitting for her sister, a job she had previously dodged to hang out with her friends, so that she can be alone with Ciarán. They gradually feel their way to teenage romance and full sexual contact, despite her mother's fretful concern that she's too young to go steady.

Their relationship takes a grim turn when Ciarán is lifted by the British army. The notorious supergrass trials (a miscarriage of justice that sent many innocent people to jail in Northern Ireland) are clogging the courts and Ciarán is locked up on remand for an indefinite period. Goretti is distraught to find that the visiting rights for his mother and brothers don't extend to her. She is further devastated to find that she is pregnant. She desparately tries to send him the news by letter, keeping it secret by writing in Irish. Letters in Irish are forbidden to prisoners lest they contain coded messages, and he never receives it. Feeling alone and abandoned, the secret pregnancy takes precedence over everything else in Goretti's life.

Her parents send her away to Irish college in the Donegal Gaeltacht, where she is tormented by internal conflicts of Catholic upbringing and burgeoning child, made worse by Irish media debates about the recent abortion referendum. She experiences lurid visions of the Virgin Mary (at odds with the film's realist format), during moments of hormonal volatility. Goretti keeps the big news from her parents on her return, and the first they hear of it is the sound of her screaming in agony as she gives birth in her bedroom in the middle of the night.

Shot in Donegal and Derry's Catholic Bogside and Creggan housing estates, Harkin's film treats its difficult subject with a deft touch and features strong, natural performances from a cast of unknown actors (the bewigged Sinéad O'Connor, already a highly regarded singer and the composer of the spare, elegant soundtrack being the exception). The deep Derry accents may prove inscrutable to audiences outside of Ireland, but the frank dialogue and solid teamwork by local talent make this low-budget feature a compelling study of a problem for which there are no easy solutions.

MY LEFT FOOT
(1989) IRL/UK colour 103 mins

(Still courtesy of the Irish Film Archive of the Film Insititue of Ireland)

Production Team

Producer .... Ferndale Films/Granada
TV Int/RTÉ/Noel Pearson/
Paul Eller/Steve Morrison
Director .... Jim Sheridan
Screenplay .... Jim Sheridan and Shane
Connaughton, adapted from the
autobiography of Christy Brown,
My Left Foot
Cinematography .... Jack Conroy
Editor .... J Patrick Duffner
Musical Score .... Elmer Bernstein

Cast

Daniel Day Lewis .... Christy Brown
Brenda Fricker .... Mrs Brown
Ray McAnally .... Mr Brown
Ruth McCabe .... Mary Carr
Fiona Shaw .... Dr Eileen Cole
Hugh O'Conor .... Young Christy Brown
Cyril Cusack .... Lord Castlewelland
Phelim Drew .... Brian
Adrian Dunbar .... Peter
Martin Dunne .... Waiter
Milt Fleming .... Mourner
Declan Croghan .... Old Tom
Julie Hale .... Rachel
Tom Hickey .... Priest
Simon Kelly .... Liam
Patrick Laffan .... Barman
Conor Lambert .. Punch and Judy puppeteer

186

MY LEFT FOOT
(1989) IRL/UK colour 103 mins

In the early-1960s, in a working class neighbourhood of Dublin, a disabled boy suffering from cerebral palsy learned to communicate with the world through the only functioning appendage of his immobile body: his left foot. Treated as a vegetable through infancy and early childhood, the seven-year-old Christy Brown (Hugh O'Conor) stares out at the world unable to move, but absorbs everything he sees. When he struggles to write on the floor with a piece of chalk held between his toes, his parents realise that his mind is fully functional. He undergoes intensive therapy and develops skills and talents previously locked inside by his incurable condition. Through the indomitable courage and love of his mother (Brenda Fricker) and the care of a sympathetic doctor (Fiona Shaw), he overcomes the limitations of his physique, and grows up to become an accomplished author and painter.

The autobiography of the same name by disabled Dublin writer Christy Brown inspired Connaughton and Sheridan's Oscar-nominated screenplay for *My Left Foot*, and led to Daniel Day Lewis' most extraordinary performance to date in the lead role. Renowned for total immersion in every part he plays, Day Lewis reached new levels of sensitivity and engagement in this astounding performance. Far from taking the soft approach and painting Christy as a wholesome example for us all, triumphing serenely over his difficulties, Day Lewis tackles head-on the anger and frustrations of living with a sharp, argumentative mind in an unco-operative body. As the irrepressible Christy, Day Lewis hurls his physically frail character into activities that cerebral palsy would deny to a less stubborn individual – playing street soccer in goals with the Brown brothers, starting a fight in a pub and romancing a nurse (Ruth McCabe) bemused by his caustic sense of humour.

Brenda Fricker is outstanding as Christy's stoic mother, determined to give her son every possible chance to live as a normal human being, despite having more than a dozen of his siblings to look after as well. She won an Oscar for her performance in the Best Supporting Actress category. The Academy gave Day Lewis the Best Actor statuette, and the makings of a great weekend in Dublin. Jim Sheridan racked up three nominations from the Academy, for Best Picture and Best Director, as well as the joint nomination with Shane Connaughton for Best Adapted Screenplay.

In the less fêted roles, the cast of supporting players give *My Left Foot* substance and depth. Hugh O'Conor, top Irish child actor and star of *Lamb*, gives a remarkable performance as the young Christy. Cyril Cusack makes a cameo appearance as Lord Castlewelland, a wealthy patron of Christy Brown's work, 70 years after he made his screen debut as a child actor in *Knocknagow*. The great Ray McAnally, the distinguished veteran of Irish stage, screen and television who plays Christy's father, Paddy Brown, died shortly after the film was made. He received the BAFTA Best Supprting Actor Award posthumously for his performance as the hard-drinking bricklayer who slowly comes round to seeing his son as a complete and capable human being.

Jim Sheridan's skilled direction of these impressive performers, and the awards that followed, combined to make *My Left Foot* an unforgettable cinematic experience and bring Irish film-making to a new level.

HIDDEN AGENDA
(1990) UK colour 108 mins

(Still courtesy of the Irish Film Archive of the Film Insititue of Ireland)

Production Team

Producer .... John Daly/Derek Gibson/
                Hemdale Film Corp/Initial Film
Director .... Ken Loach
Screenplay .... Jim Allen
Cinematography .... Clive Tickner
Editor .... Jonathan Morris
Musical Score.................... Stewart Copeland

Cast

Brian Cox .... Kerrigan
Frances McDormand .... Ingrid
Maurice Roëves ....Harris
Robert Patterson .... Ian Logan
Bernard Bloch ....Henri
Brad Dourif .... Paul
Mai Zetterling .... Moa
George Staines .... Tall man
Michelle Fairley .... Teresa Doyle
Brian McCann .... Molloy
Jim Norton .... Brodie
Des McAleer ....Sergeant Kennedy
John Benfield .... Maxwell
Patrick Kavanagh......................... Alec Nevin
John McDonnell .... Labour MP
Victoria D'Angelo .... Journalist
Ian McElhinney ....Cunningham

HIDDEN AGENDA
(1990) UK colour 108 mins

In *Hidden Agenda*, left-wing British film director Ken Loach confronted one of the more controversial government misdeeds of the Thatcher era: the shoot-to-kill policy in Northern Ireland. This policy saw civilians gunned down by British soldiers in circumstances completely at odds with military and judicial protocol. An independent inquiry conducted by a senior British police officer, John Stalker, disclosed evidence that high government officials had sanctioned these unlawful actions. Attempts were made to suppress Stalker's findings, discredit him, and clear the government of any perceived wrongdoing. In Loach's film, investigations into these fatal shootings begin when the British army kills an American lawyer named Paul Sullivan.

Sullivan (Brad Dourif) is in Ireland with his partner, civil rights activist Ingrid Jessner (Frances McDormand), to examine allegations of brutality against republican prisoners by British authorities. He becomes dangerously involved when a fugitive ex-British intelligence officer, Harris (Maurice Roëves) slips him a cassette tape containing classified government information. When Paul travels by car to a meeting with Harris near Dungannon with a republican named Molloy (Brian McCann), a speeding car overtakes them and three gunmen inside open fire. They stop and shoot them again at point-blank range, and take Harris' tape from the dead Sullivan's pocket.

The official line is that they were fired on after refusing to stop at an army checkpoint. A special inquiry is set up, headed by a Criminal Investigation Department Inspector, Kerrigan (Brian Cox), because Sullivan was an American. Kerrigan's inquiry is thwarted by RUC Inspector Brodie (Jim Norton), who resents an English officer "meddling" in Northern Ireland affairs. Kerrigan discovers that the CID interim report was faked, and learns from former colleague and Ulster native Jack Cunningham (Ian McElhinney), that the hit was carried out by a covert anti-terrorist group, codenamed Echo-4-Alpha. Despite death threats, Kerrigan perseveres with Ingrid's help to find the truth about Sullivan's murder. He meets Harris at a republican club and the ex-army captain tells an outlandish tale of his activities with Psy-Ops (MI5's Psychological Warfare Unit), substantiated, he claims, by the mysterious tape. In a joint CIA/MI5 plot in the 1970s, Harris spread propaganda that portrayed Prime Minister Harold Wilson as a Soviet agent to bring down his Labour government and facilitate Thatcher's election. The beneficiaries of this plot exert pressure on Kerrigan to scapegoat the gunmen and end his investigation. Kerrigan, a career officer who came to Ireland believing he couldn't be bought, must choose between his job, pension and family, and his belief in truth and justice. Convincing himself it's a political, not a police matter, he leaves Ingrid to bring the truth to light on her own.

Strong performances by Cox, McDormand and Morton propel an edgy thriller rooted initially in volatile factual subject matter. But for director Loach and screenwriter Allen, any stick will do to beat the British government, and their anti-establishment fervour soon gets the better of them. This daring scrutiny of real Northern Ireland soon turns into the sort of Hollywood fiction that loves to fit KGB, CIA and MI5 into the same conspiratorial line of dialogue, squandering an opportunity to bring to the screen injustices greater than those they normally address in their more familiar left-wing dramas.

THE FIELD
(1990) IRL/UK colour 110 mins

Production Team

Producer .... Noel Pearson/Granada
Director .... Jim Sheridan
Screenplay ..... Jim Sheridan, from the play of
the same name by John B Keane
Cinematography .... Jack Conroy
Editor .... J Patrick Duffner
Musical Score .... Elmer Bernstein

Cast

Richard Harris .... 'Bull' McCabe
Sean Bean .... Tadhg McCabe
Frances Tomelty .... Young widow
Brenda Fricker .... Maggie McCabe
John Hurt .... Bird O'Donnell
Ruth McCabe .... Tinker woman
Jer O'Leary .... Tinker girl's father
Tom Berenger .... Peter the Yank
Noel O' Donovan .... Tomas
John Cowley .... Flanagan
Ronan Wilmot .... Tinker
Jenny Conroy .... Tinker girl
Joan Sheehy .... 2nd tinker woman
Sean McGinley .... Father Doran
Malachy McCourt .... Sergeant
Frank McDonald .... Quarryman
Eamonn Keane .... Matchmaker

THE FIELD
(1990) IRL/UK colour 110 mins

Playwright John B Keane's powerful 1965 drama *The Field* dealt with an issue that has been at the heart of Irish conflicts for centuries: the ownership of the land. Since the displacement of the old clans from their traditional holdings by English planters to make tenants of them on their ancestral soil, the struggle to regain control of the land has been a key component of Irish nationalism. Keane's play presents this volatile national issue in microcosm, focusing on a single three-acre patch of ground in County Kerry. *The Field* provided one of the great stage roles for Irish actors in the form of Bull McCabe, the tenant farmer who rents this piece of land. Abbey Theatre veteran Ray McAnally was one of the major forces involved in bringing the play to the screen, and was due to play McCabe in Jim Sheridan's adaptation, but died before shooting began. Richard Harris emerged from a decline to play the role instead, giving one of the most powerful performances of his career.

Harris plays the Kerry minotaur Bull McCabe, an aged but ferociously overbearing farmer in the village of Carrickthomond. He rents from a young widow (Frances Tomelty) a field that he has cultivated from bare rock to green sward during the course of his lifetime, carrying creels of kelp on his back from the shore to fertilise it. He regards the field as his, and, if the widow ever wants to sell it, he can rely on the fear he strikes into his neighbours to discourage them from making her an offer. When the village idiot Bird O'Donnell (John Hurt) comes to tell him that the widow has arranged with local pub owner and auctioneer Flanagan (John Cowley) to sell the field, he heads down there with his emotionally stunted son Tadhg (Sean Bean) to let everyone know that he's buying it and doesn't want any competition. Dark mutterings about 'outsiders' taking an interest in the field prompt a tirade from Bull about the British and his heroic role in despatching them from that part of the country during the troubles. But the outsider with his sights on Bull's field isn't British, he's American (referred to in the film as 'the Yank'). To add insult to the injury of presuming to buy that which Bull believes is rightfully his, the American (Tom Berenger), plans to cement over the surface of Bull's patch of green to gain vehicular access to quarries beyond and excavate rocks "to build highways all over Ireland".

The Bull first meets his rival as he returns via the cemetery from selling his winter supply of turf to raise cash to buy the field (and pay blood money to the tinkers for Tadhg's killing of their donkey after it wandered into the field). Bull is praying at the grave of his son Sheamie, (located, tellingly, outside the graveyard walls) when the sharp-dressed Yank arrives in search of his roots. He makes another appearance later at a dance where Bull has arranged with a matchmaker (Eamonn Keane) for Tadhg to meet an eligible young woman with child-bearing hips. A brash tinker girl (Jenny Conroy) dares the local youths to dance with her and Bull intervenes just when Tadhg seems to be summoning the courage to take her up on it. The matchmakers's fix-up turns into a fiasco when Tadhg dances with the girl in question at manic speed, urged on by his father, and accidentally knocks her out. He runs from the hall in shame.

THE FIELD
(1990) IRL/UK colour 110 mins

The auction is held in the village and Bull and the Yank bid vigorously against each other. The widow announces that the auction must be postponed, as her reserve price of one hundred pounds has not been reached. The Yank is willing to pay the money on the spot, but Bull threatens him with trouble if he persists. The reserve price is a stretch for Bull and he has to sell some cattle to raise the money.

The widow arranges with the parish priest, Father Doran (Sean McGinley), to have the Garda sergeant (Malachy McCourt) remove Bull's cattle from the field and put up a 'No Trespassing' sign. Bull is livid at this affront and storms the presbytery for an explanation. He finds the Yank there visiting his pal the priest and is informed by Father Doran that his son Tadhg has been terrorising the widow nightly for ten years – done to please his father, but giving the widow cause to deny Bull the field at any price. Tadhg admits it, receiving a reprimand from the Bull who sends him from the room and lectures the priest on meddling in things he doesn't understand.

The Bull realises that his situation is worse than he thought – the Yank wants to buy the land upriver from Bull's field and redirect the waterfall, cutting off his supply. He decides that the only way to eliminate the Yank is to scare him off with threats of physical violence. On a rainy night he arranges an alibi with the complicity of the drinkers in Flanagan's, and tries to keep it airtight by banishing the Bird, who he knows to be untrustworthy. Bull and Tadhg go to the waterfall to threaten the Yank. Their adversary is unimpressed, and Tadhg starts a fight with him in which he comes off the worse. Disgusted with Tadhg and consumed by land-lust and hatred for the outsider, Bull wades in, bashing the Yank's head against a rock until he's dead. Overcome by the enormity of what he has done and unwilling to admit it, his transition from obsession to madness is well underway (and observed by the ubiquitous Bird).

The auction resumes the next day, and Bull buys the field unopposed, his henchman Bird (who lets slip that the Yank isn't coming) bidding on his behalf. Bull's triumph is hollow as he realises that his son has no interest in the three-acre kingdom that he coveted all his life and killed to obtain. Bull's wife Maggie (Brenda Fricker) breaks her eighteen-year silence – they haven't uttered a word to each other since Sheamie's death – begging the Bull to stay strong for Tadhg's sake; she doesn't want to lose another son. Tadhg heads out the bedroom window to visit the tinker girl, daughter of a nomadic class that Bull despises for their rootless relationship to that which he holds most dear, the land. Tadhg impresses her by claiming that he killed the Yank (the camera cuts to a shot of the dead Yank in the same watery grave to which Bull and Tadhg had earlier dropped the tinker's dead donkey – Berenger is the one in the suit) and will do the same to her father if he lays a hand on her. One night of love in the tinker girl's caravan is enough to convince Tadhg that he should hit the road with her, driving his father completely over the edge into a madness that makes him destroy everything he values in the world.

In this return to form as a man called Bull, Harris dominates the entire film from opening scenes to final credits with an uninhibited ferocity that shoves everyone else out of the frame, and earned him a well-deserved second Oscar nomination. His fellow cast members barely get a look in, leaving the film more than a little unbalanced. The authority figures that usually subdue unruly peasants in Irish films – the Garda sergeant and the parish priest – hold little terror for the mighty Bull, and the only real rival he faces, the American land buyer, is underwritten by Keane and Sheridan and underplayed by an actor who emotes like he's a bystander that walked onto the set. Brenda Fricker, a fine actress and Oscar winner for Sheridan with *My Left Foot* two years previously, is under-utilised and doesn't open her mouth until the final reel. Sean Bean hardly gets a word in either as the tormented Tadhg (no bad thing – when he does speak it sounds like he never set foot outside Sheffield). Harris' Kerry accent is flawless, as to be expected from the Limerick man, born one county away from where the film is set. The film inevitably belongs to Harris, and is a treat for his fans who have had to get by for years with *Orca* and *Horse* remakes. By corollary, it's a must-to-avoid for anyone who finds the actor a bit much. Harris maintained the larger-than-life persona off-camera, and the film crew affectionately dubbed the bearded actor 'the Ayatollah', a nickname earned for his similarity to the charismatic Iranian leader Khomeini. Harris hogs each and every frame of the film in which he appears, dwarfing everybody and everything in sight except for the awe-inspiring Connacht landscapes around Leenane and Killary Harbour where the *The Field* was shot.

DECEMBER BRIDE
(1990) IRL/UK colour 88 mins

(Still courtesy of the Irish Film Archive of the Film Insititue of Ireland reproduced courtesy of Little Bird)

Production Team

Producer .... Jonathan Cavendish/
Channel 4/Little Bird
Director .... Thaddeus O'Sullivan
Screenplay .... David Rudkin,
from the novel of the
same name by Sam Hanna Bell
Cinematography .... Bruno de Keyzer
Editor .... Rodney Holland
Musical Score .... Jürgen Knieper

Cast

Donal McCann .... Hamilton Echlin
Saskia Reeves .... Sarah Gilmartin
Ciarán Hinds .... Frank Echlin
Patrick Malahide .... Rev Sorleyson
Brenda Bruce .... Martha Gilmartin
Michael McKnight .... Fergus
Dervla Kirwan .... Young Martha
Peter Capaldi .... Young Sorleyson
Geoffrey Golden .... Andrew Echlin
Cathleen Delaney .... Agnes
Gabrielle Reidy .... Bridie
Frances Lowe .... Victoria
Catherine Gibson .... Mother Pentland
Julie McDonald .... Molly
Roy Heybeard .... Auctioneer
Karl Hayden .... Young Andrew
Miche Doherty .... Joe

DECEMBER BRIDE
(1990) IRL/UK colour 88 mins

Thaddeus O'Sullivan switched from cinematography to directing his first feature after shooting a series of visually accomplished films for new Irish directors in the 1980s. *December Bride* fulfilled the aesthetic promise of *Anne Devlin* and *Pigs* to establish him as Ireland's top visual stylist. The screenplay is adapted by David Rudkin from Sam Hanna Bell's 1951 novel, and set in County Down in the early-20th century. The narrative marks a significant departure from portrayals of Catholic nationalist Ireland (in which Protestants exist only in opposition roles if they exist at all), by focusing on life in a rural Protestant community in which an unorthodox household defies social convention.

Sarah Gilmartin (Saskia Reeves) and her widowed mother Martha (Brenda Bruce) work as servants for Andrew Echlin (Geoffrey Golden) and his two sons Hamilton (Donal McCann) and Frank (Ciarán Hinds). The Echlins are prosperous landowners in a predominantly Presbyterian part of rural Northern Ireland, typified by the serious demeanour of its people and their solid work ethic. Tragedy befalls them when Andrew is drowned saving Sarah and his sons after their boat capsizes. Their minister, Sorleyson (Patrick Malahide), offers solace, saying it was God's will, but independent-minded Sarah is sceptical. The minister is vexed by her remarks, and by the brothers' failure to attend church.

The brothers take charge of the farm, and both take an interest in Sarah. Frank's romantic overtures cause trouble with Martha, who storms out of their godless house, but can't persuade Sarah to leave with her. A shopping trip to Belfast with Sarah gives Hamilton his chance to get close to her. Soon the brothers are sharing her affections in a way that suits all three, after some initial jealousy. Sarah begins to influence the running of the estate and she is clearly no longer a mere servant or paramour of the Echlin brothers. She is ambitious for them and for herself. She becomes pregnant, and shocks the community by stubbornly refusing to identify the father or marry either brother. Sorleyson pressures the Echlins and Sarah to resolve this immoral situation. Sarah ignores him, and Hamilton says he'd marry her but she won't marry him. Sarah defies convention when her baby is born by registering the girl in her name, with no father cited. Both brothers seem equally devoted to mother and child, but gradually Frank becomes morose, realising that Sarah prefers Hamilton. When July 12th comes, he dons suit and bowler hat to join the Orange celebrations. He is snubbed by the community, but meets a girl he likes (Julie McDonald). She insists their courtship be kept secret because of his pariah status. On his way home, he is set upon by a mob and beaten so badly that he's disabled. Their household remains unchanged, until Sarah's daughter Martha comes of age and wants to marry. Sarah is moved by Martha's distress at not having a legal father to give her away in church, and finally marries Hamilton, giving the film its title.

O'Sullivan found a sympathetic ally for his visual objectivese in Bruno de Keyzer, cinematographer on four Tavernier films, and a former cameraman for Bergman's director of photography Sven Nykvist. De Keyser's measured compositions and slow pacing match O'Sullivan's established painterly approach to depicting landscapes and interiors, and complement this sensitive portrayal of a heretofore hidden Irish community. O'Sullivan continued his exploration of Protestant Northern Ireland less successfully five years later with *Nothing Personal*.

195

THE COMMITMENTS
(1991) UK colour 121 mins

(Still courtesy of the Irish Film Archive of the Film Insititue of Ireland)

Production Team

Producer .... Lynda Myles/Roger Randall-
Cutler/David Wimbury
Director .... Alan Parker
Screenplay .... Ian La Frenais and
Dick Clement
Cinematography .... Gale Tattersall
Editor .... Gerry Hambling
Musical Arrangement .... Paul Bushnell

Cast

Robert Arkins .... Jimmy Rabbitte
Michael Aherne .... Steve Clifford
Angeline Ball .... Imelda Quirke
Maria Doyle .... Natalie Murphy
Dave Finnegan .... Mickah Wallace
Bronagh Gallagher .... Bernie McGloughlin
Felim Gormley .... Dean Fay
Glen Hansard .... Outspan Foster
Dick Massey .... Billy Mooney
Johnny Murphy .... Joey 'The Lips' Fagan
Kenneth McCluskey .... Derek Scully
Andrew Strong .... Deco Cuffe
Colm Meaney .... Mr Rabbitte
Anne Kent .... Mrs Rabbitte
Andrea Corr .... Sharon Rabbitte
Gerard Cassoni .... Darren Rabbitte
Maura O'Malley .... Joey Fagan's mother

When the call went out to cast the band members for Alan Parker's film version of Roddy Doyle's book, *The Commitments*, almost every young musician in Dublin showed up at the auditions hoping to be discovered. The book had been enormously popular in Ireland and abroad, and the prospect of being in the film generated a lot of excitement in the city in which it was set. More than 3,000 contenders tried out in all, including a few who couldn't play, but thought they looked the part posing in front of a mirror with a tennis racket. From this multitude, twelve were chosen to play the manager, singers, and players of instruments that made up the fictional Dublin soul band that gave the book and the film their titles.

The story in the film follows this real-life beginning as sharp Northsider and music head Jimmy Rabbitte (Robert Arkins) puts together a new group from the ashes of AndAnd!And, a wedding band torn apart by conflict over where to put that pesky exclamation mark. Band members Derek (Kenneth McCluskey) and Outspan (Glen Hansard) have great faith in Jimmy's music knowledge, and ask him to manage them and help them put together a band. Jimmy puts an ad in the paper for musicians with real soul: Northsiders only need apply. Despite his strict specifications, all kinds of folkies, trad fiddlers, hippies, metalheads and shoegazers show up on his parents' doorstep, causing hilarity for his siblings and exasperation for his Ma (Anne Kent) and Da (Colm Meaney). Jimmy soon completes the band line-up with some of the ad candidates, a guy he heard singing drunk at a wedding, a girl he fancies, and two of her friends. Charismatic Jimmy convinces the new band members that soul music is the true sound of the Dublin working class. Two among them need no convincing – the trumpet player, Joey 'The Lips' Fagan (Johnny Murphy), a soul veteran who claims to have toured with Memphis legends Wilson Pickett, Otis Redding and Joe Tex; and the junior Joe Cocker vocalist, Deco Cuffe (Andrew Strong), a bus conductor with a voice like nutty slack getting shovelled into a roaring cast-iron furnace.

The band goes through the usual phases – arguing over the band name, learning their instruments, and developing into a tight, confident outfit with cheering fans and favourable press coverage. Then comes the inevitable acrimonious split over personality clashes and musical differences. The Commitments are only held together by Jimmy's hard work, cajoling and plain old-fashioned lying, but he finally gives up on them. His cocky lead singer Deco has a repellent personality and bad personal hygiene, but he's too good at what he does for Jimmy to get rid of him. The drummer, Billy (Dick Massey), can't stand Deco and has to quit before he thumps him, taking the band's transport with him. He is quickly replaced by their psychotic head of security, Mickah Wallace (Dave Finnegan), a head-butting bruiser well qualified to give the drum kit a brutal beating. Mystical, mature trumpeter Joey 'The Lips' causes some unrest when the young lads in the band realise that the back-up singers Imelda (Angeline Ball), Natalie (Maria Doyle) and Bernie (Bronagh Gallagher) have all been hitting on unsuccessfully are drawn to his sensitive nature and have been sampling

197

(Still courtesy of the Irish Film Archive of the Film Institute of Ireland)

his palpitating embouchure. The other horn player, tenor saxophonist Dean (Felim Gormley) achieves a mastery of his instrument that makes him want to experiment beyond soul. He goes all cerebral on them and adds jazz licks to his performance, to the consternation of purist manager Jimmy. The band problems really come to a head when they get a little acclaim from the press and the public. The excitement and ego inflation of their modest success, combined with the letdown on Joey's promise that his old pal Wilson Pickett would jam with them at their gig, pushes the band members over the edge. They start a huge brawl in their dressing room, and Jimmy storms out on them. The mission to bring their blue-eyed soul to the people of Ireland is at an end.

Not alone are they credible actors, but The Commitments are no Monkees – they played all their own instruments in the film and did all their own singing. Several of them had band projects underway in their own right before impressing Parker at the auditions, and most went on to professional careers in rock music and film afterwards. None had much in the way of acting experience prior to making *The Commitments*, but they more than made up for it in freshness and sheer exuberance.

Director Alan Parker, who made a cameo appearance in the film as a record pro-

THE COMMITMENTS
(1991) UK colour 121 mins

ducer (at the studios of Eeejit Records where The Commitments lay down a few tracks), shot the film entirely on location in the less Georgian parts of Dublin city. His search for urban grit took him around the graffiti-covered breeze blocks and high-rise towers of Kilbarrack, Darndale and Ballymun flats to recreate visually the world of Barrytown that Roddy Doyle had described in his book. Only Joey 'The Lips' Fagan gets a more upmarket location for the house in which he lives with his dotty mother (Maura O'Malley). The facade shots for the Fagan residence were taken in Pembroke Road, and the garden scenes were shot at Gardiner Street. The band rehearsal space is the upper level of Ricardo's poolhall in Camden Street, and their biggest, and final gig, is shot at The Waterfront on Sir John Rogerson's Quay.

Seasoned sitcom writers Ian La Frenais and Dick Clement adapted Roddy Doyle's first book of his bestselling Barrytown trilogy to create a boisterous white soul musical under versatile Parker's fast-paced direction. The other two Barrytown books, *The Snapper* and *The Van,* were adapted by Doyle himself and remain truer to his use of language than La Frenais and Clement's reworking. To international audiences, it may seem that the cast members of *The Commitments* curse like sailors who caught Tourette's Syndrome on shore leave, but the screenwriters actually toned down the language from Doyle's original all-out assault on lexicographers' delicate sensibilities. As a misguided sop to film audiences' expectations of Holy Catholic Ireland, the scriptwriters included a confessional exchange between a soul-fan priest and the band's piano player (Michael Aherne) – a medical student, chosen, Jimmy rationalised, because it would be good to have someone who can bandage heads in some of the places they'd be playing – that didn't exist in a book quite devoid of religious iconography and personnel.

The Commitments went on to become a worldwide sensation, based on the irresistible hook of the familiar soul hits (leaning towards the raw Memphis R and B end more than the overplayed Detroit style) and the unfettered energy of the rowdy young cast. On the strength of the film's success, The Commitments went on tour in Europe and the US, with a line-up that featured highly variable combinations of the original members, just like a real soul hits group.

THE MIRACLE
(1991) UK colour 98 mins

Production Team

Producer .... Stephen Woolley/
Redmond Morris/Promenade FP/
Palace Pictures
Director .... Neil Jordan
Screenplay .... Neil Jordan
Cinematography .... Philippe Rousselot
Editor .... Joke Van Wijk
Musical Score .... Anne Dudley

Cast

Beverly D'Angelo .... Renée Baker
Donal McCann .... Sam
Niall Byrne .... Jimmy
Lorraine Pilkington .... Rose
J G Devlin .... Mr Beausang
Cathleen Delaney .... Miss Strange
Tom Hickey .... Tommy
Shane Connaughton .... Rose's Father
Mikkel Gaup .... Jonner
Sylvia Teron .... Muscular Lady
Anita Reeves .... Ballroom Singer
Ruth McCabe .... Wardrobe Lady
Jer O'Leary .... Barman
Sam's Band
Earl Gill .... Trumpet
Johnny Devlin .... Saxophone
Chris Keveney .... Piano
Tommy Donoghue .... Drums

THE MIRACLE
(1991) UK colour 98 mins

Neil Jordan followed a pair of big-budget Hollywood features, *We're No Angels* and *High Spirits*, with *The Miracle*, a more modestly scaled and personal work about youthful imagination and fractured familial relationships, shot on location in Dublin and Bray, County Wicklow. The film begins with a bright cheerful disposition, but takes a darker turn when an innocent game played by two teenagers stirs painful emotions from the past for one of them.

Sardonic, literary-minded Rose (Lorraine Pilkington) and her friend Jimmy (Niall Byrne) pass the time during their summer holidays from school making up stories about people they see on the promenade – a flock of nuns bathing, an old man who may be in love with a dainty old lady who he's too shy to approach – in the resort town where they live. This harmless pursuit gives them an escape from the difficulties of their home lives. Motherless Jimmy lives with his father Sam (Donal McCann), a grouchy musician and sorry bandleader, jealous of his son's talent on the saxophone and overly fond of his drink. Rose's father is a cold creature more concerned about his golf swing than his precocious daughter. The creative teens spot a new specimen for their storytelling when a glamorous blonde woman, much older than either of them and probably a foreigner, arrives at the local railway station to stroll at the seafront. Her return visits make her an object of fascination for Jimmy, beyond the normal level that their stories require. He follows her into Dublin on the train and sees her entering the Olympia Theatre. He finds out that she is Renée Baker (Beverly D'Angelo), American, and starring in a stage version of the old western, *Destry Rides Again*. Rose takes a dim view of this new development – the previous subjects of their stories had their lives fully imagined on the promenade and didn't need this kind of in-depth research. Twinges of jealousy compel Rose to find a boy with whom to be fascinated, and she makes it her mission to humanise the brutish young elephant trainer Jonner (Mikkel Gaup) from the circus near the promenade.

Renée seems curious about Jimmy, but holds back for reasons he doesn't understand. He enlists Rose's eloquence in a church to pray to God for a miracle – that he will seduce Renée before the summer is out. His determination wears Renée down a little and when he gets to know her better, he is shocked to find that she knew his father very well back when he played sax better and drank less. Jimmy revisits the church to complain to God about the way things turned out, and finds that a miracle has indeed occurred – not the one he asked for, but a different one of Rose's devising that gives the film its surreal ending.

Lorraine Pilkington makes an outstanding debut, playing Rose with effortless charm and getting all the best lines. The winning innocence she and Niall Byrne manifest in their roles brings freshness and vitality to a film that is on surer footing with their lively imaginings than it is with the warped relationship between Renée, Jimmy and his father. Donal McCann impresses as always, playing the contrary dad hopelessly lost to the bottle. *The Miracle* showcases the seaside delights of Bray, at Dawson's Amusements, Fossett's Circus, and the promenade at Martello Terrace, to provide a cheerful backdrop to Neil Jordan's darker obsessions.

THE CRYING GAME
(1992) IRL/UK colour 112 mins

Production Team

Director .... Neil Jordan
Producer .... Palace Pictures/Channel Four
Films/Stephen Woolley
Cinematography .... Ian Wilson
Screenplay .... Niel Jordan
Editor .... Kant Pan
Musical Score .... Anne Dudley

Cast

Stephen Rea .... Fergus
Jaye Davidson .... Dil
Miranda Richardson .... Jude
Forest Whitaker .... Jody
Adrian Dunbar .... Peter Maguire
Breffni McKenna .... Tinker
Joe Savino .... Eddie
Birdie Sweeney .... Tommy
Jim Broadbent .... Col
Ralph Brown .... Dave
Tony Slattery .... Deveroux
Jack Carr .... Franknum
Josephine White .... Bar performer
Shar Campbell .... Bar performer
Brian Coleman .... Judge
Ray De Haan .... Security man
David Cronnelly .... Security man

THE CRYING GAME
(1992) IRL/UK colour 112 mins

A war-weary IRA man named Fergus (Stephen Rea) is detailed to guard a British soldier named Jody (Forest Whitaker), held hostage as part of an exchange deal for a republican prisoner in police custody in Castlereagh RUC station. The terrified Jody, lured into the hands of the IRA by Fergus' girlfriend Jude (Miranda Richardson) at a fairground, knows he has little chance of surviving his ordeal. Hoping that his life might be spared, he desperately tries to strike up a rapport with the sensitive Fergus. Jody tells him about his life back home in London, and Dil (Jaye Davidson), the lover he left behind to serve with his army unit in Northern Ireland. He shows Fergus a picture of his sweetheart, and implores him to go to London and convey his love to Dil if the hostage exchange goes wrong and he gets killed. Fergus is fascinated and develops a liking for his charge, to the annoyance of his commander Peter Maguire (Adrian Dunbar). When Fergus is directed by Maguire to shoot the hostage, he hasn't the stomach for it. Jody tries to escape and is killed accidentally by a British army patrol. Two of Fergus' comrades are also killed, and, sickened by the incident, Fergus leaves Belfast and the IRA behind and heads for London. He starts work in construction under an assumed name, and tries to forget what happened.

Fergus' fascination with the dead soldier's lover proves hard to shake. He seeks out the alluring hairdresser whose snapshot he had seen in Jody's wallet. He becomes obsessed with the sultry siren – and finds that love can blossom in the most extraordinary places. But he can't escape his violent past, and before long Jude tracks him down in London. She lets Fergus know that he has been courtmartialled in Belfast for deserting the organisation. Finding his new identity a useful cover, Jude and Maguire pressure him into carrying out another operation which fails disastrously for all of them. As the perpetrators of violence come to realise that they have let loose forces over which they have no control, the love of Fergus and Dil undergoes the severest of tests and prevails.

Neil Jordan won international acclaim and an Academy Award for a fiendishly clever screenplay that reads like a warped update of the Frank O'Connor story *Guests of the Nation*. *The Crying Game* received a total of six nominations including Best Director, Best Picture and Best Editing. Stephen Rea, in his third Jordan feature, was nominated for Best Actor. Newcomer Jaye Davidson received a nomination for outstanding work in the supporting role as the sultry singer/hairdresser. Numerous awards and nominations followed from the Writers Guild of America, BAFTA and the LA Film Critics' Association, establishing Neil Jordan as a top international screenwriter and director.

The Crying Game features many components that were fast becoming Jordan trademarks: fairground scenes, the wickedly clever soundtrack selections and a complex tangle of human emotions that range far outside romantic norms. From modest beginnings, *The Crying Game* became a worldwide success, thanks to a secret in the plot that cinema audiences kept to themselves with extraordinary conspiratorial zeal.

INTO THE WEST
(1992) IRL colour 102 mins

(Still courtesy of the Irish Film Archive of the Film Insititue of Ireland reproduced courtesy of Little Bird)

Production Team

Producer .... Jonathan Cavendish/
Tim Palmer/Little Bird/
Parallel/Majestic/
Film Four/Newcomm
Director .... Mike Newell
Screenplay .... Jim Sheridan,
from a story by Michael Pearce
Cinematography .... Tom Sigel
Editor .... Peter Boyle
Music .... Patrick Doyle

Cast

Gabriel Byrne .... Papa Riley
Ellen Barkin .... Kathleen
Ciarán Fitzgerald .... Ossie
Ruaidhrí Conroy .... Tito
David Kelly .... Grandfather
Johnny Murphy .... Tracker
Colm Meaney .... Barreller
John Kavanagh .... Hartnett
Brendan Gleason .... Inspector Bolger
Jim Norton .... Superintendant O'Mara
Anita Reeves .... Mrs Murphy
Ray McBride .... Mr Murphy
Dave Duffy .... Morrissey
Stuart Dannell .... Conor Murphy
Becca Hollinshead .... Birdy Murphy
Bianca Hollinshead .... Angela Murphy
Owen O'Gorman .... Cafferty

INTO THE WEST
(1992) IRL colour 102 mins

Mike Newell shot the charming fantasy feature *Into the West* on location in Ireland from a script by Jim Sheridan, to create a touching story of two traveller boys coming to terms with their mother's death and reconciling with their alcoholic father.

A mysterious white horse follows an old man (David Kelly) travelling by caravan from the west of Ireland to Dublin. He arrives at a halting site at Ballymun, where his grandchildren live in high-rise squalor with their drunken, difficult father, Papa Riley (Gabriel Byrne). Papa gave up life on the road and took to the drink when his wife died giving birth. His neglected children Tito (Ruairdhí Conroy) and Ossie (Ciarán Fitzgerald) take a liking to the white horse, and the younger one, Ossie, seems to have a strong affinity with it. Grandpa calls the horse Tír na nÓg, after the legendary land of eternal youth. The boys keep the horse in their flat until health inspectors pay a visit. Tír na nÓg is taken away by Gardaí, leaving Ossie deeply upset. Papa grovels at the Garda station to get the horse back, but corrupt Inspector Bolger (Brendan Gleeson) has already sold it to a businessman named Hartnett (John Kavanagh). The boys spot Tír na nÓg on television clearing jumps at the Royal Dublin Society Horse Show, and head over to the RDS, steal the horse, and gallop away towards the west to live like real cowboys.

Two posses are formed to catch them. Hartnett, with police backing, and Papa, with the help of Barreller (Colm Meaney), Tracker (Johnny Murphy) and Kathleen (Ellen Barkin) search the country for the fugitives. Tír na nÓg's wiles and Garda incompetence help Ossie and Tito evade their pursuers, and they fulfil their cowboy dream. But cooking on the campfire and sleeping under the stars in Irish weather is not like they imagined, and soon they've had enough. They want to go back, but the mystical horse follows its own determined course and takes them to their mother's grave. Ossie wants to know why his birthday is on the gravestone.

Hartnett's team tracks Tír na nÓg with police helicopters as the horse reaches the western shores. Papa closes in as well with Grandpa's help, and both groups converge on a beach in Galway. A fight breaks out between them, and as Papa clatters all round him, Tír na nÓg gallops into the sea with Ossie on his back. Ossie almost drowns, but the spirit of his dead mother intervenes, allowing Papa to pull his near-dead body from the water. The horse is nowhere to be seen. A sober and wiser Papa finally realises that he must free his dead wife's spirit in the traditional way, by burning the caravan in which she died. As the caravan burns, Ossie and Tito are cheered up by a vision of Tír Na nÓg in the flames.

Jim Sheridan's script wears its fantasy elements lightly, and is well served by the winning charm of the juvenile leads. The baddies are drawn in broad strokes, and John Kavanagh positively revels in his cartoon villainy, pencil moustache and all. Gabriel Byrne laid aside the Dublin accent that he normally uses whether he's playing a Chicago mobster or a Danish mechanic, and essayed instead a country accent of his own devising for Papa. An actor better suited to moody, taciturn roles, he struggles with the grieving, anger and more expansive emotions the script requires of him, often with unintentionally hilarious results.

YOU, ME AND MARLEY
(1992) UK colour 84 mins

Production Team

Producer ....Chris Parr/BBC
Director...................................Richard Spence
Screenplay .... Graham Reid
Cinematography .... Graham Veevers
Editor .... Greg Miller
Musical Score.....................Stephen Warbeck

Cast

Marc O'Shea .... Sean O'Neill
Bronagh Gallagher .... Frances
Michael Liebmann .... Marley
Michael Gregory ....Hugh
Emma Moylan .... Mary
Marie Jones ....Sarah
Catherine Brennan .... Rosaleen
Stella McCusker .... Mrs Hagan
Frank Grimes ....Mr Hagan
Lorcan Cranitch............................ Father Tom
James Greene .... Father Peter
Ian McElhinney .... Reggie Devine
John Keegan ....Paul
George Shane ....Tony
B J Hogg ....PC Bill
Peter Ferris .... PC John
Tony Doyle ....Police Inspector
Gerard Crossan .... Tonto

YOU, ME AND MARLEY
(1992) UK colour 84 mins

Spence's television film *You, Me and Marley* is a harrowing drama of young lives wasted in the depressed Catholic housing estates of west Belfast. The war-battered economy offers no prospects to the youths who grow up there, and their only form of excitement is stealing cars to race around the city at night. The title refers to the main characters of the film, all three of them teenage joyriders. Frances (Bronagh Gallagher) is a convent girl with brains but no interest in her schoolbooks. She spends her evenings joyriding with her boyfriend Sean (Marc O'Shea), known as 'the Wart' because of his short stature. A surly teen at home with his mother (Marie Jones) and pregnacy-prone older sister (Catherine Brennan), Sean is a fearless runt behind the wheel of a stolen car. He hotwires motors in seconds and drives Frances and their friend Marley (Michael Liebmann) around at high speed, playing chicken with the RUC patrols. Their heroes are not the fearsome Provisional IRA men who govern their estate with an iron fist (referred to disdainfully by Sean as 'the Provies'), but legendary local joyriders – one dead already at the hands of the UDR, another one killed when he wraps a stolen bread van around a pole.

The only authority within the community besides the IRA is the Catholic Church – the police remain a threatening but distant force in armour-plated vehicles, with no connection to the people. Two priests, bearded young idealist Father Tom (Lorcan Cranitch) and jaded cynic Father Peter (James Greene) address a community meeting about the joyriders. Father Tom denounces violence as a method of dealing with the young car thieves, but fails to present a better solution. He blames the IRA for turning kids into monsters, and menacing IRA leader Reggie Devine (Ian McElhinney) tells the angry crowd that if the priest is right, they will solve this problem they caused in their own way. The crowd backs him enthusiastically.

Reggie spares Sean because his two brothers were killed on active IRA duty, and makes an example of Marley instead. His henchmen smash Marley's knees, ankles, elbows and ankles to a bloody pulp with baseball bats. Marley is hospitalised, but the beating has no deterrent effect on his reckless friends. Sean, Hugh (Michael Gregory), and Tonto (Gerard Crossan) avenge the beating by vandalising Reggie's car. Reggie's frighteners arrive at Sean's house, and Reggie announces that Sean has 24 hours to leave the country. As Sean ponders his fate, his joyriding crew smuggles Marley out of the hospital to go driving with Hugh at the wheel. Hugh panics at an army road block with fatal consequences for the occupants of the car, and, lost without his friends, Sean resigns himself to a future alone in England.

Graham Reid's taut screenplay captures all the adrenalin-charged excitement of no-future teens stoked on lager and glue and their addictive need for speed. He also tackles the controversial issue of punishment beatings by the IRA, in their capacity as shadow police force in areas where the RUC has little control. Director Spence draws terrific performances from his young leads: Marc O'Shea as Sean, the blocky bantam-weight whose battered face announces that he lost every fight he ever started; Bronagh Gallagher as the cheeky but kind Frances, and Michael Liebmann as the gawky, be-spectacled Marley who remains exuberant despite his horrific injuries.

IN THE NAME OF THE FATHER
(1993) IRL/UK/US colour 133 mins

Prouction Team

Producer .... Hell's Kitchen/Gabriel Byrne/
Universal Pictures/
Jim Sheridan/Arthur Lappin
Director .... Jim Sheridan
Screenplay .... Terry George
and Jim Sheridan
Cinematography .... Peter Biziou
Editor .... Gerry Hambling
Musical Score .... Trevor Jones/
Gavin Friday/Maurice Seezer/Bono

Cast

Daniel Day Lewis .... Gerry Conlon
Pete Postlethwaite .... Giuseppe Conlon
Emma Thompson .... Gareth Peirce
John Lynch .... Paul Hill
Mark Shepherd .... Paddy Armstrong
Beatie Edney .... Carole Richardson
Don Baker .... Joe McAndrew
Marie Jones .... Sarah Conlon
Corin Redgrave .... Robert Dixon
Britta Smith .... Annie Maguire
Paterson Joseph .... Benbay
John Benfield .... Chief PO Barker
Frank Harper .... Ronnie Smalls
Alison Crosbie .... Girl in pub
Philip King .... Guilford soldier
Nye Heron .... IRA man
Seamus Moran .... IRA man

IN THE NAME OF THE FATHER
(1993) IRL/UK/US colour 133 mins

Based on Gerry Conlon's book *Proved Innocent* about his wrongful imprisonment for the IRA bombing of a pub in Guildford, near London, in 1974, *In the Name of the Father* brings to the screen one of the greatest miscarriages of British justice in recent times. The (largely) true film follows Conlon's fate after he's arrested in Belfast and held in police custody in England, along with several friends, in a sweep by the British police. Beaten and tortured during days of questioning, the weakened Conlon (Daniel Day Lewis) confesses to being involved in the bombing, implicating friends, acquaintances, and members of his own family. His father, Giuseppe Conlon (Pete Postlethwaite) travels from Belfast to London to sort out the situation and finds himself arrested as well. Despite a lack of credible forensic or circumstantial evidence against them, father and son are tried and convicted of a crime with which they had no connection. Both Conlons receive life sentences. Gerry's former London squatmates, Paul Hill (John Lynch), Patrick Armstrong (Mark Shepherd), and Carole Richardson (Beatie Edney), are also convicted and sentenced to life based on their coerced confessions. This group would become known as 'the Guilford Four', and their cause was taken up in a massive civil rights campaign conducted in Britain and Ireland in the 1970s and 1980s. Gerry Conlon spent a total of fourteen years in jail for a crime he didn't commit, but was eventually freed after a lengthy battle by lawyer Gareth Pierce (Emma Thompson) to prove his innocence. His father died in prison before the guilty verdict was overturned.

In the Name of the Father was faulted by the British media for its distortion of facts relating to the case, *Sight and Sound* tartly pointing out that Conlon spent all that time behind bars precisely because stories were fabricated about him. Screenwriters Sheridan and George added some cinematic 'improvements' to the facts, making cellmates of the father and son (in reality Gerry and Giuseppe had little contact in jail), and swapping the dreary and dragged-out bureaucratic conclusion of Conlon's appeal for a more dramatically impressive courtroom finale.

But neither these changes, nor the short cuts required to compress a decade and a half of Conlon's life into two hours, can detract from Sheridan's extraordinary artistic achievement. *In the Name of the Father* burns with all the anger and passion that drove the Guildford Four campaign, and consolidates the reputation for being a great director of actors that Sheridan established with *My Left Foot* four years earlier. He draws from his leads performances of tremendous sensitivity, as Day Lewis and Postlethwaite convey the changes in the father-son relationship from anger and filial hostility to closer mutual understanding. The minor players also impress under Sheridan's direction, among them Dublin blues musician Don Baker, deserves a special mention for his menacing portrayal of Joe McAndrew, a formidable IRA leader in Conlon's cellbock.

Seven Academy Award nominations followed for this gripping prison drama, shot on location in Dublin's Kilmainham Gaol, including Best Picture, Best Actor for Day Lewis, Best Director for Sheridan and Best Editing for Gerry Hambling. Thompson and Postlethwaite were nominated in the supporting roles, as were Sheridan and Terry George in the Best Adapted Screenplay category. The film won the Golden Bear at the Berlin Film Festival in 1994.

THE SNAPPER
(1993) UK colour 91 mins

(Still courtesy of the Irish Film Archive of the Film Insititue of Ireland)

Production Team

Producer .... Lynda Myles/BBC Films
Director .... Stephen Frears
Screenplay .... Roddy Doyle,
              from his novel of the same name
Cinematography .... Oliver Stapleton
Editor .... Mick Audsley
Musical Score .... Stanley Myers

Cast

Tina Kellegher .... Sharon Curley
Colm Meaney .... Dessie Curley
Ruth McCabe .... Kay Curley
Eanna MacLiam .... Craig Curley
Peter Rowen .... Sonny Curley
Joanne Gerrard ....Lisa Curley
Colm O'Byrne .... Darren Curley
Ciara Duffy .... Kimberley Curley
Fionnula Murphy .... Jackie
Deirdre O'Brien .... Mary
Karen Woodley .... Yvonne
Pat Laffan .... George Burgess
Virginia Cole .... Doris Burgess
Denis Menton .... Pat Burgess
Brendan Gleeson .... Lester
Ronan Wilmot .... Paddy
Stuart Dunne ....Bertie

THE SNAPPER
(1993) UK colour 91 mins

The second book of Roddy Doyle's Barrytown trilogy, *The Snapper*, was adapted by Roddy himself to make a film smaller in scale but no less enjoyable than its boisterous predecessor, *The Commitments*. Colm Meaney reprises his role as the Dublin dad, but the Rabbitte family of which he was the feckless patriarch is renamed Curley (the original family name being the property of the previous film's producers). The focus of the action shifts to his daughter, as *The Snapper* follows the turbulent journey of twenty-year-old Sharon Curley (Tina Kellegher) through her pregnancy, from drunken conception to happy birth. Her father Dessie goes through dramatic changes himself during her gestation, and learns a lot about what he missed out on while he was off down the pub with the lads during the births of his own children.

Frear's film gets straight to the point with Sharon announcing to her shocked parents that she's pregnant. She refuses to name the father, much to Dessie's annoyance. Her mother Kay (Ruth McCabe) is more sympathetic, but Dessie breaks the tension by inviting Sharon down to the pub for a drink. Dessie is horrified to hear that Burgess (Pat Laffan), an obnoxious middle-aged neighbour, has been boasting in the pub about having sex with Sharon. When Dessie confronts her about this, she denies it, but later threatens Burgess that she'll tell his wife on him if he doesn't shut up. But the harm is done, and the menfolk in Sharon's family go about defending her honour. Dessie confronts Burgess in the men's jacks in the pub but decides he's not worth hitting. Her elder brother Craig (Eanna MacLiam), a soldier back from UN service in the Lebanon, tosses a dustbin through the front window of Burgess' house and gets a night in jail for his trouble. At the Garda station, Sharon concocts a story for Dessie about sleeping with a Spanish sailor to deflect the insults and slags she is forced to endure about Burgess. Her scheme is complicated by Burgess doing a runner on his wife and kids, then stalking her professing his love, even though she is repulsed by the sight of him.

Sharon is disgusted with Dessie when he starts a pub brawl with Burgess' soccer cronies over perceived insults to her and she threatens to move out. Trying to understand what she's going through, Dessie borrows books from the library about women's anatomy, incensing his wife because he took no interest in her five pregnancies, then delighting her with new foreplay skills. When Sharon's big day comes, Dessie takes her into the Rotunda hospital and frets like a worried dad in the waiting room. When the baby is born, Sharon nurses and burps her in the hospital ward, and proud Dessie suckles on a celebratory pint across the road in the Parnell Mooney, and burps himself.

Frears captures perfectly the Irish social anarchy of big families in small houses, where every serious conversation between parents is interrupted by rowdy kids and pets barging in one door and out the other, and there's always a chaotic queue for the bathroom in the morning. Frears' lively pace never lets up during the nine-month timeframe of the film, and both Meaney and Kellegher are outstanding in this provocative comedy about the woes and joys of unplanned pregnancy.

WAR OF THE BUTTONS
(1994) UK/FRA colour 93 mins

(Still courtesy of the Irish Film Archive of the Film Insititue of Ireland reproduced courtesy of Warner Bros)

Production Team

Producer .... David Puttnam/
Enigma Productions/
Productions de la Guéville
Director .... John Roberts
Screenplay .... Colin Welland,
based on Louis Pergaud's
novel *La Guerre des Boutons*
Cinematography .... Bruno de Keyser
Editor .... David Freeman
Musical Score .... Rachel Portman

Cast

Gregg Fitzgerald .... Fergus
Gerard Kearney .... Big Con
Darragh Naughton .... Boffin
Thomas Kavanagh .... Riley
Anthony Cunningham .... Little Con
Eveanna Ryan .... Marie
Danielle Tuite .... Fionnuala
Helen O'Leary .... Helen
Yvonne McNamara .... Maeve
John Coffey .... Geronimo
Paul Batt .... Gorilla
Karl Byrne .... Mickey Moon
Barry Walsh .... Willie
Niall Collins .... Chick
Colm Meaney .... Geronimo's dad
Bairbre Dowling .... Geronimo's mum
Jim Bartley .... Fergus' dad
Ger Ryan .... Fergus' mum
Liam Cunningham .... The teacher

212

WAR OF THE BUTTONS
(1994) UK/FRA colour 93 mins

Louis Pergaud's 1912 novel *La Guerre des Boutons* transferred successfully from pre-World War I France to modern west Cork as *War of the Buttons*, a *Lord of the Flies* adventure film in which pre-pubescent young fellas engage in tribal conflict and still get home in time for dinner and homework.

The boys of adjacent villages Ballydowse and Carrickdowse are divided into rival gangs, The Ballys and The Carricks. Their rivalry turns ugly when a Bally, Little Con (Anthony Cunningham) is called a 'tosspot' and dangled off a bridge by Carricks' bruiser Gorilla (Paul Batt). That night, the Ballys carry out a fiendish reprisal for calling their member a name they don't understand. They spraypaint the worst insult they can devise on the Carrickdowse church noticeboard.

The Carricks plan an attack which backfires, as the Ballys are expecting them. Gorilla is captured, and in a scene which inspires the film's title, Ballys' leader Fergus (Gregg Fitzgerald) cuts off the hefty boy's buttons, tie, braces and laces, to get him in big trouble with his parents. Thus a war begins and soon Carricks' leader Geronimo (John Coffey) gets revenge on Fergus by removing *his* buttons and ruining his clothing. Fergus gets a beating from his abusive father (Jim Bartley), who threatens him with borstal for refusing to admit who destroyed his outfit. This leads Fergus to plan a bizarre attack. When the Carricks arrive to face their foes they are ambushed by naked, howling Ballys, and retreat in disarray across a footbridge sabotaged by Ballydowse girls. It is a decisive victory for the Ballys, though they get embarrassed when the girls see them naked.

Fergus, inspired by a Battle of Kinsale history lesson from their teacher (Liam Cunningham), organises The Ballys as a feudal army complete with brightly painted standards, and leads them into battle on a piebald pony. Again they defeat the Carricks, this time capturing Geronimo, who cuts off his own buttons to deny Fergus the satisfaction. The Ballys keep Geronimo's school uniform jacket and shirt as war trophies.

Riley (Thomas Kavanagh), a disgruntled Bally, helps the Carricks by giving them a weapon to defeat the resourceful Fergus. While the Ballys celebrate in their boathouse HQ, Riley's father's new tractor roars onto the scene driven by Geronimo, who is determined to beat Fergus if not by smart tactics, then by sheer horsepower. Geronimo jumps from the speeding tractor which crashes through the Ballys HQ and plummets into a hole in the ground. Fergus is blamed by the adults of both villages for this mayhem, and fearful of their revenge and of his father's temper he flees to the hills. A manhunt ensues complete with gesticulating mobs of villagers and air rescue helicopter, as Fergus tries to escape up a craggy cliff face. Siding with his former adversary, Geronimo follows Fergus and eventually they are hoisted from the cliff by the helicopter crew. Both Fergus and Geronimo are sent to a reformatory for their misdeeds.

Shot on location in scenic West Cork in the villages of Castletownshend and Union Hall, *War of the Buttons* is a gritty children's film full of robust characters that are far from angelic. Mercifully free of the sappy sentimentality that coats the equivalent Hollywood product, this lively drama may give cause for alarm to parents of older boys about what their lads get up to when they go out to play.

AILSA
(1994) IRL colour 75 mins

(Still courtesy of the Irish Film Archive of the Film Insititue of Ireland reproduced courtesy of Temple Films)

Production Team

Producer ...... Temple Films/Emperor Films/
IFB/RTÉ/Ed Guiney/
Stephen Bradley/Kathryn Lennon
Director .... Paddy Breathnach
Screenplay ....Joseph O'Connor,
based on his own short story
Cinematography .... Cian de Buitléar
Editor .... Emer Reynolds
Musical Score .... Dario Marianelli

Cast

Brendan Coyle .... Miles Butler
Andrea Irvine ....Sara
Juliette Gruber .... Campbell Rourke
Gary Lydon .... Jack
Blanaid Irvine .... Vera
Brendan Cauldwell .... Moloney
Niall O'Brien .... Counsellor
Conor Mullen .... Emperor
Frankie McCafferty .... Post office assistant
Brendan Conroy .... Mr Johnson Jr
O Z Whitehead .... American tourist
Darragh Kelly .... Sean
Anne McGeown .... Mrs Foley
Simon Walsh .... Punk
Stuart Dunne .... Workman
Paddy Ashe .... Man in post office
Ned McLoughlin .... Postman

214

AILSA
(1994) IRL colour 75 mins

One of the first films released following the reinstatement of the Irish Film Board in 1993, Paddy Breathnach's aesthetically ambitious feature debut is a bold break from the visual conventions of Irish dramas of the time. With its slow pacing, limited dialogue and an absence of Irish iconography, *Ailsa* belongs more in the European art-film tradition than contemporary native releases. In essence a tale of fatal obsession, the film won the Best New Director award at the 1994 San Sebastian film festival for its creators – a cash prize that helped finance *Guiltrip* for producer Ed Guiney and *I Went Down* for director Breathnach.

Miles Butler (Brendan Coyle), a quiet, disaffected twenty-something, lives in a south Dublin flat with his more outgoing girlfriend Sara (Andrea Irvine), in a relationship devoid of emotion. The couple is on first-name terms with their neighbours in the shabby Edwardian house: Vera (*This Other Eden* scriptwriter Blanaid Irvine), an old lady with an exotic flapper past; and, in the flat below, their elderly landlord, Mr Johnson. Miles works as a calligrapher for a genealogy company in a Dickensian attic office in the city, and leads a stable if humdrum life.

When Mr Johnson electrocutes himself in his bath, Miles' stability starts to wobble. Nosing around Johnson's empty flat, he finds cash and a revolver, which he takes home. Attractive American Campbell Rourke (Juliette Gruber) moves into Johnson's flat soon after, and Miles immediately becomes fascinated with her, causing him to neglect Sara. As his relationship with Sara declines, his obsession with Campbell escalates from staring at her on the train, to stealing her letters. The changes in himself are so gradual that he scarcely notices, and soon he is paying her bills without her knowledge, and entering her name on the electoral register, claiming she's his wife. Miles' preoccupation makes him negligent at work and his boss, Mr Moloney (Brendan Cauldwell), a self-described "reasonable man", fires him. Miles malingers at home for days on end, agonising intensely about Campbell. He eventually snaps, severing ties with Sara, Campbell and, ultimately, with life itself.

Ailsa is a dark and moody piece that may be too slow-paced and uneventful to sustain viewers' attention on video, and deserves to be seen on the big screen. More downbeat and ultimately less histrionic than Polanski's obsessive flat-dweller shocker, *The Tenant*, it's a testament to Breathnach's assured hand that *Ailsa* doesn't come off as just another stalker-by-numbers feature. O'Connor, making his feature script debut (he had previously written Breathnach's 1991 short, *A Stone in the Heart*), charts Miles' claustrophobic descent in an unconventional fashion instead of using a series of sign-posted incidents. This claustrophobia is heightened by Miles' cramped working and living quarters, given relief only by the view through the windows of the DART as he commutes. Such is the impact of the eerie house (in Belgrave Square, Monkstown) on its residents that it looms like an additional inanimate character. Dario Marianelli's haunting score heightens the sense of loneliness and dread that permeate the film. Cian de Buitléar's striking cinematography and bold use of colour filters works in synthesis with the soundtrack and the whispered confidences of Miles' internal monologues, to create a brooding and absorbing debut feature.

215

THE SECRET OF ROAN INISH
(1994) US colour 101 mins

Production Team

Producer .... Sarah Green/Maggi Renzi/
Skerry Movies Corp
Director .... John Sayles
Screenplay .... John Sayles,
adapted from the book
The Secret of Ron Mor Skerry
by Rosalie K Fry
Cinematography .... Haskell Wexler
Editor .... John Sayles
Musical Score .... Mason Daring

Cast

Jeni Courtney .... Fiona Conneely
Mick Lally .... Hugh
Eileen Colgan .... Tess
John Lynch .... Tadhg
Richard Sheridan .... Eamon
Susan Lynch .... Selkie
Pat Slowey .... Priest
Dave Duffy .... Jim
Declan Hannigan .... Oldest brother
Máiréad Ni Ghallchóir .... Barmaid
Mícheál MacCartaigh .... Schoolmaster
Fergal McElherron .... Sean Michael
Brendan Conroy .... Flynn
Frankie McCafferty .... Tim
Gerald Rooney .... Liam
Suzanne Gallagher .... Selkie's daughter
Cillian Byrne .... Jamie

THE SECRET OF ROAN INISH
(1994) US colour 101 mins

American director John Sayles brought his considerable storytelling skills to Ireland in 1994 to make *The Secret of Roan Inish*, about a little girl's quest to find her lost baby brother and make her grandparents happy by returning to Roan Inish, their former island home. His adapted screenplay combines elements of fantasy and folklore with beautiful Donegal scenery to create a warm, sentimental drama for children and adults.

Jeni Courtney stars as Fiona Conneely, a young girl sent by her father to live with her grandparents by the sea after her mother dies. There she listens enthralled to fantastic tales her grandfather Hugh (Mick Lally) tells of how their family came to be living on Roan Inish. Fiona's gruff grandmother Tess (Eileen Colgan) dismisses his yarns as superstition and discourages Fiona from heeding him.

Fiona's mother's death and her brother Jamie's disappearance are painful subjects for her grandparents, but her frank questioning makes Hugh reveal how Jamie's cradle was washed out to sea and never seen again, just before the family was evacuated from Roan Inish. He believes that the sea took Jamie as punishment for the Conneely's abandonment of the island. Superstitious fishermen won't go near the place, but the Conneelys, Hugh and cousin Eamon (Richard Sheridan) still go there to set lobster pots. They take Fiona along, and leave her alone on the island while they work. In the derelict cottage that had once been her family home, she is surprised to find signs of life. On the beach she sees the footprints of a small child.

Fiona is told that she's not one of the 'dark ones' by a shopkeeper, comparing her with her cousin Tadhg (John Lynch), a swarthy young man gutting fish in the yard. Tadhg tells her the story of Liam Conneely (Gerald Rooney), who fell in love with a selkie, the human form taken by seals on the island. They started a family but she missed the sea and returned to it, leaving Liam and their children behind. Her descendants carry the dark strain and are happiest on the ocean. Fiona is fascinated by the family affinity with seals and by the baby footprints at Roan Inish, and persuades Eamon to take her back there again. There she sees Jamie playing in a field by the sea, and has trouble convincing Eamon that this vision is real. They return to the mainland to find that the grandparents have received an eviction notice. Fiona travels alone to Roan Inish, guided by a seal, and sees Jamie again. Realising how downhearted her grandparents are about the eviction, she devises a plan to cheer them up and get Jamie back. The determined little miss works with Eamon to restore the family cottage on the island and make it habitable for her grandparents, knowing this will make Jamie leave his life with the seals and live with his family on Roan Inish once more.

Jeni Courtney gives a physically pellucid but emotionally opaque performance as the fearless Fiona, in a film told very much from her enchanted viewpoint. Mick Lally plays Hugh with the warmth and sincerity that typifies his Irish television work over the years, delighting in his character's raconteurial delivery. The Donegal landscapes around Port Noo and Rosbeg are beautifully filmed by veteran cinematographer Haskell Wexler, and complemented by a soundtrack of simple, effective traditional music free of the lush synth-wash often used in films to boost their mystical quotient.

GUILTRIP
(1995) IRL/FRE/IT/SP colour 89 mins

(Still reproduced courtesy of Temple Films)

Production Team

Producer .... Temple Films/Ed Guiney/
Fandango/Giuseppe Pedersoli/
Stephen Bradley/David Collins/
IFB/Rod Stoneman
Director .... Gerard Stembridge
Screenplay .... Gerard Stembridge
Cinematography .... Eugene O'Connor
Editor .... Mary Finlay
Musical Score .... Brendan Power

Cast

Jasmine Russell .... Tina
Andrew Connolly .... Liam
Peter Hanly .... Ronnie
Pauline McLynn .... Joan
Michelle Houlden .... Michele
Frankie McCafferty .... Frank
Mikel Murfi .... Petey
Rebecca Chapman-Murphy .... Baby
Eamonn Hunt .... Armoury Seargent
Fintan Lee .... Kid
Victor Wheatly .... Brady's barman
Jimmy Keogh .... Man in toilet
Dave Bell .... Man in shop
Bríd ní Chumhaill .... Sadie
Ray McBride .... Security man

218

Noted Irish theatre and television director Gerry Stembridge wrote and directed *Guiltrip*, a harrowing account of an unhappy marriage between a domineering army corporal and his docile wife in small-town Ireland. The corporal, Liam Meagher (Andrew Connolly) may be a non-commissioned officer at the barracks, but he's a general in his own house, terrifying his unfortunate wife Tina (Jasmine Russell) by questioning her every movement on any given day, and keeping a military-style book of standing orders by which he commands her to live. He forbids Tina the company of a gregarious neighbour, Joan (Pauline McLynn), who he dislikes, and ruthlessly keeps her under his control. The action in the film takes place in a single day and night, during which Tina tries to please Liam by buying him an expensive gift, and finds herself amenable to the friendly overtures of a gormless hi-fi shop owner, Ronnie (Peter Hanly); and Liam pursues a much sleazier agenda with Ronnie's tarty wife Michele (Michelle Houlden). By the night's end, Tina and Liam each have a guilty secret to hide, hers a minor criminal act done on impulse, his darker and more brutal.

Made in Ireland at a time when divorce was still illegal, *Guiltrip* exposes the trap of the bad Irish marriage to severe critical scrutiny. The prevailing Irish laws permitted bullied wives like Tina very few avenues of escape, and many women in this hopeless situation lived in fear of regular beatings and worse from their husbands. Some relief seemed possible when a national referendum on divorce was held in the same year that *Guiltrip* was released. When the electorate voted by a tight margin to allow divorce, many people, including the writer/director Stembridge, felt that the film had been influential in tipping the balance towards a 'yes' vote.

Stembridge's solid directorial experience on stage and in the Irish broadcast media allowed him to draw very impressive performances from several cast members with limited film experience. Jasmine Russell is sympathetic as the uncomplicated soul Tina who faintly hopes to mend her marriage, and hasn't the confidence to leave her psychotic thug of a husband. Andrew Connolly plays the husband Liam with extraordinary control, as a study in loathing and menace that needs little physical force to intimidate his subordinates at the army barracks and the pub and to terrify his wife at home. Peter Hanly is tremendously effective as the cheerful, cliché-spouting idiot in the hi-fi shop who befriends lonely Tina. The fact that he's so annoying throughout is a testament to his acting ability, as he suffers insults and humiliations from almost every character in the film. His thick skin worn through by his wife's rejection of him, he finally breaks down near the end, becoming more sympathetic than repellent.

Stembridge shot his modestly scaled realist drama in the towns of Leixlip and Maynooth, County Kildare, with a suitably naff Irish showband soundtrack. He steers his difficult theme to its grim conclusion with a steady momentum, marred only slightly by his overuse of flashback. Stembridge's script for *Guiltrip* won the award for Best Screenplay at Thessaloniki Film Festival in 1995.

A MAN OF NO IMPORTANCE
(1995) IRL/UK colour 99 mins

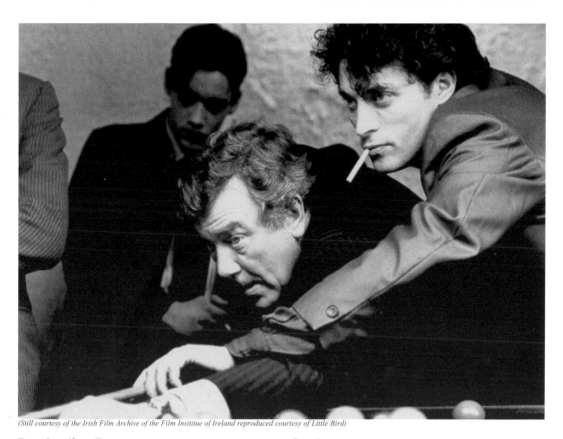

(Still courtesy of the Irish Film Archive of the Film Insititue of Ireland reproduced courtesy of Little Bird)

Production Team

Producer .... Majestic Films/BBC Films/
               Little Bird/Jonathan Cavendish
Director .... Suri Krishnamma
Screenplay .... Barry Devlin
Cinematograpéhy .... John Ward
Editor .... David Freeman
Musical Score .... Allan Wilson

Cast:

Albert Finney .... Alfie Byrne
Brenda Fricker .... Lily Byrne
Michael Gambon .... Carney
Tara Fitzgerald .... Adele Rice
Rufus Sewell .... Robbie Fay
Patrick Malahide .... Carson
David Kelly .... Baldy
Mick Lally .... Fr Kenny
Anna Manahan .... Mrs Grace
Joe Pilkington .... Ernie Lally
Brendan Conroy .... Rasher Flynn
Joan O'Hara .... Mrs Crowe
Eileen Reid .... Mrs Rock
Eileen Conroy .... Mrs Curtin
Maureen Egan .... Mrs Dunne
Paddy Ashe .... Mr Ryan
Paudge Behan .... Alfie's attacker

A MAN OF NO IMPORTANCE
(1995) IRL/UK colour 99 mins

In Dublin in 1963, lonely middle-aged bus conductor Alfie Byrne (Albert Finney) subsumes his homosexuality in an abiding passion for the dramas of Oscar Wilde. He regales his regular passengers on the number 34 with passages from Wilde's plays, and cajoles them to join his amateur drama troupe to perform *Salome* – amusing his driver Robbie Fay (Rufus Sewell), of whom he is more than a little fond. Undaunted by his failure to get beyond rehearsals in previous attempts at mounting a play, Alfie only needs a Salome to complete his cast. In the role of Herod he casts his vulgar neighbour, the butcher Carney (Michael Gambon), "the backbone, the guts, the very tripes" of the production. The pious boor Carney decides that *Salome* is a salacious play, and bullies the parish priest (Mick Lally) to stop Alfie just when he finds his lead, Adele Rice (Tara Fitzgerald). Alfie's sister Lily (Brenda Fricker), with whom he lives above Carney's butcher shop, is delighted to hear about Adele, thinking that confirmed bachelor Alfie fancies her for more than the play.

Adele seems an innocent Roscommon girl, and Alfie invests a lot of faith in this perception of her even as he prepares her to play the biblical bellydancer. When he discovers that she's no angel, the naïve conductor is devastated. He seeks comfort and cuddles in a gay bar (shot at The Stag's Head in Dublin), dressed in a grim caricature of Wildean flamboyance, and gets beaten and robbed by some rough trade (Paudge Behan) for his trouble. He bravely explains his loneliness to his sister, who shows him some badly needed sympathy. His oddball cast on the bus sticks by him despite thunderous denunciation by Carney, as does Robbie, who finally consents, to Alfie's unspeakable joy, to join the acting troupe. Alfie loses a Salome, but gains a Jokanaan.

The strengths of this film lie in the intelligent, sensitive scriptwriting by Celtic rock legend Barry Devlin, and the central performance by the inestimable Albert Finney. Devlin handles Alfie's late-in-life sexual awakening with delicacy and understatement, and his rich dialogue for the minor parts forgives his excess cleverness in character-naming (the butcher is called Carney, and Alfie's bus inspector nemesis Carson is named after the lawyer who tore Wilde apart on the witness stand at his 1895 trial). Finney warmly engages as the ageing innocent who understands little of his own sexuality and feels deep hurt at the anger that others direct at something he considers beautiful and good. Despite occasional lapses in accent – the sounds of his native Salford surface at impassioned moments in his speeches about art and the love that dare not speak its name – Finney is a joy to watch throughout. The same cannot be said of the objects of his affection; Rufus Sewell and Tara Fitzgerald flounder with their Irish accents, and fit awkwardly in the roles of alluring youth that the script accords them. Fitzgerald, credible neither as the naïve farm girl that Alfie wants her to be, nor the wanton that Carney decides she is, delivers a hammy performance, more salami than Salome. Director Suri Krishnamma keeps a faint hand on the controls, and seems content to let the film's characters drive more than the bus. But Devlin's script takes up the slack, and fulfils the promise of his feature screenwriting debut the previous year with *All Things Bright and Beautiful*.

THE ELIMINATOR
(1996) IRL colour 72 mins

(Still courtesy of the Irish Film Archive of the Film Insititue of Ireland)

Production Team

Producer .... Enda Hughes/Denis O'Hare/
Michael Hughes/Cousins Pictures
Director .... Enda Hughes
Screenplay .... Enda Hughes
Cinematography .... Enda Hughes
Musical Score .... Stuart Neville
and Chris Corrigan

Cast

Barry Wallace .... Stone
Michael Hughes .... O'Brien
Mik Duffy .... Hawk
Edward Hughes .... Johnson
Paul McAvinchey .... Scorpio
Tom Lenagh .... Mooney
Pat Quinn .... Torturer
Dermot Hughes .... Crazy Priest
Donna Crilly .... Mrs Hawk
Simon Donnelly .... Cuchulainn
Jacky Murphy .... McCool
Fergal French .... St Patrick
Pauline Andrews .... Crash Helmet Guard
Shirley Sheik .... Sui Young Chen
Denis O'Hare .... McDavitt

THE ELIMINATOR
(1996) IRL colour 72 mins

Resourceful director and Armagh native Enda Hughes harvests the guts of teenage boys' favourite films, puts them under the steamhammer of his imagination and gives them a good pounding to make his first feature *The Eliminator*. Vietnam, vampires, car chases, torture chambers, and flesh-eating zombies are all packed into an action-shocker with a budget of less than ten grand (a few quid more and an extra day's shooting, and Hughes would probably have added cowboys, pirates and space aliens to the mix). This fearless young director cuts the brake cables and puts a brick on the accelerator from the word go, making his film feel like a fast-forward videotape. The plot is as flimsy as it is lurid, but provides cast and crew with ample opportunity to indulge in high-speed mayhem.

A brainy young Irishman, O'Brien (Michael Hughes), is kidnapped from his Oxford research lab by the evil Scorpio (Paul McAvinchey), brought to a quarry in Cornwall, and tortured to make him reveal secrets of his design for a military assault vehicle, the Viper. A sinister organisation known as 'the Organisation' sends Vietnam vet Stone (Barry Wallace) to save the scientist. Stone swoops down in his little black plane, despatches Scorpio's goons with his enormous guns and rescues O'Brien. They retrieve the Viper, only to see it destroyed in a shuddering car chase. They fly back to Ireland and Stone explains how he came to be in Nam with the Organisation's eye-patched and prosthetic-armed bionic mutant Hawk (Mik Duffy).

Stone realises that Hawk gave him dodgy maps for the rescue mission, sending him into maximum danger. Back in Ireland, the demented Hawk, who has borne a grudge against Stone since their Nam days (green filters and over-exposure turn the local Keady countryside tropical for this flashback scene), shoots Stone dead after an argument. That night Hawk is devastated by psychotic nightmares about a zombie Stone, his head wrapped in bandages, attacking him in his bed. Hawk demands protection from the Organisation to keep the undead Stone at bay.

The next day the Stone zombie attacks Hawk's house, but is repelled by the Organisation's troops. At a graveyard, Stone uses incantations from the apocryphal 'Celtic Book of the Dead' to raise a zombie army to defeat Hawk's forces. The maggotty corpses devour the flesh of Hawk's men but fail to eat them all. Stone invokes the spirits of more formidable warriors, Cuchulainn and Finn McCool, and raises St Patrick from the dead. St Patrick, with his aversion to serpents, beats Stone about the head with his crozier for mentioning the Viper. The saint persuades Hawk to lay down his weapons but not Stone, who sets off a cataclysmic explosion that kills them all. The film then fades to black with Stiff Little Fingers' Belfast punk classic 'Alternative Ulster'.

Hughes kept costs down by having his actors wear their own clothes, improvise their own lines and crash their own cars. Working with an economy that makes Roger Corman look like Erich von Stroheim, Hughes' film is a resounding rebuttal to wannabe film-makers in Ireland who complain they can't finance their pet project about guns, car chases and girls without governmemt help. For sheer exuberance, from start to graveyard ghoulfest finale, *The Eliminator* marks Hughes down as a one of the most promising Irish directors of his generation.

MICHAEL COLLINS
(1996) IRL/UK colour 132 mins

Production Team

Producer .... Stephen Woolley
Director .... Neil Jordan
Screenplay .... Neil Jordan
Cinematography .... Chris Menges
Editor .... J Patrick Duffner,
Tony Lawson
Musical Score .... Elliot Goldenthal

Cast

Liam Neeson .... Michael Collins
Aidan Quinn .... Harry Boland
Julia Roberts .... Kitty Kiernan
Alan Rickman .... Eamon De Valera
Stephen Rea .... Ned Broy
Ian Hart .... Joe O'Reilly
Richard Ingram .... British Officer
John Kenny .... Patrick Pearse
Roman McCairbe .... Thomas McDonagh
Jer O'Leary .... Thomas Clarke
Michael Dwyer .... James Connolly
Martin Murphy .... Captain Lee-Wilson
Sean McGinley .... Smith
Gary Whelan .... Hoey
Frank O'Sullivan .... Kavanagh
Frank Laverty .... Sean McKeoin
Jonathan Rhys-Myers .... Collins' assassin

MICHAEL COLLINS
(1996) IRL/UK colour 132 mins

Of all the formidable heroes and statesmen who came to prominence during Ireland's War of Independence, the character most worthy of a lavish film biography is undoubtedly Michael Collins. The dashing young Corkman who masterminded the guerilla war against the British on the streets of Dublin and negotiated the 1921 Anglo-Irish Treaty in London led a life rich in romance, courage and intrigue, tragically cut short at the age of 31 by a sniper's bullet. A handsome and charismatic figure, his appeal for film-makers yielded several screen interpretations with varying degrees of accuracy, before Irish director Neil Jordan finally did justice to the man almost 75 years after his death. The Collins character played by Brian Aherne in *Beloved Enemy* in 1936 had little to do with reality in a war film in which the heaviest artillery is Cupid's arrow; Michael Redgrave's portrayal of Ireland's treaty negotiator in *Shake Hands with the Devil* in 1959 served more as a rational foil to James Cagney's volatile republican than a Collins character of any significance in his own right (ironically, Redgrave was knighted for his services to theatre and film in the same year that he played this enemy of the Crown). Neil Jordan's *Michael Collins* adheres far more closely to the facts of Collins' life and, with limited use of dramatic licence, provides a fascinating insight into the events leading up to the bitter Civil War that became a taboo subject for two generations of Irish people. His accomplishment in making this epic film, working with a crew and cast that are almost all home-grown Irish, was rewarded with the Best Picture prize at the 1996 Venice Film Festival. Liam Neeson won the Best Actor award at the same festival for his performance in the title role.

Jordan both directed and wrote the script for a project that he had been striving to bring to the screen for years. And if his screenplay makes the sort of compromises that must be made to compress the life of a man into two hours, he remains true to the story that he wants to tell. Jordan's central concerns are Collins' passionate devotion to the cause of Irish independence, his friendship forged and sundered with fellow freedom fighter Harry Boland and their romantic rivalry over Kitty Kiernan. The forces of the crown and Eamon De Valera fill the villain roles.

This approach inevitably simplifies or omits a wide range of historic events, and may annoy some viewers with a detailed knowledge of those times, but the broader audience can view the film as a gripping, slightly fictionalised drama and history primer taking us through the years 1916-1922 in Dublin. And for the audience that doesn't know or care about history, it succeeds on its own terms as a rollicking wartime adventure.

Jordan's depiction of these turbulent times is solidly acted for the most part by a stellar cast. Liam Neeson plays the role of Collins with the right balance of exuberance and delicacy that made up this complex character. He gives the performance of his career, topping his Oscar-nominated work in *Schindler's List*. Playing a figure who was a hunted gunman, a gallant lover and a boyish prankster all at once, Neeson is every inch the man described in his day as 'The Minister for Bloody Mayhem' of the

225

Free State Government, and very likely to cause disaffection to His Majesty George V.

Aidan Quinn, as Boland, gives a more understated performance that explodes into angry fission over his belief that Collins sold Ireland short in the London negotiations – with the bitter subtext that Collins had also stolen his true love.

The third corner of Michael Collins' romantic triangle is less securely pinned down. Julia Roberts as Kitty Kiernan is ineffectual at best, and there is nothing about her performance that makes her seem irresistible to her formidable suitors. Kitty Kiernan was by all accounts a capable woman who ran her family's extensive business interests from the time her parents died, when she was still in her teens. A vivacious socialite, she was much sought after by the eligible young men of Dublin society. But Julia Roberts contrives a two-dimensional Kitty, a spoiled coquette who enjoys playing her two admirers against each other when they have much more important things to worry about, like the destiny of a small nation. Leaving aside gripes about her deplorable attempt at an Irish accent, she does little justice to a strong, independent woman and an underrated exemplar of Irish womanhood.

A much larger figure pops up from the history books to get the 2D treatment as well. Jordan clearly has little sympathy for the Dev, and the portrayal of the Long Fella as a prissy manipulator with an unconcealed dislike for the rough gunslingers under his command is more than a little one-sided. Actor Alan Rickman does a fine job of the De Valera part as written, and is completely convincing in appearance, voice and mannerisms. But if Dev had been the tricky, irritable character of Jordan's devising, and nothing more, he would hardly have commanded such fierce loyalty from his men, Collins included, until they fell out over the Treaty. Collins had risked his life travelling to England to spring a disguised De Valera (dressed in furs and a daffy hat – a transformation which Rickman's Dev carries off without much gusto) from Lincoln Jail in 1919. And when De Valera was in America on a fundraising tour that same year, Collins' loyalty to his commander compelled him to go to Wicklow once a week to personally bring his wife and children their stipend from the Volunteers. Collins would hardly have taken the same risk for Jordan's Dev.

The screenplay may do Dev a disservice in presenting him as petty and conniving, but Jordan's greatest distortion of facts is the implication that, as leader of the anti-Treaty faction, De Valera actively directed the assassin (Jonathan Rhys-Myers) who killed Collins with a single shot to the head at Béal na Bláth, County Cork, in 1922. The entire film is set in Ireland, but the crucial events that sealed Collins fate and made him a martyr take place in London. A reluctant diplomat, Collins was seconded to the delegation sent to London in 1921 to negotiate the terms of Ireland's independence. De Valera, the head of state, stayed in Dublin. It is widely held that De Valera knew in advance that the negotiations would not go well for the Irish delegates, and by keeping his distance from the negotiating table he could deflect blame for the outcome from himself onto Collins. The compromise solution arrived at fell well short of full independence, making Collins a scapegoat and a target. In his own words, he signed his death warrant when he signed that Treaty.

Viewers who are unfamiliar with these details of Irish history might know the protagonists sitting across the table from Collins in London. Lloyd George, Churchill, Chamberlain and Birkenhead spent five months with Collins' team before arriving at a result that would plunge Ireland into civil war. Given that the schism caused by this Treaty continued to shape Irish politics for the rest of the century, it would have helped viewers to understand both the pressures that Collins was under and the calibre of people he was dealing with, by showing a few scenes from the Downing Street talks. These minor criticisms aside, however, the film conveys superbly the tone of the era, and takes sides as it must on a subject about which there will never be a consensus. Jordan has made more intriguing films, but he may never make a more important one. This unflinching stare at the lofty idealism and the harsh reality of nation building is a powerful testament to a man whose short life had immense influence on the course of modern Irish history. Michael Collins, a warmonger turned peacemaker, is finally given due tribute by a master film-maker.

SOME MOTHER'S SON
(1996) IRL colour 112 mins

(Still courtesy of the Irish Film Archive of the Film Insititue of Ireland reproduced courtesy of Arthur Lappin)

Production Team
Producer .... Edward Burke, Arthur Lappin
Director .... Terry George
Screenplay .... Terry George, Jim Sheridan
Cinematography .... Geoffrey Simpson
Editor .... Craig McKay
Musical Score .... Bill Whelan

Cast
Helen Mirren .... Kathleen Quigley
Fionnuala Flanagan .... Annie Higgins
Aidan Gillen .... Gerard Quigley
David O'Hara .... Frank Higgins
John Lynch .... Bobby Sands
Tom Hollander .... Farnsworth
Tim Woodward .... Harrington
Ciarán Hinds .... Danny Boyle
Geraldine O'Rawe .... Alice Quigley
Gerard McSorley .... Father Daly
Dan Gordon .... Inspector McPeake
Grainne Delany .... Theresa Higgins
Ciarán Fitzgerald .... Liam Quigley
Robert Lang .... Government Minister
Stephen Hogan .... Young Turk

SOME MOTHER'S SON
(1996) IRL colour 112 mins

Terry George's directorial debut is a harrowing drama charting the lives of two mothers from different backgrounds, and their relationship with their sons, during Northern Ireland's lowest ebb of despair – the 1981 hunger strikes by IRA prisoners in the Long Kesh Prison in Belfast. The strike lasted 217 days, during which ten prisoners starved themselves to death for the right to be treated as political prisoners instead of common criminals. The mothers are played by Helen Mirren, as Kathleen Quigley, a widowed teacher, who has ignored 'the Troubles' for years, but finds herself involved when her son Gerard (Aidan Gillen) is arrested and convicted of firearms charges; and Fionnuala Flanagan as Annie Higgins, a farmer and active republican, whose son Frank (David O'Hara) is jailed at the same time as Quigley's, following the sons' shootout with the British army.

The two mothers are drawn closer together as their sons join the H-Block protests; first on the blanket, then the so-called 'dirty protest' (the prison authorities denied the use of bathroom facilities to prisoners refusing to wear uniforms), through the final horror of the hunger strike. They become friends, in spite of Mrs Quigley's hatred of violence and all that the IRA represents, and the differences that divide them are forgotten in their mutual concern for their children.

George, who co-wrote the screenplay with Jim Sheridan, recreates the anguish of those months through the experiences of ordinary people who were directly affected by the tragic waste of life. The wrenching images in the hospital wing of the prison and the pietà of distraught mothers and their near-comatose sons make for very harrowing viewing, and bring back all too vividly the feelings of abject pessimism that pervaded Ireland during the political deadlock. He also demonstrates how the feelings of people who had ignored the Troubles could calcify into a hard, bitter cynicism during the course of the hunger strike.

Given Terry George's republican background – he did time in jail in the 1970s for his involvement in the nationalist cause – considerable effort is made in the film to humanise both sides of the drama; certainly more than he is given credit for, by those who see this film as a one-sided, pro-IRA propaganda piece. When two prison officers are murdered by the IRA, the devastation of their families as they witness the shootings is clearly shown, as is the condemnation of the murders by the Catholic Church. A botched attempt by Kathleen to teach Annie Higgins to drive on the strand ends with the car being bogged down in sand as the tide comes in; their unlikely rescuers is a platoon of squaddies on patrol in the dunes. The soldiers lift them out of trouble, forcing the die-hard republican Higgins to reluctantly concede to the pacifist Quigley that she doesn't hate them all. And within the British government, George devises a fictional diplomat sincerely committed to ending the appalling conditions in the jail without loss of life, in contrast with a two-dimensional villain from the Foreign Office who wants the strike defeated regardless of cost.

George is not uncritical of the IRA. While the film goes further than most to show what the organisation is about in terms of objectives and strategy, it doesn't gloss over their less heroic activities, such as robbing banks and using funerals to enlist the undecided to support their cause. Ciarán Hinds as the leader of Sinn Fein in Belfast presents a sinister, manipulative character. The IRA is generally depicted on-screen through the eyes of a gunman who's had enough and wants out, whether it be Stephen Rea in *The Crying Game*, Mickey Rourke in *Prayer for the Dying* or James Mason in *Odd Man Out*. George's depiction of a highly organised paramilitary and political machine is a rare depiction of the IRA than runs a lot closer to reality than Hollywood usually allows.

Some Mother's Son stumbles on the issue of Unionism, and little effort is made to explain the phenomenon to the uninitiated. A British government without a sizeable majority in parliament is inevitably reliant on the backing of Northern Ireland's Unionist MP's to stay in power; this fact is central to the difficulty of solving the Northern Ireland problem. But with the exception of a crowd waving Union Jacks at the polling station on the night hunger striker Bobby Sands (John Lynch) was elected MP, Unionists are conspicuously absent from the film; to a viewer who doesn't know the details, it seems yet again that the problem is polarised between Catholic Irish

(Still courtesy of the Irish Film Archive of the Film Insititue of Ireland reproduced courtesy of Arthur Lappin)

nationalists on one side, and the British government in London and its armed forces in Ulster on the other. A film as ambitious as this in its attempts to show the political complexity and the human drama might have shown more of the Unionist involvement in the political stalemate.

George's film may strive for balance, but his slant remains inevitably nationalist – when starvation gives each hunger striker the beatific face of an El Greco Messiah, you know that this is no documentary. But it confounds the imagination to think that there is a corollary to this grim version of events, in which the British government and its method of dealing with the protests can be shown in a favourable light. As George unfolds this traumatic saga of hopes raised and dashed and young lives lost, the most frightening scene in this disturbing film is not that of a blind and skeletal Bobby Sands (John Lynch) convulsing and dry retching as he lies near death in his hospital bed, nor the sight of a military superpower with helicopters, night-vision goggles and hi-tech weaponry, descending on an Irish farmhouse during Christmas dinner. It is instead the opening scene of the film, showing actual news footage of Margaret Thatcher, quoting St Francis of Assisi as her role model on the subjects of harmony and compassion, whilst pursuing a callous policy of intransigence that led to the deaths of ten men.

THIS IS THE SEA
(1996) UK colour 104 mins

(Still courtesy of the Irish Film Archive of the Film Insititue of Ireland)

Production Team

Producer .... Michael Garland/Pembridge
Director .... Mary McGuckian
Screenplay .... Mary McGuckian
Editor .... Kant Pan
Cinematography .... Des Whelan
Editor .... Kant Pan
Musical Score .... Mike Scott/
Brian Kennedy

Cast

Samantha Morton .... Hazel Stokes
Ross McDade .... Malachy McAliskey
Dearbhla Molloy .... Ma Stokes
Ian McElhinney .... Da Stokes
Marc O'Shea .... Jef Stokes
Richard Harris .... Old Man Jacobs
John Lynch .... Padhar McAliskey
Stella McCusker .... Ma McAliskey
Mary McGuckian .... Cathy
Gabriel Byrne .... Rohan
Des McAleer .... Inspector Wilson
James Nesbitt .... Constable Hubert Porter
Richard Leaf .... Pastor Lamthorn
Caolan Byrne .... Ezekiel Lamthorn
Liam Bradley .... Bass player in bar
Margery McGuckian .... Mrs Pready
Jim Sheridan .... Station master

THIS IS THE SEA
(1996) UK colour 104 mins

Writer/director Mary McGuckian devised a lively Romeo-and-Juliet update in a Northern Ireland setting for her second feature, *This is the Sea*. Filmed in her native province during the 1994 ceasefire, the romance that provides the charm and heart of the story involves a happy-go-lucky teenage boy from Belfast and a sheltered girl from a remote farm in the country.

Malachy McAliskey (Ross McDade) spots Hazel Stokes (Samantha Morton) at Balmoral Agricultural Show, where he's selling hot dogs with his brother Padhar (John Lynch), a taxi driver. She's there with her elderly neighbour, Jacobs (Richard Harris), selling cattle. Malachy is more than smitten, and the naïve Hazel clearly feels the first flush of attraction to the opposite sex. The pair begin an innocent relationship, neither one realising that they come from different religions, and neither one caring when they do find out. Malachy's family is Catholic, and Hazel belongs to the Plymouth Brethren, a Protestant sect. Hazel doesn't get out of the house much because her parents are strict, but with the complicity of the cryptic Jacobs she gets to meet Malachy in Belfast at the weekend by pretending she's going to prayer meetings in the city. Hazel's volatile brother Jef (Marc O'Shea) doesn't believe her cover story and follows her into town to discover the truth.

Malachy, meanwhile, is under pressure from a sinister IRA leader Rohan (Gabriel Byrne, hamming uproariously like it's a mafia comedy, all wicked grins, exaggerated swaggers, and invasions of personal space) to join the allegedly off-duty organisation. Malachy is a good driver, and the 'ra needs him. His older brother Padhar looks out for him, but gets in trouble himself when the IRA 'borrows' his taxi, stuffs it with semtex, and tries to blame the loyalists for disrupting the ceasefire. As the romance intensifies between the young lovers, so does the will to end their forbidden love, and once again Jacobs is the catalyst. The elderly farmer helps Jef get his hands on a bomb from an unspecified loyalist paramilitary outfit. But Jef's botched attempt at getting rid of his sister's lover goes wrong, devastating both Malachy's family and his own.

As often happens in films about Northern Ireland, the contrasts between the two communities are presented in such a way as to favour the Catholics. The raucous McAliskey household is warm and hearty, with a loving mother and foodfights at teatime; the grim Stokes' farmhouse is a place of austerity and loaded silences. Having piled on these differences, McGuckian then draws from them a very credible love affair between her two charming leads, who show a depth and delicacy in their relationship uncommon in such young actors. Samantha Morton delights as the ingenue Hazel, not yet a woman nor still a child, but full of curiosity about the world beyond the farm. And Ross McDade plays Malachy with real charm, as the light-hearted messer who takes love seriously when he meets the girl from the glens. John Lynch, one of the outstanding Irish actors of his generation, is impressive as always as the brother Padhar.

This is the Sea also features a cameo from director Jim Sheridan, who had played Jonathan Swift in McGuckian's directorial debut the previous year, *Words on the Window Pane*. The son of a railway man himself, Sheridan plays the station master who provides an alibi for Jacobs when his bomb goes off in Belfast.

I WENT DOWN
(1997) IRL/UK colour 105 mins

(Still courtesy of the Irish Film Archive of the Film Insititue of Ireland)

Production Team

Producer .... Robert Walpole/Treasure/
BBC/Buena Vista/Euskal Media/
Irish Film Board/RTÉ
Director .... Paddy Breathnach
Screenplay .... Conor McPherson
Cinematography .... Cian De Buitléar
Editor .... Emer Reynolds
Musical Score .... Dario Maranelli

Cast

Brendan Gleeson .... Bunny Kelly
Peter McDonald .... Git Hynes
Peter Caffrey .... Frank Grogan
Tony Doyle .... Tom French
Donal O'Kelly .... A friendly face
David Wilmot .... Anto
Antoine Byrne .... Sabrina Bradley
Michael McElhatton .... Johnner Doyle
Joe Gallagher .... Steo Gannon
Liam Regan .... Little boy at Teresa's
Kevin Hely .... Petrol station attendant
Eamonn Hunt .... Cork barman
Frank O'Sullivan .... Cork man number 1
Jason Byrne .... Cork man number 2
Eamonn Kelly .... Cork man number 3
Carly Baker .... Caroline

I WENT DOWN
(1997) IRL/UK colour 105 mins

The prospect of watching yet another violent indie crime caper, buddy flick and road movie all rolled into one might repel audiences already pulped once too often by Tarantino imitators. And if this plotline sounds way too familiar – two minor criminal types sent on a vague mission by a sinister gang boss find themselves out of their league, but within striking distance of a lot of money, if only they can outwit the bigtime mobsters – it's because we're in a vein already mined to the point of exhaustion by the Coen Brothers and Quentin himself. Tarantino may not have patented the idea of two idiots talking rubbish to pass the time en route to robbing, kidnapping, or killing someone they've never met, but he did perfect it. And anyone who uses this as a premise for a film must inevitably be compared with him.

But what makes Paddy Breathnach's *I Went Down* different from the rest of the Tarantino homages are screenwriter Conor McPherson's ripe Dublin dialogue, set in a bluntly realist depiction of the less glamorous parts of Ireland, and the shocking disclosure that young Irish people are as hormonally propelled into guilt-free sexual escapades as their counterparts anywhere else in the world. Add to the mix the terrific performances director Breathnach gets from his lead actors Peter McDonald and Brendan Gleeson, and *I Went Down* constitutes a fresh and very Irish take on an American movie genre, as seen through the eyes of two incompetent criminals.

The ill-matched duo Git Hynes (Peter McDonald), a languid individual who won't put two words together where one will do, and braindead motormouth Bunny Kelly (Brendan Gleeson), sporting monumental sideburns and shoes made from several species of lizard, are thrown together on a mission by sinister gang leader Tom French (played with stubbly menace by Tony Doyle). French has got something on both of them, and if they carry out this little job for him, they're off the hook. Git is dragged into French's scheme by his mate Anto (David Wilmot) over some gambling debts that French's henchmen Steo (Joe Gallagher) and Johnner (Michael McElhatton) try to settle the hard way. Bunny's involvement in the job comes about for more delicate reasons that become clear as the plot goes along.

Git and Bunny hit the road to Cork in a stolen car to fetch French's business associate Frank Grogan (Peter Caffrey), bring him to meet 'a friendly face', and retrieve some missing funds for the Dublin gang leader. Things don't go according to plan, but when they finally rescue Frank from what looks a lot like captivity, Frank doesn't seem too happy to be rescued. This causes Git some confusion. Frank is a loquacious rogue who has a much clearer idea of what's going on than Bunny or Git, but quickly realises that he'll get more mileage out of feigning ignorance to French's agenda, and where the hidden money might be. Nasty encounters with Frank's associates force Git and Bunny to look out for each other, and a friendship of sorts evolves between them. They resolve to tackle the mob head-on and and track down the missing loot together, risking their lives in the process.

As the older and more experienced of the two, Bunny fancies himself a mentor to

I WENT DOWN
(1997) IRL/UK colour 105 mins

the fledgling criminal Git, renting him a gun for the duration of the job, but charging him an extortionate rate per bullet to keep things professional and business-like between them. He throws in a free firearms lesson for Git, showing him how to behave like a psycho and make the perp at the business end of the gun barrel believe that he's just crazy enough to use it.

Bunny possesses a certain amount of street cunning, but when he tries to operate at a higher level, he gets stuck. Cogent thoughts are so foreign to him they need a visa to get into his head. Bunny's trouble is not just that he won't shut up, but that he keeps talking when he has no idea what he's trying to say. Theories on romance are best avoided by the hard of thinking, but Bunny is undeterred by his lack of mental firepower on the subject. He lectures Git on the nuances of women until they're both thoroughly confused, and the audience is rolling around the place laughing. Brendan Gleeson's Bunny is consistently hilarious, and his comedic performance fortifies his reputation as one Ireland's most versatile actors. Making his screen debut, Peter McDonald delivers an assured performance as the reluctant criminal Git, recently released from jail for a crime in which he was barely involved, and roped into the caper for reasons outside his control. The supporting cast is just as impressive – Peter Caffrey as the captive whose inability to shut up finds him relegated to the boot of the car for much of the journey, and Tony Doyle as the gang leader, a walking five o'clock shadow of tired hatred.

I Went Down is as low key as its title suggests. And as screen criminals go, the two main charcters Bunny and Git are probably the most inept that ever stepped – if they fired their guns at the ground they'd probably miss. The narrative through which they bumble appears loose and shapeless, going nowhere in particular and in no hurry to get there. But this shaggy mutt of a story settles into its own pace, gliding with ease from ribald comedy to raw violence to nail-biting tension. McPherson evolves a complex storyline that is shot through with spot-on banter every meandering step of the way. He's a smart enough writer to simultaneously quote Plato and make reference to his lead character's jail time and sexual preferences, all in the innocous title of the film, and too tongue-in-cheek about it to seem pretensious. The quality of his monologue writing had already been proven in his award-winning stage dramas *The Weir*, *This Lime Tree Bower* and *St Nicholas*. In this, his first screenplay, his ear for film dialogue is as finely tuned as it is for the stage, as he deftly skips around the trap of putting overly polished words in the mouths of thick-tongued galoots like Git and Bunny.

But *I Went Down* is not entirely without flaws – anytime romance rears its beautiful head, the quality of the dialogue dips down into sentimental mush. The romance sub-plot that opens and closes the film adds nothing to the overall plot, except to underline the fact that Git is a big sap, stuck on a girl (Antoine Byrne) who ran off with his best friend. This might pass unnoticed but for the fact that it bookends the hole story. In his other romantic encounter in the film, Git makes a frank disclosure in bed the morning after to the girl who picks him up at a hotel disco. It's the sort of rubbish guys make up to get girls in between the sheets, not when they're already there. And while it may not be necessary to end a circuitous story with a resounding finale, the punchline of Git and Bunny's mission for the Dublin mob don is lame enough to do an injustice to the strong scenes that precede it. But the skill with which those scenes are put together by Breathnach, McPherson and their leads make the journey well worthwhile, and of greater value than the destination.

I Went Down enjoyed enormous critical acclaim in Ireland, and the punters turned out in droves, making the film the most successful Irish indie feature ever. On mainland Europe, Breathnach once again won the New Director Award at the San Sebastian Film Festival, the first to do so twice in a competition open to directors submitting their first or second film. McPherson's script won the Best Screenplay Award at the same festival.

(Still courtesy of the Irish Film Archive of the Film Insititue of Ireland)

THE BUTCHER BOY
(1998) IRL colour 106 mins

Production Team

Producer .... Redmond Morris/
Stephen Woolley
Director .... Neil Jordan
Screenplay ...... Neil Jordan and Pat McCabe,
adapted from McCabe's
book of the same name
Cinematography .... Adrian Biddle
Editor .... Tony Lawson
Musical Score .... Elliot Goldenthal

Cast

Eamonn Owens .... Francie Brady (boy)
Stephen Rea .... Da Brady
and Francie Brady (adult)
Aisling O'Sullivan .... Annie Brady
Fiona Shaw .... Mrs Nugent
Alan Boyle .... Joe Purcell
Ardal O'Hanlon .... Mr Purcell
Andrew Fullerton .... Philip Nugent
John Olohan .... Mr Nugent
Ian Harte .... Uncle Alo
John Kavanagh .... Dr Boyd
Sean McGinley ....Sergeant
Rosaleen Linehan .... Mrs Canning
Milo O'Shea .... Father Sullivan
Brendan Gleeson .... Father Bubbles
Sinéad O'Connor .... Our Lady
Patrick McCabe .... Jimmy the Skite

THE BUTCHER BOY
(1998) IRL colour 106 mins

Director Neil Jordan succeeded in filming the unfilmable, in this darkly comic drama adapted from Pat McCabe's book and set in Monaghan in the early-1960s. The internal monologue of a cheerful psychopath gave the book a puddle-of-consciousness structure that seemed impossible to translate to film. But Jordan, collaborating with McCabe on the script, made that translation very successfully and to great critical acclaim, winning the best Director Award at the 1998 Berlin Film Festival.

In this hilarious and unsettling film, a long-term psychiatric patient named Francie Brady (Stephen Rea) tells the grim story of his early life – the suicide of his depressed mother (Aisling O'Sullivan) after he ran away from home to escape his parents' arguments, the drunken squandering of musical talent by his alcoholic father (Stephen Rea) and his own torments at the hands of cruel neighbours. Though decades have passed since these events occurred, time stands still for Francie in the hospital, and he tells of insults received, losses suffered, and revenge meted out as though they just happened. His brain works like a pinball machine, thoughts and perceptions bouncing from the ugly reality of his life to his fantasy world of cowboys and comics, with neither the capacity nor the interest to tell one from the other.

Jordan took a big risk in making a film that relies heavily on a character played by a thirteen-year-old Killeshandra schoolboy with no prior acting experience. But the risk pays off, and Eamonn Owens delivers an adrenalin-charged performance that is nothing short of astonishing. He inhabits the skin and the mind of the psychotic Francie so convincingly as to give concern for his sanity, and the safety of his classmates, when the cameras stop and Owens goes back to school and normal life.

Shot in Clones, Pat McCabe's hometown, *The Butcher Boy* script captures perfectly the Monaghan twang of the book, featuring catchphrases of the 'up-she-flew-and-the-cock-nailed-her' variety – gibberish that passes for witty banter in the midlands, and spares people the trouble of ever talking about anything serious. Complementing the language and the early-1960s context, Jordan's soundtrack utilises obscure but perfectly chosen tunes of the era, from Kim Fowley's demented Tchaikovsky knockoff, 'Nut Rocker' (blaring while Francie undergoes shock treatment), to a wacky 'Mack the Knife' cover by Santo and Johnny. Sinéad O'Connor lends her sublime vocal talents to the suicide ballad of the film's title, sung plain and unadorned. She also has a cameo role as Francie's friend Our Lady, chosen for the part because her bone structure reminded Jordan of plaster statues of the BVM in Irish country churches.

This horrific account of childhood is shot through with flashes of outrageous humour that protect Francie from the harshness of the world and enable him to survive, even after he loses his only friend Joe (Alan Boyle) to nerdhood and exacts a bloody retribution on his perceived nemesis, Mrs Nugent (Fiona Shaw). Jordan treats Francie as neither victim nor villain, but takes the lid off this child-psychopath's mind to look at the mess inside with savage humour and compassion. Jordan brilliantly illustrates how a wicked sense of fun can help a disturbed boy bear the worst that life can dump on him and see the lighter side of the darkness that surrounds him.

DIVORCING JACK
(1998) IRL/UK colour 110 mins

Production Team

Producer ....Robert Cooper/
StephenWoolley/Chris Craib/
Nick Powell
Director.....................................David Caffrey
Screenplay .... Colin Bateman,
from his own book
of the same name
Cinematography .... James Welland
Editor .... Nick Moore
Musical Score........................ Adrian Johnston

Cast

David Thewlis .... Dan Starkey
Rachel Griffiths ....Lee Cooper
Jason Isaacs ....Cow Pat Keegan
Laura Fraser .... Margaret
Richard Gant...........................Charles Parker
Laine Megaw .... Patricia
Robert Lindsay .... Michael Brinn
Kitty Aldridge .... Agnes Brinn
Bronagh Gallagher ....Taxi Driver
Barbara Adair .... Old Woman
Sean Caffrey .... Joe
Robert M Cooper .... Civil Servant
Brian Devlin .... Dan's workmate
Patrick Duncan .... Waiter
Jim Duran .... Hood
Paddy Rocks .... Mad Dog
Derek Halligan ....Frankie

DIVORCING JACK
(1998) IRL/UK colour 110 mins

David Caffrey's feature debut *Divorcing Jack* is a black comedy set in Northern Ireland in the near future, and an equal opportunity offender to both sides of the divide in the politically deadlocked province. The film features a superlative performance from David Thewlis in the lead as a dissolute hack who writes a sarcastic political column for a Belfast newspaper. A magnet for trouble, Dan Starkey (Thewlis) attracts more than he can handle when he meets Margaret (Laura Fraser), a vivacious wine-swilling student, while drinking in the park on the way to a party at his own house. His wife (Laine Megaw) isn't impressed when he shows up drunk with Margaret, even less so when when she catches them later sharing a polo mint after he's been on the great white telephone.

Kicked out of the house, Starkey shacks up with Margaret. He goes out for chips the next night, and comes back to find her horribly mutilated, near death, and bloodily burbling the only clue as to who did it: "Divorcing Jack". In an unfortunate misunderstanding, Starkey kills her mother immediately afterwards and goes into hiding, accused of both murders. The dead women are the wife and daughter of a top adviser to Northern Ireland's likely next prime minister, Michael Brinn (Robert Lindsay), and soon Starkey is on the run from the British army, RUC, IRA and UVF.

Screen thrillers usually convert ordinary citizens into gun-toting super sleuths when faced with deadly odds – they can out-drive, out-shoot and outsmart professional killers who've been making their living despatching slobs just like them for years. Thewlis' Starkey, however, acts like any normal person would on becoming the target of Ulster's top military and paramilitary organisations: he falls completely to pieces, drinks a lot of whiskey, beats up a bad comedian, and spends the rest of the film hanging onto his sanity by his filthy fingernails. If he gets the upper hand or escapes the traps that open in front of him, it's more through blind luck than knowing how to beat the pros at their own game. His jittery reprobate Starkey is hilarious throughout the film, always quick with the smart mouth even as he's staring down the wrong end of a gun barrel. Actors from outside the province rarely achieve such mastery of the Northern Irish accent, and his tone and timing never falter in a central performance which keeps him on-screen for almost the entire film. Colin Bateman's script, adapted from his book, deftly mixes a bizarre lineup of foul-mouthed grannies, a gun-slinging nunagram, an aversion to Jim Reeves, and a corrupt political system, flirting constantly with implausibility without ever being seduced by it.

David Caffrey, directing with a firm but relaxed hand, takes chances with audience reactions to violence. Numbed by 25 years of bombing on television news, Irish viewers still remain sensitive as to how it's portrayed in films. It's quite an achievement, albeit a cynical one, to make a cinema audience laugh when major characters in the film are blown to bits by a car bomb. Caffrey plays his explosions not for shock value but as comedy, and gets away with it. In *Divorcing Jack* he gives the finger to any delicate sensibilities audiences might have about Northern Ireland, using the sort of black humour in the face of tragedy for which natives of the Province are renowned.

THE GENERAL
(1998) IRL/UK b&w cinemascope 129 mins

(Still courtesy of the Irish Film Archive of the Film Insititue of Ireland reproduced courtesy of Merlin Films Group Ltd)

Production Team

Producer ....John Boorman
Director......................................John Boorman
Screenplay ....John Boorman
Cinemtography .... Seamus Deasy
Editor ....Ron Davis
Musical Score...........................Richie Buckley

Cast

Brendan Gleeson .... Martin Cahill
Adrian Dunbar .... Noel Curley
Sean McGinley .... Gary
Maria Doyle Kennedy .... Frances
Angeline Ball .... Tina
Jon Voight .... Inspector Ned Kenny
Eanna McLiam .... Jimmy
Tom Murphy .... Willie Byrne
Paul Hickey .... Anthony
Tommy O'Neill .... Paddy
John O'Toole ....Shea
Ciaran Fitzgerald .... Tommy
Ned Dennehy ....Gay
Vinnie Murphy .... Harry
Roxanna Williams .... Orla
Eamonn Owens .... Young Martin Cahill
Colleen O'Neill .... Patricia

THE GENERAL
(1998) IRL/UK b&w cinemascope 129 mins

A few weeks before its 1994 ceasefire, the IRA took care of some unfinished business on a suburban street in Dublin. It was to be the paramiltary organisation's final hit before declaring an end to its campaign of violence. The target was neither British nor loyalist, nor did he have any known political affiliations. He was a rotund diabetic Dubliner, a father of nine children, and a keen pigeon fancier. He was also the most notorious gangster in a Dublin underworld that had grown from petty thievery into heavily armed factions, well able to match the firepower of the paramilitaries.

His name was Martin Cahill, but the people of Ireland knew him better as 'The General'. Cahill was very different from the flashy thugs and drug dealers who typified the Dublin crime scene, and therein lay the fascination for the media and the public. He neither drank nor smoked, and he took a dim view of drug use after several of his brothers became addicts. He lived quietly in a middle-class neighbourhood near the site of the demolished slums in which he had grown up. The car he drove was a modest two-door sedan, and his only material indulgence was a fondess for motorbikes. A lack of enthusiasm for school left this abstemious criminal barely literate. But if he couldn't spell, he knew how to count – wads of cash in large amounts. From an early career as a housebreaker he moved up to daring raids, jewellry heists and bank robberies that racked up £40 million worth of loot over a twenty-year period. He often left clues at the crime scene as a calling card for the Gardaí, to let them know who had done it. Cahill would give himself an airtight alibi by hanging out at the police station to register complaints against particular officers while his gang carried out robberies that he had meticulously planned. Despite round-the-clock surveillance by dozens of Gardaí, detectives couldn't make the charges stick for any of his crimes, and Cahill continued to elude his pursuers and rob the homes of the wealthy around Dublin.

Those omniscient hounds, the dogs in the street, knew the General's real name and where he lived, but nobody knew what he looked like. Whether decked out in a balaclava helmet, anorak hood, or smearing his face with fingerprint ink when the Gardaí took him in for questioning, he kept his features hidden from the the law, the press and the public. The son of an alcoholic lighthouse keeper, Cahill was himself a devoted father and an unlikely stud – he had five children with his wife and four more with her sister, in an arrangement that seemed to suit all parties involved. If Cahill had never existed, fiction couldn't have devised a credible facsimile of this bizarre Godfather. John Boorman's *The General* was the first to be completed of three Cahill biopics. Boorman also wrote the screenplay, based on the best-selling biography of the same name by Dublin journalist Paul Williams. Boormans' film of the colourful gang leader is made, oddly enough, in black and white. The film has a shimmering, irridescent quality, particularly in the exterior scenes, an effect achieved by shooting with colour film and processing it in monochrome. The director follows the pattern of the source book closely, opening with the General's demise at the hands of the IRA. A tacky rewind follows, in which the bullet that killed Cahill returns to the gun, and the triggerman runs backwards into the bushes in which he had been hiding. Boorman then takes us back to Cahill's childhood (Eamonn Owens of *The Butcher Boy* plays the young Martin), showing the hardship and deprivation that convinced the Cahill boys that there was no point in trying to make a living honestly. The slum scenes of their early life are filmed on the same set that director Jim Sheridan used for *The Boxer* several months before, and Sheridan himself makes a cameo appearance in *The General*, as a protester from Concerned Parents Against Drugs.

Having sown the seeds of sympathy for the young Cahill and his cheerful attempts to subvert authority, Boorman returns to the adult criminal, played with extraordinary conviction by Brendan Gleeson. Gleeson revels in the role of the charming rogue, as he devises outrageous schemes that have as much to do with embarrassing the police force as making himself rich. The film centres on two of Cahill's most notorious strokes, a jewellery heist on the southside of Dublin, and the theft of paintings by Vermeer, Goya, Rubens and Gainsborough from the collection of Sir Alfred Beit at Russborough House in County Wicklow. Boorman sees Cahill as an iconoclast who despised all the pillars of authority in Irish society – the Catholic Church, the police and the government. For the General, the IRA was just one more intrusive organisation to be defied and ignored. When the IRA wanted a cut of his haul from the O'Connor jewellry heist, he told them to get lost. And when Cahill got involved with the Ulster Volunteer Force in an attempt to off-load the paintings he stole from the Beit collection, he saw the arrangement as strictly business. But the republicans didn't see it that way, and when the Gardaí lifted their round-the-clock surveillance of Cahill, the General soon found himself in the crosshairs of an assassin's Magnum 357.

Boorman has been accused of glamourising the gang leader, but there's nothing glamourous about the portly patriarch in baggy jeans and comb-over driving his Renault 5 around Rathmines. And Boorman doesn't shy away from the sadistic side of Cahill. When a gang member is supected of taking more than his fair share from a robbery, Cahill nails him to a pool table to get him to admit it. The intimidation of witnesses and the crippling of a forensics expert with a car bomb balance out the audience's amusement at the same genial practical joker who digs craters in the greens at the Garda golf club in Stackstown to make it easier for them to get a hole-in-one. Boorman strives to show the many sides of this enigmatic character, and for the most part stays close to the facts. Only at the end of Cahill's life does he play loose with the truth, when he shows the assassination of Cahill occurring the same day that the Gardaí stopped the 24-hour watch on his house, implying an unlikely collusion between the police and the IRA. In reality, the Garda surveillance made Cahill a difficult target and ironically kept him alive longer than the 'ra would have liked. The shooting of the General actually occurred several weeks after the police returned to their normal duties.

The women in Cahill's life, his wife Frances and sister-in-law Tina, are played with stoic understatment by Maria Doyle Kennedy and Angeline Ball from *The Commitments*. The General's gang is comprised of an assortment of up-and-coming and es-

THE GENERAL
(1998) IRL/UK b&w cinemascope 129 mins

(Still courtesy of the Irish Film Archive of the Film Insititue of Ireland reproduced courtesy of Merlin Films Group Ltd)

tablished television actors from the Irish scene, among them Adrian Dunbar and Sean McGinley. Dunbar, too patrician by far to play a professional frightener from the same tenements as Cahill, seems a little bewildered with how little he's been given to do in the film. He looks like he'd be a lot more at home tied to a chair with gaffer tape around his mouth, playing one of the toffs whose homes get burgled by the stealthy Cahill. McGinley is better as the accomplice who cracks from the twenty-four/seven monitoring of the gang by the Gardaí. The cast is given some international starpower by Oscar winner and three-time Oscar nominee Jon Voight, reunited with Boorman on their first project together since *Deliverance* in 1970. The veteran actor plays Cahill's nemesis, Inspector Ned Kenny, a compound character based on several officers who dedicated their careers to bringing in the elusive crook. Voight chews down on his character's Kerry accent like it was a wad of tobacco, and spits out his lines at the devious General with a peculiar restraint that implies more sympathy for his enemy than a senior officer in an embarrassed police force would manifest. But he brings a tweedy dignity to a film heavily populated with gougers, thugs and thieves, and his star presence in the project was a necessary component in drawing financial support and festival exposure for Boorman's film.

Accustomed as we are to seeing the mob depicted as Armani-clad high-rollers, Boorman's hoodlum drama may be too small-scale and downbeat to fascinate mafia aficionados abroad, but in Dublin's contribution to the gangster film genre, Gleeson gives the performance of his career as the scheming gang leader, to whom he bears an uncanny physical resemblance. Boorman resisted pressure from investors to use a bigger 'name' in the lead role because he felt very strongly that Gleeson was perfect for the part, and his faith in the actor has been amply rewarded. *The General* won the Best Director award for John Boorman at Cannes in the year of its release.

THIS IS MY FATHER
(1998) US/CAN/UK/IRL colour 120 mins

Production Team

Producer ..... Nicolas Clermont/Philip King/
Filmline Intl/Hummingbird Comm.
Director .... Paul Quinn
Screenplay .... Paul Quinn
Cinematography .... Declan Quinn
Editor .... Glen Berman
Musical Score .... Donal Lunny

Cast

Aidan Quinn .... Kieran O'Day
Moya Farrelly .... Fiona Flynn
James Caan .... Kieran Johnson
John Cusack .... Eddie Sharp
Colm Meaney .... Seamus Kearney
Moira Deady .... Mrs Kearney
Gina Moxley .... Mrs Flynn
Donal Donnelly .... Mr Maney
Maria McDermottroe .... Mrs Maney
Stephen Rea .... Father Quinn
Eamon Morrissey .... Father Mooney
John Kavanagh .... Liam
Jacob Tierney .... Jack
Brendan Gleeson .... Garda Jim
Marian Quinn .... Dolores
Pauline Hutton .... Maria

THIS IS MY FATHER
(1998) US/CAN/UK/IRL colour 120 mins

Irish-American film director Paul Quinn made his feature debut with *This is my Father*, a remarkable cinematic collaboration involving four members of the Quinn family. The film stars the director's brother Aidan Quinn as a luckless farm worker who falls for a much younger woman above his social station. His brother Declan is the director of photography, and a cameo performance by their sister, actress Marian Quinn, completes the sibling quartet. Their combined talents create a moving romantic drama about a man's search for the father he has never known, and the ill-fated teenage romance that his mother kept secret from him throughout his life.

Paul Quinn developed the screenplay from a true story that his mother had heard as a child growing up in Ireland. The film is an accomplished first outing, in which the director boldly mines a stratum of Irish lore that had previously shown serious signs of audience fatigue. Another film about malevolent monsignors meddling in the love-life of their parishioners, set in pre-electric, pre-war rural Ireland, doesn't exactly make the punters turn up in droves at the cinema turnstiles. But Paul Quinn deftly side-steps the traps and pitfalls of this clichéd terrain to produce a feature lifted above the ordinary by polished story-telling, the simple beauty and economy of Declan's cinematography, and a lead performance by Aidan Quinn that ranks as the finest of his career to date. The star is ably supported by a strong cast of top Irish and American actors, among them John Cusack as a flamboyant aerial photographer, Colm Meaney as a swishy traveller who runs a B&B, and Stephen Rea as a prurient priest obsessed with the carnal desires of his flock. Even the very minor roles in the film are played by top Irish actors of the calibre of Brendan Gleeson and John Kavanagh.

Veteran actor James Caan also stars, as a forlorn Chicagoan named Kieran Johnson who travels to Ireland to solve the mystery of his father's identity after he finds an old photograph of his mother with a handsome young man. Caan's character is a jaded high school teacher worn down on the outside by years of teaching history to bored suburban teenagers, and hollowed out from within by a childless marriage, his wife's early death, and the pain of never knowing his father. He drags himself into school each day to try and make his disinterested pupils appreciate the past, knowing that he may never unravel the details of his own – his elderly mother is debilitated by a stroke and couldn't tell him about his father even if she wanted to. He resolves to go to Ireland, taking his half-sister's troubled teenage son Jack (Jacob Tierney) with him for company.

The presence of the nephew gives the director a second, lighter tier to the film, as the lad meets with skittish Irish teenage girls, gets slagged about his dance stylings at the local disco, and feels the first flush of romance while his uncle is uncovering the painful truth about the love that conceived him more than half a century earlier. The story switches deftly over and back between the events of the summer of 1939, when Kieran's mother fell in love with Kieran O'Day (Aidan Quinn), and the present day,

THIS IS MY FATHER
(1998) US/CAN/UK/IRL colour 120 mins

when her grandson does the same thing with a local girl, but without the same tragic consequences.

The root cause of the film's tragedy is one of the most divisive issues in the history of rural Ireland, a cause of deeper discord than the more obvious problem of religion on the island – the issue of land ownership. Kieran O'Day was, in the parlance of the time, a poorhouse bastard who had been adopted by a childless couple, Mr and Mrs Maney (Donal Donnelly and Maria McDermottroe) to work on the farm they rented from a wealthy local widow (Gina Moxley). The widow's daughter Fiona (Moya Farrelly), a free-spirited girl sent home early from boarding school in Galway after a row with the nuns, meets up with Kieran, invites him to go dancing, and they soon fall for each other. His step-parents live in perpetual dread of being evicted from the few bony acres off which they scrape a living, and if the widow finds out about the romance between the uneducated orphan and her darling daughter, she'll send the bailiffs round immediately to throw her tenants out. From her bitter perspective, the affair between the farmhand and the much younger Fiona can only be a plot to get the girl pregnant and inherit the land through the offspring, so Kieran and Fiona are compelled to keep their love secret. But in a small village secrets are hard to keep, and soon the full force of the Catholic Church is enlisted to keep them apart. The simple, earnest Kieran is more sensitive to threats of eternal damnation than the bohemian Fiona, but his efforts to stay away from her prove futile, as his love is stronger than his fear of hell. They resume the affair and suffer consequences from which neither they nor the village will ever recover.

As the socially mis-matched couple, both Aidan Quinn and Moya Farrelly are outstanding. Moya Farrelly is incandescant in her first major role as the livewire Fiona. She delivers an eager, uninhibited performance that would be unthinkable from a Hollywood actress of the same age. Aidan Quinn immerses himself without a trace of thespian vanity in the part of the shy, emotionally stunted farmer, and belies the perception from his earlier roles on screen that he was cast more for the decorative value of his azure eyes than any facility he might have with accents and nuances of character. Not many Hollywood hunks would willingly submit to a brutal haircut that looks like it was clipped with a set of sheep shears and combed with a beetfork, or costumes that suggest burlap sacks aspiring to tweed. The awkward body language and inarticulate speech of a full-grown orphan accustomed more to cutting turf in the bog than talking to people limits the actor's options in conveying the quailties that make Kieran O'Day attractive to a girl like Fiona. But Quinn projects a sincerity and decency that is believable as the two draw closer together during the course of the film. James Caan's performance conveys this same decency, but a more tired version, as befits an older man burdened with his sad history.

The Quinns' use of language is impressive throughout, both in Aidan's Irish accent and Paul's writing. As Irish-Americans who spent some of their childhood in Ireland, they both have a good feel for the differences in the use of English on either side of the ocean. And Paul's old-fashioned ability to tell a good story circumvents any likelihood of audience recoil from a tale that features clairvoyant travellers, hokey superstitions, and the bewitching of the widow as components of the plot. Modern Irish film-makers shun the scenic pleasures of Ireland, with its rustic parishes and petrifying priests, with a view to avoiding the clichés of the two Johns, Hinde and Ford, yet they rarely produce films of quality that are identifiably Irish. With *This is my Father*, this team of brothers from Chicago by way of Offaly has succeeded admirably in depicting an Ireland of the past and of the present that is credible, sentimental, and funny, as it struggles to shake free of its old prejudices and cramped emotions.

I COULD READ THE SKY
(1999) IRL/UK colour 82 mins

(Still photograph by Steve Pyke reproduced courtesy of Hot Property Films)

Production Team

Producer ...... Janine Marmot/Hot Property/
Nicholas O'Neill/ Liquid Films
Director .... Nichola Bruce
Screenplay .... Nichola Bruce,
based on the book of
the same name by
Timothy O'Grady and Steve Pyke
Cinematography .... Seamus McGarvey
and Owen McPolin
Editor .... Catherine Creed
Musical Score....................... Iarla Ó Lionáird

Cast

Dermot Healy .... The old man
Maria Doyle Kennedy .... Maggie
Brendan Coyle .... Francie
Stephen Rea .... P J
Geraldine Fitzgerald .... Eileen
Noel O'Donovan .... Tailor
Aidan O'Toole .... Dermot
Liam Ó Maonlaí .... Joe
Colm Ó Maonlaí .... Martin
Frances Burke .... Ma
Jimmy McCreevy .... Da
Iarla Ó Lionáird ....Singer at wedding
Timothy O'Grady ....
Steve Pyke ....
Pat McCabe ....
Mick Lally ....

250

I COULD READ THE SKY
(1999) IRL/UK colour 82 mins

Tales of the Irish Diaspora in the US have been screened since the earliest days of cinema, but the stories of those who emigrated to the nearest port of call, Britain, remain hidden. Nichola Bruce's feature *I Could Read the Sky* elucidates the lost social history of these men who left Ireland to find work in post-war England. Without much schooling, their fate was to shovel the rubble of Britain's decaying empire for a pittance that felt like a fortune to country boys who never had more than bed and board at home. Based on the beautiful, elegiac novel of the same name by Timothy O'Grady and Steve Pyke, Bruce's film honours the lives of those second and third sons who didn't inherit the land, wouldn't work for the brother who did, and didn't have a vocation (or a stern directive from the Ma) to study for the priesthood.

Westmeath-born author, poet and sometimes actor Dermot Healy carries the hod for the whole film as its central character, an un-named old man living in a shabby bedsit in London. He reminisces about his youth on the farm and the village he left in damp decline to work a lifetime on English building sites. No stranger to the navvy's lot himself, Healy draws on his own experience working in England to express perfectly the cadence and tone of a poorly educated but intelligent man with a fondness for words as he reflects on the past. The film takes its title from a rural skill learned in adolescence on his father's farm and listed among others with quiet pride by the white haired, rheumy-eyed old man. He could mend a shoe, make a coffin, stuff a saddle and strike a deal. He also lists the things he could never do – top of that list is 'stop remembering'.

The old man's memories are presented visually as a seamless montage that glides and floats past the camera in a swirling haze. Seamus McGarvey's diaphanous cinematography and Catherine Creed's adept editing convey beautifully the fleeting nature of memory, and combine with Healy's performance to create a wealth of deeply moving and indelible images. To cite but three from among many: the navvy's evaluation of his current financial state, finding that he had more money in his pocket when he arrived in England as a boy than he does now after a lifetime of hard work; his infinite loneliness after his beloved wife (Maria Doyle Kennedy) died, expressed in a single heartrending line – "Maggie's not here now"; and his anguished return home to bury his dead mother (Frances Burke), finding he has to do it himself, as the gravedigger is ill and there's no one else to open the ground. Having reached the right depth and moved his father's rattling coffin temporarily up out of the same plot to make room for her, he can't get back up onto the rain-sodden grass, and tries vainly to grip fistfuls of wet rushes to pull himself out.

An earlier study of Irish immigrants in Britain, Thaddeus O'Sullivan's *On a Paving Stone Mounted* also took an experimental free-form approach to its subject, a reflection of the rootless lives of the nomadic navvies, always on the move to where the work is. Nichola Bruce's beautiful, eloquent lament dignifies their humble station and is that rare cinematic achievement, a film that fully honours its remarkable source material.

251

BIBLIOGRAPHY

Cagney, J, *Cagney by Cagney* (New York: Doubleday) 1976.

Caughie, J & K Rockett, *The Companion to British and Irish Cinema* (London: Cassell/ BFI Publ) 1996.

Flynn, A, *Irish Film 100 Years* (Bray, County Wicklow: Kestrel Books Ltd) 1996.

Flynn, Errol, *My Wicked, Wicked Ways* (New York: G P Putnam & Sons) 1959.

Henry, Mike Tomkies, *The Robert Mitchum Story: It Sure Beats Working* (Chicago: Regnery Co.) 1972.

Le Giornate del Cinema Muto/BFI Publ, *Rex Ingram: Master of Silent Cinema* (London) 1993.

McIlroy, B, *Irish Cinema - An Illustrated History* (Dublin: Anna Livia Press) 1988.

McIlroy, B, *Shooting to Kill: Filmmaking and the "Troubles" in Northern Ireland* (Wiltshire: Flicks Books) 1998.

McKillop, J (ed.), *Contemporary Irish Cinema* (Syracuse, NY: Syracuse University Press) 1999.

Miles, S, *Serves Me Right* (London: MacMillan) 1994.

National Library of Ireland, *Cinema Ireland 1896-1950 From The Liam O'Leary Film Archives* (Dublin) 1990.

Pendreigh, B, *On Location: The Film Fan's Guide to Britain and Ireland* (Edinburgh: Mainstream Publishing) 1995.

Rocket, K, L Gibbons & J Hill, *Cinema And Ireland* (Syracuse, NY: Syracuse University Press) 1987.

Rockett, K, *The Irish Filmography* (Dun Laoighaire, County Dublin: Red Mountain Media) 1996.

Scéal na Scannán Prionsias î Conlœain Oifig an tSoláthair (Baile Atha Cliath) 1953.

Walsh, R, *Each Man in his Time* (New York: Farrar Stauss and Giroux) 1974.

INDEX OF FILMS

A Hard Day's Night, 87
A Man of No Importance,
  220-221
A Stone in the Heart, 215
A Taste of Honey, 125
African Queen, The, 127, 175
Ailsa, **214-215**
All Things Bright and
  Beautiful, 221
Angel, **158-159**
Angels with Dirty Faces, 45,
  70-73
Anne Devlin, **162-163**, 195
Another Shore, 21 **86-87**
Apocalypse Now, 123

Ballroom of Romance, **160-
  161**
Beloved Enemy, **60-61**, 225
Ben Hur, 3
Birth of a Nation, 36, 49
Bishop's Story, The, *see*
  Budawanny
Black Narcissus, 81, 127
Blarney, **76-77**
Blithe Spirit, 137
Bowery, The, **46-49**
Boxer, The, 244
Bridge on the River Kwai, 137
Brief Encounter, 137
Budawanny, **172-173**
Butcher Boy, The, **238-239**,
  244

Cal, **164-165**
Caoineadh Airt Uí Laoire,
  146-147
Captain Blood, **54-55**
Captain Boycott, 81, **82-83**
Circle of Friends, 161
Clash of the Ash, **178-179**
Close Encounters of the Third
  Kind, 141
Colleen Bawn, The, **6-9**

Commitments, The, **196-199**,
  211, 244
Cool Hand Luke, 130
Cradle of Genius, 97
Crying Game, The, **202-203**,
  230

Da, **182-183**
Danny Boy, *see* Angel
Darby O'Gill and the Little
  People, 77, **110-111**
Daughter of Darkness, **88-91**
Dawn, The, **62-65**, 75
Dead, The, **174-177**
December Bride, 169, **194-195**
Deliverance, 141, 245
Dementia 13, **122-123**
Divorcing Jack, **240-241**
Doctor Zhivago, 137
Doughboys in Ireland, 119

Eliminator, The, **222-223**

Field, The, **190-193**
Fighting Prince of Donegal,
  The, 130
Flight of the Doves, 113
For Ireland's Sake, **10-11**
Four Days in July, **166-167**
Four Horsemen of the
  Apocolypse, **34-37**
From the Manger to the
  Cross, 9
Fun Loving, *see* Quackser
  Fortune has a Cousin in the
  Bronx, 135

General, The, **242-245**
Girl with Green Eyes, **124-125**
Godfather, The, 123
Golden Virgin, The, *see* Story
  of Esther Costello, The
Gone with the Wind, 21
Graduate, The, 130

Greed, 35
Guests of the Nation, **56-57**
Guiltrip, 215, **218-219**

Hangman's House, 59
Happy Ever After, **100-101**
Hell Drivers, 121, 145
Hidden Agenda, **188-189**
High Spirits, 201
Home is the Hero, **112-113**
Horse, 193
Hungry Hill, 89
Hush-a-bye-baby, **184-185**

I Could Read the Sky, **250-251**
I See a Dark Stranger, **78-81**,
  89
I Went Down, 215, **234-237**
Images, **140-141**
In Cold Blood, 130
In the Days of St Patrick, **28-
  29**
In the Heat of the Night, 130
In the Name of the Father,
  208-209
Informer, The, 21, **58-59**
Into the West, **204-205**
Ireland a Nation, **12-15**, 163
Ireland's Boderline, *see*
  Blarney
Irish and Proud of it, **68-69**
Irish Destiny, **38-41**
Islandman, The, **74-75**

Jacqueline, **102-103**
James Joyce's Women, 131,
  175
Jimmy Boy, 77

Kind Hearts and Coronets, 87
Knocknagow, **24-27**, 67, 187

Lad from Old Ireland, The, **2-
  3**, 5

INDEX OF FILMS

Lamb, **170-171**, 187
Lavender Hill Mob, The, 87
Lawrence of Arabia, 137
Life and Times of Judge Roy Bean, The, 143
Luck of the Irish, The, **92-93**

M*A*S*H*, 141
Mackintosh Man, The, **142-143**
Maeve, **154-155**
Magician, The, 37
Maltese Falcon, The, 175
Man of Aran, **50-53**, 75, 153
Mare Nostrum, 37
McCabe and Mrs Miller, 141
Men of Ireland, *see* Islandman, The
Michael Collins, **224-227**
Mildred Pierce, 107
Miracle, The, **200-201**
Mise Éire, 113
Mother Machree, 59
Musketeers of Pig Alley, 17
My Left Foot, 161, 171, **186-187**, 193, 209

Nanook of the North, 51
Night Fighters, The, *see* A Terrible Beauty
No Resting Place, **96-97**, 157
Nothing Personal, 195

O'Neill of the Glen, **20-21**
Odd Man Out, **84-85**, 119, 230
Old Yeller, 111
On a Paving Stone Mounted, 251
Oracle, The, 97
Orca, 193
Ourselves Alone, **66-67**

Paddy, **132-133**

Passages from James Joyce's 'Finnegan's Wake', 175
Passport to Pimlico, 87
Pigs, **168-169**, 195
Poitín, **148-149**
Portrait of the Artist as a Young Man, 131, **148-151**, 175
Prisoner, The, 145
Prizzi's Honor, 183
Public Enemy, The, **42-45**, 71

Quackser Fortune has a Cousin in the Bronx, **134-135**
Quare Fellow, The, 113, **120-121**
Quiet Man, The, 59, 95, **98-99**, 101, 105, 149

Reefer and the Model, **180-181**
Regeneration, **16-19**
Rising of the Moon, The, 93, **104-105**
River of Unrest, *see* Ourselves Alone
Robinson Crusoe, 177
Rooney, 103, **108-109**
Rory O'More, **4-5**
Ryan's Daughter, **136-139**

Saints and Sinners, **94-95**
Schindler's List, 171, 225
Secret of Roan Inish, The, **216-217**
Secrets and Lies, 167
Shake Hands with the Devil, **114-115**, 225
Slave Girl, 101
Snapper, The 199, **210-211**
Some Mother's Son, **228-231**
Song of Scheherezade, 101

Star Wars: The Phantom Menace, 171
Story of Esther Costello, The, **106-107**
Story of GI Joe, 119

Tenant, The, 215
Terrible Beauty, A, **118-119**
Third Man, The, 86
This is my Father, **246-249**
This is the Sea, **232-233**
This Other Eden, **116-117**, 215
Three Leaves of a Shamrock, *see* Rising of the Moon, The
Traveller, **156-157**
Treasure of the Sierra Madre, 175

Ulysses, 97, **128-131**, 133, 149, 150, 175
Uncle Nick, 63

Vicar of Bray, The, 21

War of the Buttons, **212-213**
We're No Angels, 201
West of Kerry, *see* Islandman, The
When Love Came to Gavin Burke, **22-23**
Whisky Galore, 87
White Heat, 45
Wild Colonial Boy, The, 99
Willy Reilly and his Colleen Bawn, **30-33**
Willy Wonka and the Chocolate Factory, 135
Words on the Window Pane, 233

You, Me and Marley, **206-207**
Young Cassidy, 115, **126-127**

Zardoz, **144-145**

INDEX OF NAMES

20th Century Pictures, 46

Acres, Harry, 66
Adair, Barbara, 240
Addison, John, 124
Aeon Films, 162
Aherne, Brian, 64, 65, 224
Aherne, Michael, 196, 199
Alderton, John, 144
Aldridge, Kitty, 240
Alexander, Frances, 30, 31
Alexander, Ross, 54
Allan, William, 78
Allen, Anthony Havelock, 135
Allen, Ira, 28
Allen, Jim, 188, 189
Alliance, 66
Allied Artists, 132
Allwyn William 84
Allwyn, William, 78, 82, 96, 114
Altman, Robert, 140, 141
Amy, George, 54
Anders, Luana, 122, 123
Anderson, Michael, 114, 115
Andrews, Harry, 142
Andrews, Pauline, 222
Angel, Heather, 58, 59
Anthony Havelock-Allen Productions, 120
Antrim, Harry, 92
Apfel, Oscar, 46
Arden, John, 146, 147
Argosy, 98
Arkins, Robert, 196, 197
Arliss, Leslie, 94, 95
Arliss, Pam, 94
Arthur, Perry, 122
Arts Council of Ireland, 156
Arts Council, 172
Ashe, Paddy, 214, 220
Asseyev, Tamara, 132
Atwill, Lionel, 54, 55
Auberjonois, René, 140, 141
Audsley, Mick, 210
August, Joseph H, 58
Ault, Marie, 78
Auric, Georges, 86, 106
Austin, Mel, 154
Ayres, Robert, 106

Bagley, Desmond, 142, 143
Bairéad, Colm, 152
Baker, Carly, 234
Baker, Don, 208, 209
Baker, Robert S, 112

Baker, Roy, 102
Baker-Smith, Malcolm, 86
Balcon, Michael, 50, 86
Balderston, John L, 64
Ball, Angeline, 196, 197, 242, 244
Ball, Seamus, 184
Bancroft, George, 70, 71
Bannen, Ian, 142, 170, 171
Barker, David, 154
Barkin, Ellen, 204, 205
Barn, Peggy, 16
Barrat, Robert, 54
Bartley, Jim, 212, 213
Bateman, Colin, 240, 241
Bates, Granville, 60
Bates, Irene, 184
Batt, Paul, 212, 213
Baxter, Anne, 92, 93
BBC Films, 210, 220, 234
Bean, Sean, 190, 191, 193
Beatty, Robert, 84, 85, 86, 87
Beaven, Donald, 56
Beckett, Samuel, 123
Beery, Wallace, 34, 46, 47
Begley, Rita, 102
Behan, Brendan, 113, 120, 121
Behan, Paudge, 220, 221
Bell, Dave, 218
Bell, Sam Hanna, 194, 195
Benet, Marianne, 114, 118
Benfield, John, 188, 208
Benoit, Georges, 16
Berber Films, 180
Berenger, Tom, 190, 191, 193
Bergin, Emmet, 136, 148, 149
Berman, Glen, 246
Berman, Monty, 112
Bernelle, Agnes, 120
Bernstein, Elmer, 182, 186, 190
Bezencenet, Peter, 108
BFI, 154
Biddle, Adrian, 238
Bing, Herman, 46
Bischoff, Sam, 70
Biziou, Peter, 208
Black, Cathal, 168, 169
Black, Stanley, 100
Blackman, Honor, 88, 91
Blackmore, Barry, 158
Bleifer, John, 46
Bloch, Bernard, 188
Blondell, Joan, 42, 43
Blunden, Bill, 134
Bogart, Humphrey, 70, 71
Boley, May, 58

Bolster, Anita Sharp, 94, 104
Bolt, Robert, 136
Bond, Ward, 98
Bono, 208
Bono, Liz, 158
Boorman, John, 141, 144, 145, 242, 243
Booth, Roger, 170
Borradaile, Osmond, 94
Boucicault, Dion, 6, 7-9
Bourke, P J, 12
Box, Muriel, 116, 117
Boyle, Alan, 238, 239
Boyle, Peter, 204
Boyle, Robert, 162
Bozzuffi, Marcel, 140, 141
Bradley, Liam, 232
Bradley, Padraic, 146
Bradley, Stephen, 214
Bradsell, Michael, 164
Brambeld, Molly, 154
Brambell, Wilfred, 86, 87
Brame, George, 28
Brazzi, Rossano, 106, 107
Breathnach, Paddy, 180, 214, 215, 234, 235, 237
Breathnach, Seán Bán, 146, 147
Breen, Myles, 178
Breffni, Moira, 24
Brennan, Bríd, 154, 155, 161, 162, 163, 167
Brennan, Catherine, 207
Brennan, Jimmy, 168, 169
Breslin, John, 114
Bright, John, 42
British Lion, 94
Broadbent, Jim, 202
Brody, Estelle, 106
Brogan, Harry, 112, 114, 116, 118, 119, 120, 121, 124
Brown, George H, 56, 02, 108
Brown, Harry Joe, 54
Brown, Irene, 108, 109
Brown, Phil, 92
Brown, Ralph, 202
Brown, Robert, 114
Brown, Rosina, 180, 184
Brown, Rowland, 70
Bruce, Brenda, 194, 195
Bruce, Nichola, 250, 251
Buckley, Richie, 242
Buena Vista, 234
Buggy, Niall, 144, 145, 148
Burke, Brenda, 24
Burke, Edward, 228

INDEX OF NAMES

Burke, Francis, 250, 251
Burke, Frankie, 70
Bushnell, Paul, 196
Bute, Mary Ellen, 175
Byrne, Antoine, 234, 236
Byrne, Billy, 208
Byrne, Breffini, 180, 184
Byrne, C, 28
Byrne, Caolan, 232
Byrne, Cillian, 216
Byrne, Eddie, 94, 100, 108, 109, 164
Byrne, Gabriel, 204, 205, 208, 232, 233
Byrne, Jason, 234
Byrne, Karl, 212
Byrne, Niall, 200, 201
Byrne, Robert, 168

Caan, James, 246, 247, 249
Caffrey, David, 240, 241
Caffrey, Peter, 158, 159, 234, 235, 236
Caffrey, Sean, 240
Cagney, James, 42, 43, 45, 70, 71-73, 114, 115, 224
Cairney, John, 114
Campbell, Daisy, 38, 39
Campbell, Diana, 96
Campbell, Gurney, 146
Campbell, Robert Wright, 118, 122
Campbell, Shar, 202
Campbell, William, 122, 123
Cannon, Pomeroy, 34, 35
Capaldi, Peter, 194
Cardiff, Jack, 126, 127
Cardinall, Alice, 28
Carey, Brian, 74
Carey, Denis, 170
Carey, Paddy, 74
Carleton, William, 23, 30
Carr, Jack, 202
Carre, J M, 20, 21, 24, 25
Carrickford, J B, 28
Carroll, Helena, 174, 175, 177
Carroll, Paul Vincent, 94
Carruthers, Leto, 88
Casey, Cathy, 184, 185
Cass, Peggy, 132
Casson, Christopher, 144
Cassoni, Gerard, 196
Catto, Max, 88. 89, 91
Cauldwell, Brendan, 214, 215
Cavanaugh, Hobart, 54
Cave, Des, 132, 133, 148, 150
Cavendish, John, 204, 220

Cavendish, Jonathan, 194
Cellier, Antoinette, 66, 67
Challis, Christopher G, 108
Channel 4, 170, 172, 194, 202
Chapman-Murphy, Rebecca, 218
Chinsealach, Máire, 180
Choil Mhaidhc, Johnny, 156, 157
Christie, Julie, 126, 127
Cinegael, 146, 147, 149, 172
Circus Films, 178
Clancy, Joe, 146
Clancy, Nora, 20, 21, 22, 23, 24, 25
Clark, Amiee, 182
Clark, Anna, 4, 5, 6, 7
Clark, Jack J, 4, 5, 6, 7, 9, 10
Clark, Mae, 42, 43
Clark, Matt, 182
Clayton, Jack, 106
Clement, Dick, 196, 199
Clermont, Nicolas, 246
Clery, Ann, 88
Clifford, Graeme, 140
Clifford, Jack, 68
Cobb, Lee J, 92, 93
Coen Brothers, 238
Coffey, John, 212, 213
Coghlan Jr, Frank, 42, 45
Cole, George, 100, 101
Cole, Virginia, 210
Coleman, Brian, 202
Coleman, Queenie, 22
Colgan, Eileen, 134, 135, 216, 217
Collins, David, 168
Collins, Niall, 212
Collins, Tom, 158, 184
Collis, Robert, 56
Comerford, Henry, 180
Comerford, Joe, 146, 156, 157, 180, 181
Comfort, Lance, 88
Compton, Fay, 106
Compton, Fay, 84
Coneely, Big Patcheen of the West, 50
Conlon, Gerry, 209
Conmee, Marie, 162, 163
Connaughton, Shane, 167, 186, 200
Connell, Maureen, 104
Connely, Edward, 34
Conner, Rearden, 114
Connery, Sean, 110, 111, 144, 145
Connolly, Andrew, 218, 219
Connor, Tommie, 108

Connors, Kathleen, 100
Conroy, Brendan, 214, 216, 220
Conroy, Eileen, 220
Conroy, Jack, 186, 190
Conroy, Jenny, 190, 191
Conroy, Ruaidhrí, 204, 205
Cook, Donald, 42, 43
Cook, J Fielder, 112
Cookson, Catherine, 102, 103, 108
Cooney, Stephen, 178
Cooper, Jackie, 46, 47
Cooper, Merian C, 98
Cooper, Robert, 240
Cooper, Tom, 30, 61, 63
Copeland, Stewart, 188
Coppola, Francis Ford, 122, 123
Corbett, Harry, 114
Corbett, J, 66
Corman, Julie, 182
Corman, Roger, 122, 123, 222
Cornwell, Judy, 132, 133
Corr, Andrea, 196
Corrigan, Chris, 222
Corrigan, D'Arcy, 58
Courtney, Jeni, 216, 217
Cowan, Jerome, 64, 65
Cowley, John, 104, 105, 162, 163, 190, 191
Cox, Brian, 188, 189
Coyle, Brendan, 214, 215, 250
Coyle, David, 184
Craib, Chris, 240
Craig, May, 96, 98, 104, 124
Craig, Stuart, 164
Craigie, Ingrid, 161, 174, 182
Cranitch, Lorcan, 207
Crawford, Anne, 88
Crawford, Joan, 106, 107
Creed, Catherine, 250, 251
Crichton, Charles, 86
Crilly, Donna, 222
Crisp, Donald, 64
Croghan, Declan, 186
Cronnelly, David, 202
Crosbie, Alison, 208
Crossan, Gerard, 206, 207
Crowe, Eileen, 98, 104, 112, 114, 118, 119, 124
Crowley, Donnacha, 178
Crowley, Evin, 136
Crowley, Pat, 60
Crusade Films, 68
Cullinane, Paddy Dunne, 38, 39
Culver, Roland, 142
Cummins, Danny, 134

INDEX OF NAMES

Cummins, Julie, 146
Cunningham, Anthony, 212, 213
Cunningham, Cissy, 56
Cunningham, Jack, 120
Cunningham, Liam, 212, 213
Curran, Chris, 128
Curran, Eileen, 74, 75
Curtiz, Michael, 54, 70
Cusack, Cyril, 24, 25, 45, 56, 84, 85, 102, 103, 104, 105, 114, 118, 152, 153, 187
Cusack, John, 246

D'Alton, Louis, 116, 117
D'Angelo, Berverly, 200, 201
D'Arcy, Margaretta, 146
Dade, Stephen, 118
Dalton, Audrey, 116, 117
Dalton, Emmet, 112, 113, 116, 117
Daly, John, 188
Dannell, Stuart, 204
Darcy, Ita, 132, 133
Daring, Mason, 216
Darro, Frankie, 42, 45
Davidson, Jaye, 202, 203
Davies, Cedric Thorpe, 102, 118
Davies, Jack, 100
Davies, John, 154, 155
Davis, Desmond, 124
Davis, Eileen, 60, 61
Davis, Liz, 134
Davis, Ron, 242
Davy, Máirtín, 146
Day Lewis, Daniel, 186, 187, 208, 209
Day, Tilly, 76
De Brulier, Nigel, 34, 36
De Buitléar, Cian, 214, 215, 234
De Carlo, Yvonne, 100, 101
De Cordoba, Pedro, 54
De Haan, Ray, 202
De Havilland, Olivia, 54, 55
De Keyzer, Bruno, 194, 195, 212
Deady, Moira, 246
Deans, Marjoire, 66
Dearden, Julia, 164
Deasy, Séamus, 152, 172, 242
Delaney, Pauline, 108, 109, 120, 126
Delany, Cathleen, 174, 175, 177, 194, 200
Delany, Grainne, 228
Delany, Maureen, 82, 83, 84, 85, 86, 94, 102, 106
Delfgou, Peter, 170
Dell, Gabriel, 70

Dempsey, Martin, 128, 130, 162, 163, 182
Dennehy, Ned, 242
Dennigan, Jimmy, 178
Derry Film & Video Workshop, 184
Desmond, Shaun, 68, 69
Devlin, Alan, 156, 157, 158, 178, 179
Devlin, Barry, 220, 221
Devlin, Brian, 240
Devlin, J G, 110, 200
Devlin, Johnny, 200
Dhabharáin, Siobhán, 146
Dillon, Tom, 94, 95
Dirrane, Maggie, 50, 51
Dirrane, Stephen, 50
Dods, Marcucs, 126
Doherty, Miche, 194
Doherty, Sean, 184
Dolan, Michael, 94, 95
Dominguez, Beatrice, 34, 35
Donaldson, Arthur, 2, 3, 4, 5, 6, 7
Donat, Robert, 82, 83
Donn-Byrne, Dorothea, 68
Donnelly, Donal, 104, 105, 126, 174, 175, 246, 248
Donnelly, Simon, 222
Donoghue, Tommy, 200
Donovan, Judy, 156, 157
Donovan, Nora, 156
Donovan, Paddy, 156, 157
Douglas, Harold, 56
Dourif, Brad, 188, 189
Dow, Maureen, 184
Dowley, Marian, 178
Dowling, Bairbre, 144
Dowling, Rachel, 174, 176
Dowling, Vincent, 126
Downes, Bernie, 162, 168
Downing, Joe, 70
Downing, Wilfred, 118
Doyle Kennedy, Maria, 242, 244, 250, 251
Doyle, Charles, 28
Doyle, Jill, 182, 183
Doyle, Maria, 196, 197
Doyle, Patrick, 204
Doyle, Roddy, 196, 197, 199, 210, 211
Doyle, Roger, 168, 172
Doyle, Sé Merry, 168, 180
Doyle, Tony, 134, 234, 235, 236
Dreifuss, Arthur, 113, 120, 121
Dress, Michael, 134

Drew, Phelim, 186
DRM, 118
Dudley, Anne, 200, 202
Duff, Justin, 154
Duff, Warren, 70
Duffner, J Patrick, 158, 186, 190, 224
Duffy, Ciara, 210
Duffy, Dave, 180, 204, 216
Duffy, Frank, 74
Duffy, Gerard, 74
Duffy, John, 74
Duffy, Martin, 172, 184
Duffy, Mik, 222, 223
Duggan, Frank, 178
Duggan, Jim, 178
Duhan, Johnny, 180
Dunbar, Adrian, 186, 202, 203, 242, 244
Duncan, Patrick, 240
Dunne, Eithne, 96, 122, 123
Dunne, Lee, 132, 133
Dunne, Martin, 186
Dunne, Philip, 92
Dunne, Stuart, 210, 214
Dunsany, Lord, 123
Duran, Jim, 236
Dwyer, Michael, 224
Dymoke, Lionel, 56

Ealing Studios, 86
Eaton, Sidney, 74
Edney, Beatie, 208, 209
Edwards, Hilton, 56, 116, 118, 120
Edwards, Snitz, 42
Edwin, J H, 76, 77
Egan, Colette, 178
Ellenshaw, Peter, 111
Eller, Paul, 186
Emperor Films, 214
Endfield, C Raker, 121
English, Stephanie, 184
Enigma Productions, 212
Enigma, 164
Ennis, Patrick, 12
Eppel Films, 38
Eppel, Derek, 38
Eppel, Dr Isaac, 38, 40
Eppel, Simon, 38
Estabrook, Howard, 46
Euskal Media, 234
Evans, Clifford, 66, 67
Evans, David, 68
Evans, Edith, 126

INDEX OF NAMES

Fagan, Charles, 68
Faherty, Patcheen, 50
Fairley, Michelle, 188
Faithfull, Geoffrey, 68
Fallon, Gabriel, 74, 75
Fandango, 218
Faraway, 136
Faris, Alexander, 120
Farrell, Michael, 56
Farrell, Paul, 66, 67, 116
Farrelly, Moya, 246, 248
Fassbender, William, 56
Fay, W G, 84, 85
Faye, Janina, 106, 107
Fegan, Maggie, 172, 173
Fellowes, Rockcliffe, 16, 17-18
Fenton, Leslie, 42, 43
Ferndale Films, 186
Ferris, John, 112
Fields, W C, 83
Figgis, Danny, 148, 149
Film Company of Ireland, 20, 21,
   22, 23, 24, 25, 28, 30,
Film Four, 204
FilmDallas Pictures, 182
Filmline Intl, 246
Finaly, Mary, 218
Finch, Peter, 124, 125
Fine, H, 56
Finn, Mickey, 146
Finnan, Pascal, 146
Finnegan, Dave, 196, 197
Finney, Albert, 220, 221
First National Pictures, 54
Fisher, George, 6, 7
Fitzgerald, Barry, 56, 57, 98, 99,
   100, 101, 108, 109, 183
Fitzgerald, Ciarán, 204, 205, 242
Fitzgerald, Geraldine, 250
Fitzgerald, Gregg, 212, 213
Fitzgerald, Josephine, 78, 102, 103
Fitzgerald, Neil, 58
Fitzgerald, Susan, 150
Fitzgerald, Tara, 220, 221
Fitzgerald, Walter, 110, 111
Fitzgerlad, Ciarán, 228
Fitzsimmons, Charles, 98
Flaherty, Frances, 50
Flaherty, Robert, 50, 51-53, 149, 153
Flanagan, Fionnuala, 128, 129-131,
   175, 228
Fleming, Milt, 186
Flicker Productions, 170
Flood, Tom, 38
Flynn, Errol, 54, 55

Flynn, Gerard Mannix, 164
Flynn, Rita, 42
Foley, Bill, 116, 148
Foley, Don, 158
Ford, 98
Ford, Cecil, 74, 75
Ford, Francis, 58, 98
Ford, John, 21, 58, 59, 93, 95, 98, 99,
   101, 104, 105, 126, 127, 153, 249
Ford, Wallace, 58, 59
Forde, Seamus, 134, 135, 164, 165
Foreman, John, 142
Foster, Barry, 136, 138
Foster, Preston, 58
Four Provinces Productions, 104
Fox, William, 16,
Franken, Rose, 64
Fraser, Laura, 240, 241
Frears, Stephen, 210
Freeman, David, 212, 220
French, Fergal, 222
Fricker, Brenda, 161, 186, 187, 190,
   193, 220, 221
Friday, Gavin, 208
Fry, Rosalie K, 216
Fullerton, Andew, 238

Gaffney, Liam, 68, 69, 82, 83
Gainsborough, 50
Gallagher, Bronagh, 196, 197, 207,
   240
Gallagher, Joe, 234, 235
Gallagher, Suzanne, 216
Gambon, Michael, 220, 221
Gant, Richard, 240
Garfath, Mike, 170
Garland, Michael, 232
Garnett, Tay, 118, 119
Gaumont, 50
Gauntier, Gene, 2, 3, 4, 5, 6, 7, 9,
   10, 11
Gaup, Mikkel, 200, 201
Genet, Jean, 129
George, Terry, 208, 209
George, Terry, 219, 228, 229
Geraghty, Clive, 132, 133
Gerrard, Joanne, 210
Gibbs, 116
Gibson, Catherine, 164, 194
Gibson, Derek, 188
Gielgud, John, 148, 149, 151
Gill, Anna, 172
Gill, Earl, 200
Gill, Gwenllian, 68, 69
Gillen, Aidan, 228, 229

Gillen, Freda, 172
Gilliat, Sidney, 78, 81, 82, 83
Ginna, Robert Emmett, 126
Glasmon, Kubec, 42
Glazier, Sidney, 134
Gleason, Brendan, 190, 204, 205,
   210, 234, 235, 236, 238, 242, 244,
   246, 247
Gleason, James, 46, 60
Glover, Julian, 124, 125
Goff, Ivan, 114
Gogan, Jane, 178
Goldblatt, Harold, 102, 104, 108,
   109
Goldcrest, 164
Golden, Edward, 78, 82, 116, 118,
   120, 128, 148, 149
Golden, Geoffrey, 116, 117, 118,
   128, 129, 194, 195
Golden, Michael, 86
Goldenthal, Elliot, 224, 238
Goldsworthy, John, 92
Goldwyn, Samuel, 64
Gorcey, Leo, 70
Gordon, Dan, 228
Gordon, Michael, 104
Gorman, Eric, 120, 121
Gormley, Felim, 196, 197
Gorry, David, 170
Gottinger, Lislott, 124
Gough, Michael, 96, 97
Gould, Stephen, 22, 23
Graham, Sheila, 154
Grahame, Margot, 58, 59
Granada TV, 186, 190
Granger, Stewart, 82, 83
Green, F L, 84
Green, Gilbert, 28
Green, Philip, 94, 108
Green, Sarah, 216
Greenblatt, Kathy, 182
Greene, David, 88, 89
Greene, James, 207
Greenwood, John, 50
Gregg, Colin, 170, 171
Gregory, Lady, 105
Gregory, Michael, 207
Gregson, John, 102, 108, 109
Grehan, Aingeal, 154
Grehan, Carmel, 154
Gribble, Bernard, 86
Griffin, George, 28
Griffith, D W, 17, 25, 35, 36, 49
Griffiths, Rachel, 240
Gruber, Juliette, 214, 215

Guiney, Ed, 214, 215, 218
Guthridge, John, 102

Hackett, Gillian, 162
Haines, Fred, 128, 129
Hale, Alan, 34
Hale, Julie, 186
Hall, Huntz, 70
Haller, Daniel, 132, 133
Halligan, Derek, 240
Halligan, Liam, 162, 168, 169
Halop, Billy, 70
Halpin, Oonah, 22, 23
Hambling, Arthur, 88
Hambling, Gerry, 192, 208
Hamilton, Paula, 167
Hamilton, Robert, 170
Hanbury, W Victor, 88
Hanly, Peter, 182, 218, 219
Hannawalt, Charles, 122
Hannigan, Declan, 216
Hansard, Glen, 196, 197
Hanseat, 148
Harbaugh, Carl, 16, 17
Harcourt, James, 78
Harkin, Margo, 184, 185
Harlow, Jean, 42, 44
Harmer, Lillian, 46
Harper, Frank, 208
Harpur, Joan, 168, 169
Harris, Richard, 114, 118, 119, 190,
    191, 193, 232, 233
Harrison, Cathryn, 140
Harte, Ian, 224, 238
Hartnell, William, 84
Harvey, Forrester, 54
Harvey, Grizelda, 58
Harvey, Walter, 66
Hassell, George, 54
Hastings, Máire, 128
Haybeard, Roy, 194
Hayden, Karl, 182, 183, 194
Hayden, Maria, 174
Hayes, Máirín, 56
Hayes, Tom, 162
Hayward, Richard, 68, 69
Heale, Patrick Keenan, 74
Healy, Dermot, 250
Healy, Gerald, 96
Healy, Tommy, 146
Heffernan, Honor, 158, 159
Heffernan, William, 178, 179
Hell's Kitchen, 208
Hely, Kevin, 234
Hemdale Film Corp, 188

Henchey, Evelyn, 38, 39
Hennessey, Michael, 124
Hennessy, Michael C, 112, 124
Hennessy, Peter, 120
Hennessy, Robert, 96, 97
Hepburn, Doreen, 182, 183
Herbert, Holmes, 54
Herbert, Percy, 142
Heron, Nye, 208
Herron, Alastair, 154
Hersholt, Jean, 34
Hetherington, Stuart, 148
Hewitt, John, 167
Heywood, Anne, 118, 119
Hibernia Films, 62
Hickey, Paul, 242
Hickey, Tom, 186, 200
Hickey, William, 182, 183
Higgins, Sabina, 180
Hill, Walter, 142
Hillier, Erwin, 114
Hinde, John, 249
Hinds, Ciarán, 194, 195, 228, 230
Hitchcock, Alfred, 35
Hitchcock, Reginald, see Ingram,
    Rex
Hoch, Winton C, 110
Hoey, John, 112
Hogan, Bosco, 144, 148, 149, 162,
    163
Hogan, Stephen, 228
Hogarty, David, 134
Holland, Rodney, 194
Hollander, Tom, 228
Hollinshead, Becca, 204
Hollinshead, Bianca, 204
Hollister, Alice, 6, 7
Hollister, George, 2, 3, 4, 6, 10
Holloway, Stanley, 86, 87
Holmes, Christopher, 132
Holmes, Stuart, 34
Homans, Robert E, 42, 43
Hordern, Michael, 142, 143
Hot Property, 250
Houlden, Michelle, 218, 219
Howard Productions, 64
Howard, Trevor, 78, 79-81, 136
Howley, Alan, 184, 185
Howley, Christy, 156
Huber, Harold, 46
Hughes, Barnard, 182, 183
Hughes, Dermot, 222
Hughes, Edward, 222
Hughes, Enda, 222, 223
Hughes, Hazel, 76, 77

Hughes, Michael, 222, 223
Hume, Maude, 28
Hummingbird Communications,
    246
Hunt, Eamonn, 162, 218, 234
Huntley, Raymond, 78, 79
Hurst, Brian Desmond, 66, 91
Hurt, John, 190, 191
Hussein, Waris, 134
Huston, Angelica, 174, 175-177
Huston, Anthony, 175, 177
Huston, John, 142, 143, 174, 175,
    177
Hutchinson, Harry, 66, 67, 106
Hutton, Pauline, 246
Hymer, Warren, 46

Ibañez, Vicente Blasco, 34
IFB, 214, 216
Individual Pictures (UK), 78, 82
INFC, 74
Ingram, Rex, 34, 36-37
Ingram, Richard, 224
Initial Film, 188
Irish Film Board, 172, 180, 234
Irvine, Andrea, 214, 215
Irvine, Blanaid, 116, 183, 214, 215
Irving, Roy, 84, 85
Irwin, Charles, 92
Issacs, Jason, 240

Jackson, Barry, 136
Jackson, Cyril, 56
Jackson, Mary, 154, 155
James, Sidney, 106, 107
Jamison, Lucie, 154
Jannan, Reginald, 144
Jarre, Maurice, 136, 142
Jeakins, Dorothy, 179
Jefford, Barbara, 128, 129-131
Jennings, Dev, 42
John of Aran, 50
Johns, Glynis, 114, 115
Johns, Mervyn, 82
Johnson, Denis, 66
Johnson, Fred, 96, 97, 100
Johnson, Georgina, 56
Johnson, Stanley, 110
Johnston, Adrian, 240
Johnston, Audrey, 164
Johnston, Denis, 56, 57
Johnston, Luke, 148, 149
Jones, Christopher, 136, 137
Jones, Marie, 184, 207, 208
Jones, Trevor, 208

Jordan, Bobby, 70
Jordan, Neil, 156, 158, 159, 200,
    201, 202, 203, 224, 225, 227, 238,
    239
Joyce, James, 128, 149, 150, 174, 175
Justine, R V, 20

Kalem Company, 2, 3, 4, 5, 6, 7, 11
Kane, Billy, 154
Kaufman, Charles, 106
Kavanagh, H T, 110
Kavanagh, John, 132, 133, 161, 164,
    165, 204, 205, 238, 246, 247
Kavanagh, Patrick 188
Kavanagh, Thomas, 212, 213
Kay, Kwesi, 168, 169
Kean, Maire, 102, 103, 108, 109,
    112, 120, 124, 125, 136, 158, 174,
    176, 177
Keane, Desmond, 86
Keane, Eamonn, 190, 191
Keane, John B, 190, 191, 193
Kearney, Gerard, 212
Keating, Alice, 24, 26, 28, 29
Keating, Arthur, 162
Keating, Henry, 112, 113
Keegan, Barry, 102, 103
Keegan, John, 154, 155
Kellaway, Cecil, 92, 93
Kellegher, Tina, 210, 211
Kelly, Darragh, 214
Kelly, David, 124, 128-130, 134,
    148, 150, 162, 163, 204, 205, 220
Kelly, Dermot, 86, 112, 120
Kelly, Eamonn, 234
Kelly, P J, 64
Kelly, Simon, 186
Kelly, Skeets, 78
Kelly, Trudy, 154
Kelly, W A, 86
Kelton, Pert, 46
Kemplen, Ralph, 106
Kennally, Eileen, 170
Kennedy, Arthur, 112, 113
Kennedy, Brian, 232
Kenny, John, 224
Kent, Anne, 196, 197
Keogh, Jimmy, 218
Kerr, Deborah, 78, 79-81, 89
Kerrigan, J M, 20, 21, 92, 93
Kestelman, Sara, 144, 145
Keveney, Chris, 200
Kibbee, Guy, 54
Kickham, Charles, 24, 25
Kidder, Margot, 134, 135

Kildare, Owen, 16
Killanin, Lord, 104
King, Claude, 64
King, Coleman 'Tiger', 50, 51
King, Ivan, 88
King, Philip, 208, 246
Kinnell, Murray, 42, 43
Kirwan, Dervla, 194
Kirwan, Kitty, 84
Kirwan, Patrick 102, 108, 116, 183
Kitty the Hare, 123
Kivilo, Alar, 182
Knieper, Jürgen, 194
Knopfler, Mark, 164
Knowlden, Marilyn, 70
Koch, Winton, 98
Kohlmar, Fred, 92
Korngold, Erich Wolfgang, 54
Koster, Henry, 92
Krasker, Robert, 84, 104, 106
Krishnamma, Suri, 220, 221
Kubrick, Stanley, 163

La Frenais, Ian, 196, 199
Lacambre, Daniel, 132
Laffan, Patrick, 124, 125, 186, 168,
    169, 210, 211
Lally, Mick, 161, 216, 217, 220, 221,
    250
Lalor, Leslie, 148
Lamb, Peadar, 172, 173
Lambert, Conor, 186
Lane, Charles, 46
Lang, Robert, 142, 228
Lappin, Arthur, 208, 228
Larchet, George, 24, 25
Lashelle, Joseph, 92
Launder, Frank, 78, 81, 82
Laverty, Frank, 224
Lawler, Iris, 120
Lawler, James B S, 60
Lawless, Eddie, 28
Lawlor, Sean, 180, 181
Lawrence, Christy, 96
Lawson, Charles, 167
Lawson, Tony, 224, 238
Lawton, Frank, 104
Lawton, Kieran, 146
Layde, Pat, 112, 132
Leaf, Richard, 232
Leahy, Eugene, 74
Lean, David, 136, 137-139
Leavy, Pat, 162
LeBlanc, Donal, 132, 133
Lee, Fintan, 218

Leigh, Mike, 167, 168, 169
Lenagh, Tom, 222
Lennon, Kathry, 214
Leonard, Hugh, 182, 183
Leslie, Dudley, 66
Lesslie, Colin, 96
Levy, Edward, 56
Lewenstein, Oscar, 124
Lewis, J Gordon, 28
Liebman, Michael, 184, 185
Liffey Films, 174
Lilburn, James, 98
Lillis, John, 180
Limehouse Pictures, 170
Lindo, Olga, 78
Lindsay, Robert, 240, 241
Linehan, Rosaleen, 128, 148, 238
Lines, Graham, 128
Lionsgate, 140
Liquid Films, 250
Lister, Moira, 86, 87
Little Bird, 194, 204, 220
Lloyd Russell, 142
Loach, Ken, 169, 188, 189
Loder, John, 66, 67, 106
Lodge, John, 66, 67, 63
London Films, 94
Lord, Derek, 158
Lorimer, Louise, 92
Love, Bessie, 106
Lover, Samuel, 4
Lowe, Frances, 194
Lunny, Donal, 246
Lycett, Eustace, 111
Lydon, Gary, 214
Lynch, Joe, 118, 124, 126, 128
Lynch, John, 164, 165, 208, 216,
    228, 230, 231, 232, 233
Lynch, Susan, 216
Lysaght, W T, 20

Mac Donnacha, Máirtín, 146
Mac Iomhair, Seán, 146
Mac Lochlan, Tomás, 146
MacAn, Tony, 56
MacAulay, Tom, 78, 79
MacBlante, Séamus, 30, 31
MacCabe, Leo, 58
MacCartaigh, Mícheál, 216
MacDarby, John, 142, 143
MacDonagh, John, 30, 31
MacDonnell, Barrett, 30, 31
MacEoin, Tomás, 152
MacFhlannchada, Máirtín, 146
MacGabhann, Brendan, 184

INDEX OF NAMES

MacGarvey, Cathal, 38, 39
MacGinnis, Niall, 66, 67, 82, 83, 116, 117, 118
MacGowran, Jack 96, 97, 98, 99, 104, 108, 109, 110, 126
Macken, Walter, 112, 113, 120, 121
MacLaverty, Bernard, 164, 165, 170
MacLiam, Eanna, 210, 211, 242
MacMurrough, Dermot, 76
MacNamara, Frances, 38, 39
MacNamara, Walter, 12, 13, 14, 163
Magee, Barney, 12
Magee, Patrick, 122, 123
Mageean, Jimmy, 68, 69, 100
Magowan, Brian, 20, 21, 22, 23, 24, 25, 30, 31, 38, 39
Majestic Films, 204, 220
Malahide, Patrick, 194, 195, 220
Malcolmson, Rodney, 76, 77
Malone, Kay Rae, 178, 179
Manahan, Anna, 128, 220
Manahan, Sheila, 86, 94, 95, 106, 107
Manning, Joe, 56
Manning, Mary, 56
Manning, Wolfe, 142
Mapes, Agnes, 2, 3, 6, 7
Maranelli, Dario, 234
Marcus, James A, 16, 17
Marianelli, Dario, 214
Marks, Owen, 70
Marmot, Janine, 250
Marsh, Garry, 78, 79
Martin, Edie, 86
Marvin, Mia, 42, 44
Marwyn, J Miles, 68, 69
Mason, James, 84, 85, 142, 143, 230
Massey, Dick, 196, 197
Mathis, June, 34, 35
Matthews, A E, 100, 101
Matthews, Brendan, 134
Matthewson, Ernest, 28
Mayne, Herbert, 28
McAleer, Des, 162, 167, 232
McAlinney, Patrick, 100
McAnally, Ray, 114, 115, 158, 159, 164, 165, 186, 187, 191
McAuliffe, Michael, 178, 179
McAvinchey, Paul, 222, 223
McBride, Ray, 180, 181, 204, 218
McCabe, Leo, 64
McCabe, Mary, 172
McCabe, Pat, 238, 239, 250
McCabe, Ruth, 186, 187, 190, 200, 210, 211

McCafferty, Frankie, 214, 216, 218
McCairbe, Ronan, 224
McCann, Brian, 188, 189
McCann, Donal, 142, 143, 152, 153, 158, 164, 165, 172, 173, 174, 175, 177, 194, 195, 200, 201
McCann, Johnny, 16, 17
McCann, Nuala, 154
McCarthy, Dermot, 28
McCarthy, Hugh, 154
McCarthy, Mary, 178
McClory, Sean, 174
McCluskey, Kenneth, 196, 197
McCormick, F J, 84, 85
McCourt, Emer, 184, 185
McCourt, Malachy, 190, 192
McCoy, Harry, 16
McCreevy, Jimmy, 250
McCusker, Stella, 232
McDade, Ross, 232, 233
McDermott, Edward M
McDermottroe, Maria, 174, 176, 246, 248
McDonald, Frank, 182, 190
McDonald, Julie, 184, 194, 195
McDonald, Peter, 234, 235, 236
McDonnell, Fergus, 84
McDonnell, John, 188
McDonnell, Patrick, 28
McDonough, Pat, 50
McDormand, Frances, 188, 189
McElhatton, Michael, 234, 235
McElherron, Fergal, 216
McElhinney, Ian, 158, 162, 163, 170, 180, 181, 188, 189, 207, 232
McGarvey, Seamus, 250, 251
McGeown, Anne, 214
McGill, Barney, 46
McGinley, Sean, 190, 192, 224, 238, 242, 244
McGlynn Sr, Frank, 54
McGoohan, Patrick, 120, 121
McGowan, J P, 2, 4, 5, 7
McGuckian, Margery, 232
McGuckian, Mary, 232, 233
McGuinness, Mr, 28
McHugh, Martin J, 105
McKay, Craig, 228
McKenna, Bernadette, 170
McKenna, Breffni, 202
McKenna, Sí obhan, 88, 89, 91
McKenna, T P, 118, 124, 125, 126, 128, 129-130, 148, 149, 150
McKenzie-Bary, Sarah, 146
McKern, Leo, 136, 137-138

McKnight, Michael, 194
McLaglen, Victor, 58, 59, 98, 99
McLaughlin, Declan, 184
McLoughlin, Lise-Anne, 158
McLoughlin, Ned, 214
McLynn, Pauline, 218, 219
McManus, Kate, 154
McNeill, Allen, 46
McNulty, Sonny, 161
McPherson, Conor, 234, 236, 237
McPolin, Owen, 250
McSorley, Gerard, 158, 228
Meade, Walter, 86
Meadows, Jayne, 92, 93
Meaney, Colm, 174, 196, 197, 204, 205, 210, 211, 212, 246, 247
Measor, Beryl, 84
Medwin, Michael, 86, 87
Meegan, Paddy, 158
Meek, Donald, 54, 58, 59
Megaw, Laine, 240, 241
Mendoza, David, 42
Menges, Chris, 158, 224
Menton, Denis, 210
Mercer, Beryl, 42, 43
Merrit, George, 88
Metro, 34
MGM, 136
Middleton, Noelle, 100
Miles, Sarah, 136, 137-139
Millais, Hugh, 140, 141
Millane, Michael, 50
Miller, David, 106
Mills, John, 136, 137-139
Mills, Reginald, 128
Mirren, Helen, 164, 165, 228
Mitchell, Mary, 122, 123
Mitchum, Robert, 118, 119, 136, 137-138
Mockridge, Cyril J, 92
Molloy, Dearbhla, 132, 133, 232
Molloy, John, 132, 133
Monsarrat, Nicholas, 106
Montagu, Ivor, 86
Montgomery, Bruce, 112
Montgomery, Niall, 56
Moody, Ron, 113
Mooney, Ria, 116
Moore, Kieron, 94, 95, 110, 111
Moore, Nick, 240
Moran, Seamus, 208
Moriarty, Dr D A, 30, 60
Morley, John, 140
Morley, Karen, 64, 65
Morris, Adrian, 70

INDEX OF NAMES

Morris, Jonathan, 188
Morris, Oswald, 142
Morris, Redmond, 200, 238
Morrison, Steve, 186
Morrison, Van, 170
Morrissey, Eamon, 246
Morse, Barry, 88
Morton, Samantha, 232, 233
Morven, Myrette, 76, 77
Motion Picture Company of
    Ireland, 158
Moxley, Gina, 178, 179, 246, 248
Moylan, Tiffy, 156, 157
Moynihan, Séamus, 74
Muir, Esther, 46
Mulhall, Jack, 64
Mulholland, Mark, 154
Mullen, Conor, 214
Mullin, Pat, 50
Munier, Ferdinand, 46
Munn, Brian, 164, 165
Munro, Janet, 110
Munrow, David, 144
Murfi, Mikel, 218
Murnane, Mary, 28
Murphy, Bill, 60
Murphy, Daisy, 74
Murphy, Fionnula, 210
Murphy, Fred, 174
Murphy, J J, 164
Murphy, Jacky, 222
Murphy, Johnny, 168, 169, 196,
    197, 204, 205
Murphy, Kathleen, 22, 24, 25, 78
Murphy, Martin, 224,
Murphy, Pat, 154, 155, 162, 163
Murphy, Paul, 134
Murphy, Tom, 242
Murphy, Vinnie, 162, 178, 179, 242
Murray, Brian, 148, 150
Murray, Don, 114, 115
Murray, Jack, 98
Myers, Stanley, 128, 148, 210
Myers, Thelma, 78, 82
Myles, Lynda, 196, 210

Naish, J Carroll, 54
Natwick, Mildred, 98, 99
Naughton, Darragh, 212
Nee, Little John, 180
Neeson, Liam, 170, 171, 224, 225-
    226
Neil-Brown, J, 74
Nesbitt, James, 232
Neville, Stuart, 222

Newcomm, 204
Newell, Mike, 204, 205
Newhouse, David, 94
Newman, Alfred, 64
Newman, Paul, 142, 143
Newton, Robert, 84, 85
Newton, Sally Anne, 144
Ní Balustrum, Bairbre, 146
Ní Chonghaile, Mairead, 152, 153
Ní Chumhaill, Bríd, 218
Ní Dhonncha, Bairbre, 152
Ni Dhonnchú, Caitlín, 146
Ní Dhrisceoil, Máire, 146
Ní Fhlatharta, Bernadette, 146
Ní Ghallchóir, Máiréad, 216
Ní Shúilleabhain, Síobhan, 146
Niall, Ian, 96, 97
Nichols, Dudley, 58, 59
Nieter, Hans, 68
Nilsson, Anna Q, 16, 17-18
Niven, David, 64, 100, 101
Nolan, Anto, 168
Nolan, Larry, 168
Noone, Máire, 168
Norden, Christine, 94, 95
Norina, Madam, 10, 11
North, Alex, 174
Norton, Fletcher, 46
Norton, Jim, 188, 189, 204
Nugent, Frank S, 98, 104
Nuttall Beyda, Nancy, 180
Nykvist, Sven, 195

Ó Bríain, Míchéal, 112, 116, 124
Ó Coisdealbha, Seán, 152, 172, 180
Ó Colaí, Máirtain, 146
Ó Fátharta, Macdara, 152
Ó Fathartha, Máirtín, 146
Ó Finneadha, Colm, 146
Ó Flaithearta, Tomás, 172
Ó Flatharta, Tomás, 152, 153
Ó hAinle, Gearóid, 146
Ó Lionáird, Iarla, 250
Ó Maollalaí, Micheál, 152
Ó Maonlaí, Colm, 250
Ó Maonlaí, Liam, 250
O'Brien, Barry, 12, 13
O'Brien, Deirdre, 210
O'Brien, Edna 124, 125
O'Brien, Niall, 136, 162, 163, 214
O'Brien, Pat, 70, 71-73
O'Brien, Ronald, 122
O'Byrne, Colm, 210
O'Cahill, Donal, 60, 61, 74
O'Callaghan, Ed, 136

O'Casey, Ronan, 100
O'Casey, Sean, 126, 127
O'Connell, Marian, 60
O'Connor, Eugene, 218
O'Connor, Frank, 56, 57, 105, 201
O'Connor, Joseph, 214, 215
O'Connor, Pat, 161, 164, 165
O'Connor, Robert Emmett, 42, 43
O'Connor, Sinéad, 184, 185, 238,
    239
O'Connor, Stuart, 170
O'Connor, Thomas, 2, 3
O'Connor, Una, 58, 59
O'Conor, Hugh, 170, 171, 182, 186,
    187
O'D Productions, 76
O'Dea, Denis, 84, 104, 105, 106,
    107, 110
O'Dea, Jimmy, 76, 77, 104, 105, 110,
    111
O'Dea, Joseph, 98
O'Donnell, Agnes, 156
O'Donnell, Joe, 120, 124
O'Donnell, Maire, 112, 113, 132,
    133
O'Donnell, Patrick, 24, 25
O'Donoghue, Maurice, 168, 169,
    182
O'Donovan, Derry, 122
O'Donovan, Fred, 12, 20, 21, 22, 23,
    24, 25, 58, 67, 86
O'Donovan, Harry, 60, 76, 77
O'Donovan, Noel, 162, 163, 190,
    250
O'Dowd, Dermot, 24, 30, 31
O'Farrell, Bernadette, 82
O'Flaherty, Liam, 58, 59
O'Flaherty, Susan, 172
O'Flynn, Phillip, 108, 109, 112, 113,
    116, 120, 121, 126, 127, 136
O'Gallagher, Eamonn, 104
O'Gorman, Owen, 204
O'Gorman, W, 78, 79
O'Grady, Chris, 172
O'Grady, Timothy, 250, 251
O'Hanlon, Ardal, 238
O'Hara, David, 228, 229
O'Hara, Joan, 112, 113, 182, 220
O'Hara, Maureen, 95, 98, 99
O'Hare, Denis, 222
O'Hehir, Róisín, 156
O'Herlihy, Cormac, 174
O'Herlihy, Dan, 84, 85, 118, 119,
    174, 175, 177
O'Higgins, Brian, 96, 97, 100

O'Kelly, Donal, 234
O'Leary, Helen, 212
O'Leary, Jer, 190, 200, 224
O'Mahoney, Jerry, 60
O'Mahoney, Michael, 86
O'Mahoney, Nora, 88, 110
O'Malley, Áine, 172
O'Malley, Daragh, 164
O'Malley, Dominick, 172
O'Malley, Kit, 38, 39
O'Malley, Martin, 172
O'Malley, Maura, 196, 199
O'Malley, Oliver, 172
O'Malley, Pat, 60
O'Neill, Chris, 162
O'Neill, Colleen, 242
O'Neill, Máire, 94, 95
O'Neill, Nicholas, 250
O'Neill, Tommy, 242
O'Rawe, Geraldine, 228
O'Riada, Seán, 126
O'Rorke, Brefni, 78, 79
O'Rourke, Breffni, 24
O'Rourke, Tommy, 50
O'Shea, Marc, 207, 232, 233
O'Shea, Milo, 116, 128, 129-130,
    132, 133, 238
O'Sullivan, Aisling, 238, 239
O'Sullivan, Arthur, 120, 121, 126
O'Sullivan, Brian, 60, 61, 74, 75
O'Sullivan, Frank, 224, 234
O'Sullivan, Maureen, 96
O'Sullivan, Owen, 136
O'Sullivan, Richard, 102
O'Sullivan, Thaddeus, 156, 157,
    162, 163, 168, 169, 194, 195, 251
O'Toole, Aidan, 250
O'Toole, John, 242
O'Toole, Katherine, 174
O'Toole, Patrick, 172
Oberon, Merle, 64, 65
Olcott, Sidney, 2, 3, 4, 5, 6, 7, 9, 10,
    11,
Ollis, May, 134
Olohan, John, 238
Orgar, Betty, 96
Orrom, Michael, 96
Owens, Eamonn, 238, 239, 242, 244

Palace Pictures, 200, 202
Palmer, Tim, 204
Pan, Kant, 202, 232
Parallel, 204
Parker, Alan, 196, 197, 199
Parker, C S, 76

Parker, Cecil, 82, 83
Parker, Clifton, 88
Paterson, Joseph, 208
Patrick, Nigel, 142
Patterson, Frank, 174, 176
Patterson, Lee, 106, 107
Patterson, Robert, 188
Patton, Bart, 122
Patton, N F, 24, 25
Pavey, Stanley, 88, 100, 112
Pavlow, Muriel, 108, 109
Pawley, Edward, 70
Pearce, Michael, 204
Pearce, Michel, 131, 175
Pearson, Noel, 186, 190
Pedelty, Donovan, 68
Pedersoli, Giuseppe, 218
Pelly, Farrell, 110
Pembridge, 232
Pembroke, Clifford, 38
Pembroke, George, 68, 69
Pender, M T, 20
Pendleton, Gaylord, 58
Pergaud, Louis, 212, 213
Perry, Desmond, 128, 132, 148, 149
Pertwee, Michael, 100
Phillips, Joan, 108, 109
Phillips, Leslie, 116, 117
Phillips, Siân, 126, 127
Pickering, Andrew, 170
Pilkington, Joe, 156, 161, 220
Pilkington, Lorraine, 200, 201
Polanski, Roman, 215
Polito, Sol, 70
Pollock, George, 103, 108
Poole, Mabbie, 94
Portman, Rachel, 212
Portman, Rachel, 212
Postlethwaite, Pete, 208, 209
Potter, H C, 64
Potter, Maureen, 104, 105, 128, 148,
    149
Powell, Nick, 240
Power, Brendan, 218
Power, Charles, 24, 25
Power, Derry, 116
Power, Tyrone, 92, 93. 105
Pratt, Purnell, 42
Productions de la Guéville, 212
Promenade FP, 200
Pubsley, Bernard, 70
Purcell, Noel, 76, 77, 82, 83, 94, 95,
    96, 97, 102, 103, 104, 105, 108,
    109, 114, 115, 118, 119, 142
Puttnam, David, 164, 212

Pyke, Steve, 250, 251

Queally, Jim, 178
Quigley, Godfrey, 104, 108, 109,
    118
Quilligan, Veronica, 158, 159
Quinn, Aidan, 224, 225, 246, 247,
    248
Quinn, Bob, 146, 147, 152, 153, 172,
    173
Quinn, Declan, 178, 246, 247
Quinn, Marian, 246, 247
Quinn, Pat, 222
Quinn, Paul, 246, 247, 249
Quinn, Tony, 66, 67, 78, 94, 104,
    106

Raft, George, 46, 47
Ralph, Jessie, 54
Rampling, Charlotte, 144, 145
Randall-Cutler, Roger, 196
Randell, Ron, 106, 107
Rank Organisation, 102
Rascoe, Judith, 148, 149
Rathbone, Basil, 54, 55
Rea, Stephen, 158, 159, 167, 202,
    203, 224, 230, 238, 239, 246, 247,
    250
Reade Jr, Walter, 128
Reddin, Kenneth, 86
Redgrave, Corin, 208
Redgrave, Lynn, 124, 125
Redgrave, Michael, 114, 115, 126,
    127, 224
Redmond, Liam, 78, 82, 88, 89, 94,
    100, 102, 103, 108, 109
Reed, Carol, 84, 85
Reed, Maxwell, 88, 89
Reed, Peter, 122
Reeves, Anita, 158, 200, 204
Reeves, Saskia, 194, 195
Regan, Liam, 234
Reid, Eileen, 220
Reid, Graham, 207
Reidy, Gabrielle, 194
Reilly, Dominick, 12
Renzi, Maggie, 216
Republic, 98
Reynolds, Emer, 214, 234
Reynolds, T O'Carroll, 28, 29
Rhodes, Christopher, 118
Richards, C M P, 76
Richards, Shelah, 56, 57
Richardson, Henry, 116
Richardson, Marian, 156

INDEX OF NAMES

Richardson, Miranda, 202, 203
Rickman, Alan, 224, 225
Rimkus, Stevan, 164, 165
RKO, 58
Roberts, Ben, 114
Roberts, Charles, 168
Roberts, John, 212
Roberts, Julia, 224, 225
Roberts, Valentine, 22, 23, 24, 25
Robinson, Casey, 54
Robson, Flora, 126, 127
Roche, Frank, 168
Rocks, Paddy, 240
Rodway, Norman, 116, 117
Roëves, Maurice, 128, 129-130, 150, 188, 189
Rogers, Julie, 184, 185
Rohr, Tony, 158
Rolston, Louis, 164
Romulus, 106
Rooney, Gerald, 216, 217
Rooney, Miss, 24
Rosenthal, Joe, 38
Ross, Julie, 126
Roth Solomon, Bessie, 46
Roth, Arthur, 118
Rotha, Paul, 96, 97, 157
Rourke, Mickey, 230
Rousselot, Philippe, 200
Rowen, Peter, 210
RTÉ, 148, 156, 214, 234
Ruadh, Patch (Red Beard), 50
Rubinstein, John, 132
Rudkin, David, 194, 195
Russell, Jasmine, 218, 219
Ruxton, Charles, 178, 179
Ryan, Eveanna, 212
Ryan, Ger, 212
Ryan, Jacqueline, 102, 103
Ryan, Jonathan, 172, 173
Ryan, Kathleen, 82, 83, 84, 85, 102, 103
Ryan, Tim, 92

Sabatini, Gabriel, 54
Sainpolis, John, 34
Salew, John, 78
Samaniegos, Ramon, 34
Samuel, Philip, 84
Sanda, Dominique, 142
Santley, Laurene, 2
Saunders, Jessica, 170
Savage, Norman, 136
Savino, Joe, 202
Sawyer, Joe, 58

Sayles, John, 216, 217
Scaife, Ted, 126
Scanlan, Carol, 180, 181
Schanzer, Karl, 122
Schulz-Keil, Wieland, 174
Scott, Mike, 232
Sears, Heather, 106, 107
Seezer, Maurice, 208
Seitz, John, 34
Sewell, Rufus, 220, 221
Sextant Films, 126
Shane, George, 154, 164, 168, 169
Sharpe, Albert, 110, 111
Shaw, Fiona, 186, 187, 238, 239
Sheehan, Cecil, 148
Sheehy, Joan, 190
Sheen, Martin, 182, 183
Sheer, William, 16
Sheik, Shirley, 222
Sheldon, 136
Sheldon, Horace, 74
Shepherd, Mark, 208, 209
Shepley, Michael, 100, 101
Sheridan, Ann, 70, 71
Sheridan, Dinah, 68, 69
Sheridan, Jim, 186, 187, 190, 191, 193, 204, 205, 208, 209, 228, 229, 232, 233, 243,
Sheridan, Richard, 216, 217
Sheridan, Richard, 30, 31
Sheriff, R C, 84
Shields, Arthur, 24, 25, 98
Shine, Bill, 86
Sievernich, Chris, 174
Sigel, Tom, 204
Silliphant, Stirling, 130
Silvi, Roberto, 174
Sim, Alaister, 82
Simmons, Michael L, 46
Simpson, Geoffrey, 228
Sinclair, Ronald, 64
Skerry Movies Corp, 216
Slattery, Tony, 202
Slocombe, Douglas, 86
Slowey, Pat, 216
Smedley-Aston, Brian, 124
Smith, Britta, 208
Smith, J, 20,
Smith, Maggie, 126, 127
Smith, Robert, 154
Snowden, Alec C, 116
Spain, Noel, 180
Spillane, Davy, 156
Staines, George, 188
Standing, Wyndham, 64

Standún, Pádraig, 172
Stapleton, Oliver, 210
Stein, Ronald, 122, 123
Steiner, Max, 58, 59, 70
Stembridge, Gerard, 218, 219
Stephenson, Henry, 54, 64, 65
Stevenson, Robert, 110
Stoker, Bram, 123
Stoneman, Rod, 218
Stout, Archie, 98
Strick, Joseph, 97, 128-131, 148-151, 175
Strong, Andrew, 196, 197
Strong, L A G, 100
Stross, Raymond, 118
Suedo, Julie, 76, 77
Sullivan, J M, 21, 23, 24
Sumner, Robin, 126
Sundstrom, Jacqueline, 120
Suschitzky, Wolfgang, 96, 97, 128
Swanson, Maureen, 102
Sweeney, Birdy, 180, 202
Sweeney, Michael, 146
Swickard, Joseph, 34, 35
Swift, Jessica, 144
Swingley, William, 92
Syms, Sylvia, 120, 121

Talent, Julie, 88
Tanner, Peter, 118
Tarantino, Quentin, 238
Tattersall, Gale, 196
Taylor, Gilbert, 134
Taylor, Rod, 126, 127
Taylor, Victor, 74
Temple Films, 214, 218
Teron, Sylvia, 200
Terry, Alice, 34, 36, 37
Thew, Harvey F, 42
Thewlis, David, 240, 241
Thompson, Emma, 208, 209
Thompson, Marian, 114
Thompson, Tommy, 140
Thorburn, June, 108, 109
Thorndike, Sybil, 114, 115
Thorpe, George, 88
Thorpe, Herbert, 68, 69
Tickner, Clive, 188
Tierney, Jacob, 246
Tighe, Fergus, 178, 179
Toal, Maureen, 108, 109, 132, 133
Todd, James, 92, 93
Todd, Sherman, 64
Tóibín, Niall, 136, 152, 153, 161
Toland, Gregg, 64

INDEX OF NAMES

Tomelty, Frances, 170, 171, 190, 191
Tomelty, Joseph, 100, 118
Toolin, Frank, 56
Torrence, David, 54
Towb, Harry, 170
Tracey, William, 70
Treasure, 234
Trevor, William, 161
Troy Films, 114
Trubshawe, Michael, 104
Tuathail, Coilín, 146
Tubor, Mort, 122
Tuite, Danielle, 212
Tully, Caroline, 134
Tully, Mick, 156
Turner, Bowditch, 34
Turner, Yolanda, 124
Tushingham, Rita, 124, 125
Twentieth Century Fox, 92
Two Cities Films, 84
Twomey, Michael, 178
Tyler, Grant, 88, 89

Ulysses FP, 128, 148
UMC Pictures, 134
Universal Pictures, 208
Unsworth, Geoffrey, 102, 144
Urquhart, Robert, 100, 101

Valentino, Rudolph, 34, 35, 37
Van Wijk, Joke, 200
Vaughan, Peter, 142
Vernon, Mike, 154
Vestron, 174
Vignola, Robert, 2, 3, 4, 5, 6, 7
Voight, Jon, 242, 245
Von Stroheim, Erich, 35, 222
Vuolo, Tito, 92

Walker, Leslie, 148
Wallace, Barry, 222, 223
Wallace, Marjie, 170

Wallace, Oliver G, 110
Walpole, Robert, 234
Walsh, Barry, 212
Walsh, Gabriel, 134
Walsh, George, 46
Walsh, Gerry, 168
Walsh, Maurice, 98
Walsh, Raoul, 16, 17, 45, 46, 48, 49
Walsh, Simon, 214
Walt Disney, 110, 111
Ward, David, 78, 79
Ward, John, 220
Warner Brothers, 42, 70, 164
Warner, Jack, 49, 54, 55
Warrington, Ken, 76, 77
Wates, Henry, 180
Watkin, Lawrence Edward, 110
Watkinson, Eve, 180, 175
Wayne, John, 59, 95, 98, 99
Webb Jr, J Watson, 92
Webster, Donald, 142
Webster, Harry, 78
Welland, Colin, 212
Welland, James, 240
Wellman, William, 42, 45
Wells, Margaret, 92
Weston, Maggie, 16, 17
Westwood, Patrick, 100
Wexler, Haskell, 216, 217
Wexley, John, 70
Wheatly, Victor, 218
Whelan, Bill, 228
Whelan, Des, 232
Whelan, Gary, 224
Whitaker, Forest, 202, 203
White, Josephine, 202
Whitehead, O Z, 214
Whitten, Norman, 28, 29
Whitten, Vernon, 28, 29
Whytock, Grant, 34
Wild, Jack, 113
Wilder, Gene, 134, 135

Williams, Enda, 168
Williams, John, 140, 141
Williams, Margaret, 156
Williams, Paul, 243
Williams, Roxanna, 242
Williamson, W Lambert, 116
Willmot, Ronan, 170, 182, 190, 210
Wilmot, David, 234, 235
Wilson, Allan, 220
Wilson, Ian, 202
Wimbury, David, 196
Winter, Brenda, 184
Winters, Mary, 172
Winwood, Estelle, 110, 111
Woodfall F P, 124
Woodley, Karen, 210
Woods, Edward, 42, 43, 45
Woodward, Tim, 228
Woolley, Stephen, 200, 202, 224, 238, 240
Worth, Irene, 86
Wray, Fay, 46, 47
Wright, Tony, 102
Wynn, Manny, 124
Wynter, Dana, 114, 115

Yamash'ta, Stomu, 141
York, Susannah, 140, 141
Young, Frederick A, 136, 139
Young, Maura, 178
Young, Tammany, 46
Young, Victor, 98

Zadek, Gitta, 120
Zampi, Mario, 100, 101
Zanuck, Darryl F, 42, 46
Zeiger, Neil, 170
Zenith Productions, 174
Zetterling, Mai, 188
Zielinski, Jerzy, 164
Zsigmond, Vilmos, 140, 141